BUSINESS
ENGLISH
STUDIES
SERIES

商务英语
研究丛书

总主编：仲伟合　　副总主编：张武保　何家宁

语料库辅助的商务英语短语教学研究

Phraseology in Business English Teaching: A Corpus-Aided Study

胡春雨　陈丽丹　何安平　著

外语教学与研究出版社
FOREIGN LANGUAGE TEACHING AND RESEARCH PRESS
北京 BEIJING

编 委 会

　　本书系广东省高等教育教学改革项目"语料库辅助的商务英语短语教学研究"（2015256）、广东省哲学社会科学"十二五"规划2012年度学科共建项目"中国大学生商务英语词汇能力发展研究"（GD12XWW04）的阶段性成果，并获得教育部人文社会科学重点研究基地"外国语言学及应用语言学研究中心"基金资助。

总　序

仲伟合

　　中国的外国语言文学学科在过去的十年中取得了长足的发展。外国语言文学学科发展的内涵得到了深化，学科内容得到了丰富，学科的范畴得到了拓展。这样的变化一方面因应了学科自身发展的需要，更主要的是因应了国家政治、经济、文化、社会等发展的需要。外国语言文学类本科专业从1993年的38种，增加到2012年的62种，新增专业包括商务英语、翻译在内的24种。商务英语专业独立成为一门专业，商务英语学科也应运而生。

　　商务英语专业自2007年由对外经济贸易大学与广东外语外贸大学试办以来，申办商务英语专业的学校与年倍增。截至2014年9月，全国已有216多所本科院校获批开设商务英语本科专业，商务英语专业发展呈现出欣欣向荣之势。与此同时，部分院校也开设了商务英语专业的研究生点和博士点，商务英语的学科建设及高层次人才的培养也取得了较大成绩。较为完整的商务英语人才培养体系已初步建立。然而，伴随着商务英语的快速发展，也带来了一系列的问题。有的对商务英语的学科内涵认识不清，有的对商务英语专业人才培养理念理解不透，有的对商务英语的研究方法不够了解等。

　　正是在此背景之下，广东外语外贸大学国际商务英语研究中心与外语教学与研究出版社策划出版了"商务英语研究系列丛书"（下称"丛书"）。该丛书是一套专门研究国际商务英语语言的理论专著。"丛书"采用开放式，内容涵盖了商务英语学科与专业研究的多个领域：如商务英语专业与学科建设、商务英语人才培养模式创新、商务英语教学、商务英语测试、跨文化商务学、商务英语翻译、商务词汇学、商务文体学、商务语篇功能、商务语用学、商务语料库等方面的研究。我们希望借此套丛书的出版，对商务英语学科及专业的理论体系进行探索性建构，对商务英语与相关学科进行跨学科的研究，以其为刚刚发展的商务英语学科与专业做一点学术上的贡献。

该套丛书是顺应国家发展战略和学科发展需求而启动的。回顾过去商务英语专业（专业方向）教学，我们有极为丰富的经验和体会需要归纳、总结、提炼和系统化。商务英语学科的发展建设也需要建立系统的理论体系与相关标准。为此，"丛书"的宗旨包括两个主要方面：一是在探索商务英语专业教学经验的基础上，把商务英语专业系统化、专业化、规范化，从中提炼出较为体系的商务英语学科理论，建立商务英语学科的基本框架，为商务英语学科建设提供理论支持和依据；二是为商务英语学科的高端发展，尤其是硕、博层次的建设与发展提供理论保障。虽然商务英语专业的本、硕、博招生教学体系已经初步建立，但理论体系、教学体系、相互之间的衔接等，均需尽快形成或完善。商务英语理论团队也亟待培养形成。作为一门新型复合型学科，商务英语学科犹如一片蓝色海洋，有非常广袤的开发前景。对这片蓝色海洋的系统开发需要蓝图和规划，这就是写作这套"丛书"的主要目的。

商务英语讲的是商务的语言或国际商务活动中的英语。所以，"丛书"的编撰理念是以商务语言为其核心内容，以语言学理论为其主要理论基础，以复合增值理论，以及其他相关复合学科理论为其辅助理论，并在此基础上，结合商务英语教学多年的实践经验，探讨、归纳、总结商务英语自己独特的语言理论与规律，以建立商务英语学科的理论框架与体系。

我们在编撰"丛书"时同时遵循了以下的原则：以质量为核心，坚持专业内涵建设与发展；以需求为导向，探索多元人才培养模式；以创新为驱动，提升学生能力与素质；以实践为抓手，强化学生应用能力提升；以发展为统领，提高专业教师能力素养；以评估为手段，规范和提高办学水平，以提高商务英语语言教学与学习的科学性与有效性。

"丛书"的阅读对象主要是商务英语专业教师、本科生、研究生（硕、博研究生）以及英语类专业教师以及研究人员，对于从事国际商务领域的职业人士、管理人员以及商务英语爱好者，都有非常好的参考价值。

"丛书"的出版有赖于整个编撰团队的不懈努力，更有赖于外语教学与研究出版社的鼎力支持，在此衷心表示感谢！我们期望该"丛书"能作为引玉之砖，吸引更多专家、学者加入到商务英语研究的队伍中来，为该学科的发展添砖加瓦！

前　言

　　本书系2015年度广东省高等教育教学改革项目"语料库辅助的商务英语短语教学研究（2015256）"的最终成果。申报这一课题的动因主要来自两个观察。首先，近几十年语料库语言学的一个重要研究成果是：短语在人类的语言表征与使用中占据核心地位。据此，我们推理：由于在国际商务交际与实务中长期而广泛地使用，商务英语中存在大量的术语、惯用语、固定或半固定的搭配以及多词序列。

　　商务英语短语的重要性可从商务类学科（如经济学、管理学、营销学等）的核心术语的界定看出：

　　（1）*The consumer price index (CPI) is a measure of the overall cost of the goods and services bought by a typical consumer.*

　　在上例中，consumer price index自身已是一个常用短语。由于其高频使用，已变为首字母缩略词CPI。a measure of也是学术英语中的常用短语；cost 可以与许多形容词搭配，例如actual cost, annual cost, approximate cost, average cost, basic cost, carrying cost, external cost, financial cost, fixed cost, great/greater cost, high/higher cost, individual cost, low cost等等；该例中的overall cost则与功能词the和of联合构成更为拓展的商务类学科短语the overall cost of, 如：

　　（2）This chapter examines how economists measure **the overall cost of** living.

　　同样，overall也与cost, price等表示商务测量的词构成"互选"（co-selection）关系，如：

　　（3）Inflation refers to a situation in which the economy's **overall price level** is rising.

在商务语境下，goods and services则更是频繁使用的短语，如：

（4）Business is an organization that provides **goods and services** to earn profits.

仔细观察例（4）不难发现，该复合句也由几个短语构成：*Business is an organization that...* 是常用于下定义的短语构式*A is B that...* 的示例化（instantiation）；provide + goods and services惯常词汇搭配；以及earn与money，pay，profit，return，wage等商务类名词的惯常搭配。

类似例（1）–（4）中形式多样的短语单位，在商务英语中比比皆是。这些商务英语短语既富含商务专业知识信息，也构成了商务英语重要的语体识别特征，是学习者必须掌握的核心内容。因此，是否能够识别、理解并产出规范的商务英语短语，是衡量商务英语学习者语言能力及商务专业知识的一项重要指标。

然而遗憾的是，我们在教学中发现，商务英语专业大学生的短语能力并不容乐观。笔者每次在指导本科毕业论文前，习惯于让他们先用英语界定几个他们在本科阶段所学的核心术语。许多学生在界定上文提到的business时，就会说：Business is an action（activity）to make money。尽管这种表达也不为错，却存在两个缺憾。首先，学生们未能像例（4）那样把business界定为"通过提供产品与服务而盈利的组织"（即"企业"），尽管这是早在大一*Business Essentials*课程中已学过的概念。其次，学生使用短语make money，虽通俗，但不够学术。同样，我们也注意到，学生在作业或课堂展示中经常使用small enterprise来表达"小企业"的概念，而不是使用small businesses这种本族语者更常用的商务短语。类似的还有：使用increase interest rates或improve interest rates表达"提高利率"，而不使用更地道的raise interest rates；使用know financial knowledge表达"学习金融知识"，而不是本族语者经常使用的动词acquire。

基于以上两个观察，我们下决心开展语料库辅助的商务英语短语教学研究。经过几年来的教学实验，我们更加坚定了最初的信念：培养商务英语专业大学生的短语意识，提升他们使用地道的商务英语短语，既有助于他们英语水平的提升，也能帮助他们借用语言有效地建构商务知识。

作为项目主持人，我由衷地感谢参加到本项目的郭桂杭教授、何家宁教授、彭玲玲副教授、杨贝副教授、任朝旺博士。我尤其感谢陈丽丹老师，她是本次教改的实际操作者，没有她的创意和坚守，本书充其量也只是一些教改理念及零零星星的课堂实验。让我们感到非常幸运的是中途何安平教授的加盟。何老师是我国第一位语料库语言学博士（1997年毕业于新西兰惠灵顿大学），她在语料库驱动的短语研究领域以及语料库辅助的外语教学领域造诣颇深。何老师以课堂观察者的身份加入了陈丽丹老师第二轮和第三轮的教改实验，并提出了很多宝贵的指导意见。

　　本书第1–3章由胡春雨撰写，何安平审阅增删；第4–6章由陈丽丹和何安平联合撰写；第7章为三位作者联合撰写。

　　本书是迄今为止对语料库辅助的商务英语短语教学进行系统研究的首本专著，具有一定的理论价值和实践意义。但由于作者水平有限，虽经多次修改，错误仍在所难免，敬请读者指出以便作者加以修正。

胡春雨

2018年9月

目 录

表格目录

图目录

缩写词表

BEC	Business English Corpus
BTC-1	Business English Textbooks Corpus-1
BTC-2	Business English Textbooks Corpus-2
BNC	British National Corpus
CBI	Content-based Instruction
CLIL	Content and Language Integrated Learning
COCA	Corpus of Contemporary American English
DDL	Data-driven Learning
ESP	English for Specific Purposes

第1章
总论

本章简要概述商务英语的内涵和外延、商务英语专业的定位和学科属性，之后介绍短语的界定和研究范式，最后论述语料库辅助商务英语教学的优势及可行性。

1.1 商务英语

何为商务英语？这一看似简单的问题，不同的学者有着很不同的回答，从而也影响了他们研究的内容。比如，国内学者曹合建等从文体学的视角对商务英语进行了以下界定：

商务英语（business English）是一种语言现象，属于语言学的研究范畴，也是应用语言学研究的重要分支。商务英语作为一个有明显特征的语体，在现代社会和经济生活中产生了重大作用和影响。其发展历史和变迁、内在结构与规律、特别是在音韵、词法、句法、语用和语义等方面表现出来的语言学特征，值得认真探讨和深入研究。如果说文学文体曾是20世纪文体学的研究重点，在全球化时代影响越来越大的商务英语（包括其他商务语言）必将是21世纪语言学的重要研究对象（曹合建et al 2008：1）。

曹合建等在《基于语料库的商务英语研究》一书中，重点探讨了商务英语词汇特征、商务英语句型特征、商务英语的语篇衔接特征。然而，也有学者并不认为商务英语具有独特的音韵、句法特征。比如，在Pickett（1989）看来，作为一种"工作语言"（working language），商务英语仅包含语汇层次和交际层次，几乎不涉及语法层次。他重点探讨了商务英语词汇和普通英语（general English）词汇之间的关系，主要包含以下几点（参见Pickett 1989：7-9）：

- 商务词汇以普通词汇作为构词词根，有些普通词汇经常作为商务词汇使用，如percentage，loan，trade等。这类商务词汇是普通大众所能理解也普遍使用的。
- 商务词汇有普通词汇经复合或联想扩展而来，其意义可以相当准确地被推断出来，如 takeover，cheap loan，shelf-life，upmarket，downmarket，brand image等。
- 商务词汇由普通词汇构成，单个词的字面意义可以推测，但普通大众理解其含义却有一定困难，如export credit，guarantee，brand loyalty，share等。
- 商务词汇由普通词汇构成，但非业内人士从字面猜会弄错，如container，terms of trade（简称TOT，指贸易条件指数、进出口交换比率）等。
- 商务词汇由普通词汇构成，但其意义没有专业知识就不能理解，如piggy-back scheme，preference share，General Agreement on Tariffs and Trade，free on board等。
- 商务词汇由普通词汇复合而成，复合的方式基于某种联想，词汇和概念之间的关系并非是显而易见的，在一定程度上是约定俗成的，如tombstone，sweetheart contract，Chinese wall，APR，GATT等。

但是，当具体思考某些词汇（如*business*）是否属于商务英语时，我们很快就会意识到商务英语和普通英语之间的区别可能要比以上Pickett给出的要微妙得多。我们先从Business Class这个常见的短语谈起。航空公司通常把客舱分为First Class，Business Class，Economy Class三类，如中国南方航空公司的英文网页截图：

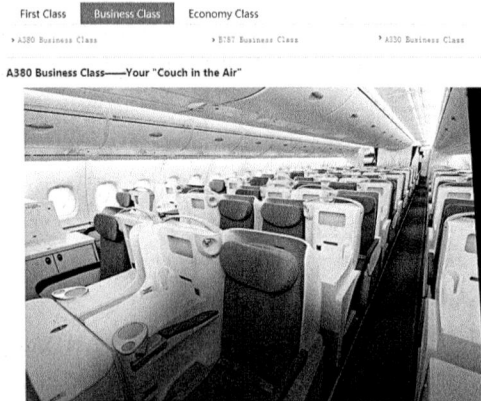

图1.1 南航客舱等级分类

（源自http://www.csair.com/en/tourguide/flight_service/cabin_features/first_business/ ）

有的航空公司会做更为细致的划分，下图是新加坡航空公司（Singapore Airlines）的客舱分类图：

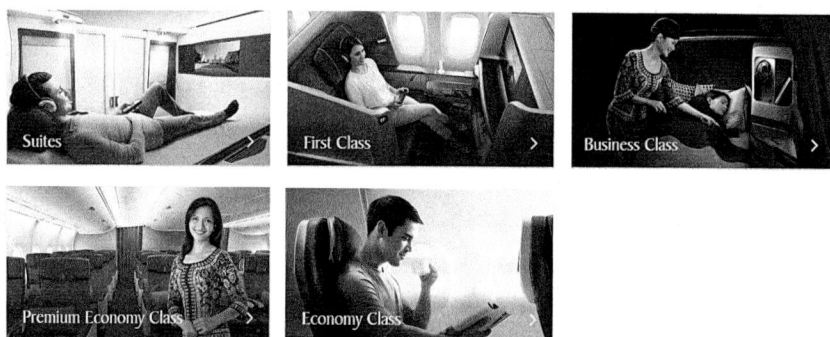

图1.2 新加坡航空公司客舱等级分类
（源自http://www.singaporeair.com/en_UK/cn/flying–withus/cabins/）

点击上图中的Business Class，跳出以下画面：

图1.3 新加坡航空公司Business舱等级分类
（源自http://www.singaporeair.com/en_UK/cn/flying–withus/cabins/business–class/）

并附有以下文字：

Business Class
A successful business plan includes sleep.

When you're travelling for business, everything must go as planned. Like the meal you reserved with Book the Cook, and the uninterrupted sleep you're looking forward to on your fully-flat bed. So you're wide awake, refreshed and ready for business as soon as you land.

以上的Business Class貌似属于商务英语的范畴，这不仅因为business似乎自带商务英语的属性，而且该短语出现在商务交际环境中，故可翻译为"商务舱"。然而，在现实中，我们会注意到很多乘坐Business Class Cabin的不一定是商业人士。而且通过上述文字，我们也很难推断出business这里到底指"公务"还是"商务"。这大概就是business一词的一大特色。为了进一步理解business一词的多义性，我们不妨再多看几个business使用的语境：

- Business is business.
- It's none of your business.
- The business of America is business.
- "It's a jungle out there" and "Business is business" should not be excuses for engaging in unethical behavior. (BTC 1_Principles of Managerial Finance)

概言之，business可以指"事业""事务""公务""商务""商业""企业"。可见，商务英语与通用英语之间并没有明晰的界限，二者类似于太极图中的阴阳鱼，在某些地方区别较大，在另外一些地方区别较小，而且可以互换。

为了更好地理解商务英语这个难以捕捉的概念，我们不妨再看看更为普通的一些英语表达是如何获得其商务内涵的。比如，我们看到Thirst Knows No Season或All the Year Round这样的表达时，很难把它界定为商务英语，但当它出现在图1.4的交际语境中时，这些短语就与红色的可口可乐文字以及棕色的瓶子一起构成了完美的商务英语语篇。

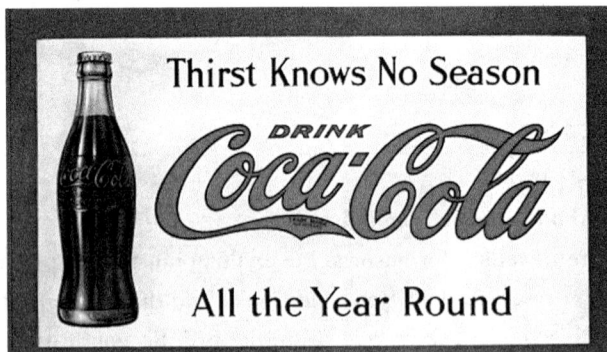

图1.4 可口可乐公司1922年广告

上述例子似乎告诉我们：（1）脱离语境而判断某一英语表示属于通用英语还是商务英语，有较大的难度；（2）商务英语的内核研究对象应为商务话语（详见1.3.2）。这里，我们可以把商务话语简单地界定为：商务话语 = 商务语境 + 商务语篇。相应地，商务英语可被简单地界定为商务交际中使用的英语。

上述界定貌似明晰，但仔细推敲，还是存在一些问题。比如，上述广告中的all，the，year，round是不是商务英语词汇呢？如果说商务英语必须在特定的商务语境下才能识别，为什么大部人都会觉得CEO，managers，customers，corporate，financial等词语属于商务英语呢？通常我们并不为这些看似简单的问题所困，似乎只需根据直觉开展研究即可。但有没有一种科学界定商务英语词汇、短语的方法呢？目前学界多采用语料库的方法（参见Nelson 2000；Hsu 2011；胡春雨 2011）。我们将在第二和第三章进一步探讨这个话题。

所以，我们最好从交际的视角把商务英语界定为"人们在商务交际中使用的专门用途英语"，本质上属于ESP范畴。按照这一界定，典型的商务英语包含英文商务广告、商务会议、商务谈判、商务合同、上市公司年报、上市公司新闻发布会等等。但是，本书所探讨的商务英语，是指在教学语境下，商务英语专业大学生所学的经济学、管理学、营销学、金融学、会计学等商务英语，本质上属于专门学术英语（EAP）的范畴。

综合上述，Business English应有三种内涵：

- 商务英语语篇：在某一特定的商务交际语境下出现的单个语篇，如图1.4中的广告语篇。
- 商务英语语类：使用语境相似、交际功能相仿的语类（genre），如商务广告、商务会议、商务谈判、商务合同、上市公司年报、上市公司新闻发布会等。
- 商务英语词汇语法系统：储存在长期记忆中的各类商务英语词汇或短语。

这三类商务英语之间存在着密切的关联。比如，某一商业人士大脑里储存有商务短语，在特定的商务交际语境下，他就会根据自己的交际意图进行话语策略选择，包括唤起记忆中的相关商务英语短语。又比如，航空公司遵循礼貌原则和客户至上的商业策略，选择First Class，Business Class，Economy Class，而不是直接把这三类客舱命名为First Class，Second Class，Third Class，犹如把不同富裕度的国家称为第一世界、第二世界、第三世界。

1.2 商务英语专业

　　商务英语教育在我国可追溯至20世纪50年代。然而，商务英语专业获得教育部批准却是半个多世纪后的事。以下简述商务英语专业在我国英语教育的定位、历史沿革、培养目标和主要教学模式。

1.2.1　专业地位与发展

　　如果从对外经济贸易大学1951年创办的"外贸英语"算起，国内的商务英语本科教育已有六十多年的历史。改革开放以来，商务英语专业更是蓬勃发展，遍地开花。然而直到2007年，教育部批准对外经济贸易大学、广东外语外贸大学、上海经贸学院试设"商务英语专业"；直到2012年，商务英语专业才正式被列入教育部《普通高等学校本科专业目录》（专业代码为050262）。商务英语专业官方地位的确立意味着该专业从自发走向了自觉。自此，商务英语本科专业蓬勃发展，截止到目前，全国共有395所高校开办了商务英语本科专业。

　　硕士研究生层面的商务英语教育在我国则有近40年的历史。自20世纪80年代初，外经济贸易大学、广东外语外贸大学、上海对外经贸大学、东北财经大学等就开始招收商务英语硕士生。近年又新增了湖南大学、上海财经大学、西南财经大学、天津外国语大学、华中农业大学等。据不完全统计，我国依托英语语言文学或外国语言学及应用语言学二级学科的商务英语方向，已先后培养出近万名商务英语研究生。其中包括2007年起国内部分高校在新设的翻译硕士专业学位点开设的商务翻译、商务口译、商务法律翻译等方向。这些新设方向旨在培养应用型和复合型的商务英语专业人才。从招生生源和就业看，商务英语一直生源充足，就业好，是研究生招生的最热门专业。

　　随着经济全球化的发展和中国成为第二大经济体，国家急需商务英语高级研究人才和师资。从2012年起，部分高校开始在一级博士学科下试设商务外语的博士点。例如，对外经济贸易大学在应用经济学一级学科下目录外自主设置了商务外语研究二级博士点，含商务英语研究、商务翻译研究、跨文化研究三个方向；广东外语外贸大学在外国语言文学一级学科下目录外自主设置了商务英语研究二级博士点，含商务英语语言研究、法商语言研究、商务英语教学研究、商务文化与交际四个方向；中国海洋大学在工商管理一级学科下目录外自主设置了国际商务语言与文化二级博士点，含国际商务语言学、国际商务跨文化两个方向；湖南大学在外国语言文学一级博士点下设立了商务英语教育方向。

如今，商务英语学科体系和人才培养体系在我国已基本建立，也形成了学段齐全的本、硕、博的学科专业，2018 年还正式出台了《高等学校商务英语本科教学质量国家标准》（教育部 2018），这都标志着商务英语正逐步由边缘走进我国英语教育的中心。

1.2.2 培养目标与教学模式

根据教育部最新制定的《高等学校商务英语专业本科教学质量国家标准》，商务英语专业"旨在培养英语基本功扎实，具有国际视野和人文素养，掌握语言学、经济学、管理学、法学（国际商法）等相关基础理论与知识，熟悉国际商务的通行规则和惯例，具备英语应用能力、商务实践能力、跨文化交流能力、思辨与创新能力、自主学习能力，能从事国际商务工作的复合型、应用型人才"（王立非 *et al.* 2015：298）。

新国标把商务英语本科课程划分为四大模块：语言知识与技能、商务知识与技能、跨文化交际能力和人文素养，具体的教学要求中列出了各个模块所包含的核心课程及相关选修课。由于办学传统的不同以及师资力量等各方面的条件局限，目前开设商务英语专业的大学在教学模式上大致可分为以下三类：

模式一：英语+商务（少量商务课程）

此模式在以英语语言文化教学为重心的基础上，开设部分商务英语课程，只给学生提供零散、笼统的商务知识。

模式二：英语+商科（汉语授课）

此模式提供语言主干课程和相对系统的商科知识，但商科课程是用中文上课，存在教材与国际接轨的问题，且学生商科的专业英语能力较差，仍难在跨文化商务交际中应用。

模式三：英语+商科（英语授课）

此模式实际上是全英双专业培养模式，同时开设英语和商科两个专业规定的系列主干课程，对师资要求高，目前只有极少数学校采用（如广东外语外贸大学）。

无疑，第三种模式是相对理想的模式，但除了多数院校未能达到师资要求外，它仍存在另一个问题，即对商务知识技能的重视程度仍然不够。而这问题放在模式一和模式二，情形更加不容乐观。正如朱万忠、刘付川

（2010：102）所言："虽然总的指导思想是把商务知识与英语知识相结合，但是在课程设置上更偏重英语知识的教学，往往只是'英语知识'和'商务知识'的简单相加、课程交叉重复、缺乏理论依据等矛盾的出现，并不能从根本上满足复合型人才培养的需要。"

我们认为，商务英语专业本科教学重在培养"商务与英语齐飞，科学与人文兼修"的创新型跨学科人才，目前的教学模式尚无法满足这一目标。保证商务英语专业的可持续发展，需探讨以下几个议题：（1）对商务英语的语言特征进行更全面、系统的描述；（2）对商务英语专业学生的需求、动机、学习策略和学习风格进行系统调查；（3）基于对上述二者的理解，设计更有针对性的教学任务和教学大纲。其中议题（1）包括要更加科学系统地描述商务英语短语的特征，并在此基础上开展语料库辅助的商务英语短语教学研究，这是促进商务英语专业高质量发展的重要推手。正如Meunier & Granger（2008：249）指出，我们现在很迫切地想搞清，短语教学路径到底对外语的教和学产生什么样的影响。

1.3 商务英语学科

商务英语专业的深入发展离不开对商英学科内涵的理性思考。以下探讨商务英语的学科属性、研究对象、研究内容及其方法。

1.3.1　学科属性

目前，国际商务英语在我国高校已从一两门课程发展成了一个自成体系的新学科（林添湖 2001）；我国商务英语教学研究的现状已基本符合独立学科的构建条件（翁凤翔 2009）。

然而，商务英语的学科归属仍是一个颇具争议的问题。有的学者，如林添湖（2005：4）认为，按"语言学→（英语）应用语言学→专门用途英语→国际商务英语"这个分级层次，可以把国际商务英语学科划归为语言学门下的一个四级学科。又如刘法公（2009：15）指出，"根据商务英语学科的研究对象，当前学界认为商务英语学科宜归于应用语言学学科之下。商务英语学科虽然涉及诸多其他学科，但它的任务是研究在国际商务领域和活动中英语的使用和以此为教学内容的教学体系，培养的是在国际商务活动中具备行为能力的专业人士。实质上，商务英语学科是一门以应用语言学为主导、以多学科知识为基础的应用型交叉学科。"

另外一些学者则提出不同看法。比如，曹德春（2011）借鉴北美的商务沟通研究和欧洲的商务话语研究传统，提出了将广义的商务沟通构建成为我国商务英语理论体系的共同核心的主张，并从实践和理论两个方面来论证这样一个共同核心。他认为，从实践上看，近年来我国企业因跨国并购和海外上市、地方政府因海外招商而催生了跨文化组织沟通和外部交流这一新兴的交流需求，而我国当前商务英语的教学和科研均缺少对这些需求的回应；从理论上讲，商务沟通可以天然地将商务英语知识体系的四个知识板块融为一体。故而有必要整合北美的商务沟通和欧洲商务话语的学术视野与资源，将广义的商务沟通构建成为我国商务英语理论体系的共同核心；构建这个共同核心，可以促进我国商务英语的理论建设提升一个层次，可以弥补我国外语教育在跨国并购、海外上市等高层次英语人才培养方面的缺憾。

我们整体上认可曹德春（2011）把商务沟通构建成为商务英语理论体系共核的提议，但更倾向于欧陆传统，把商务话语研究看作商务英语学科的共核，围绕商务话语研究可有商务翻译研究和商务英语教育研究。我们同时也注意到，商务英语的学科归属在很大程度上也取决于外部环境。有些学校（如广东外语外贸大学）因为有"外国语言文学"一级学科点，就直接把商务英语研究设为"外国语言文学"一级学科下的二级学科。有些学校（如对外经济贸易大学）因为有"应用经济学"一级学科点，就在该学科点下设立"商务外语研究"二级学科点；一旦获得了"外国语言文学"一级学科博士点，对外经济贸易大学就在2018年的招生简章中，把"商务外语研究"变成了"外国语言文学"下的二级学科。

1.3.2 研究对象

商务英语学科的研究对象也是众说纷纭，尚无定论。比如，翁凤翔（2009）认为，应把商务英语教学作为商务英语的研究对象，而且我国商务英语教学研究的现状已基本符合独立学科的构建条件。陈建平（2010）则把国际商务活动中的英语语言行为看作研究对象。张佐成（2008）认为商务英语学科的研究对象包括三个主体：商务学科本体、英语学科本体、二者结合产生的交叉本体。张武保（2014）认为，作为一个学科的研究对象，要有其独特性和不可替代性。故此商务英语学科的研究对象应有两个：商务英语语言、商务英语的专业复合。

以上观点都不无道理，但我们认为，商务英语学科的内核研究对象包括三大模块，即：商务话语、商务翻译、商务英语教育。商务话语研究是商务翻译研究的基础，二者皆可服务于商务英语教育。

1.3.3　研究内容

如果认同上述商务英语学科的内核研究对象，那么研究的具体内容还可细分为商务机构话语研究、商务媒体话语研究、商务学科话语研究和商英教育研究等。其中商务机构话语的研究主要包括企业话语研究和金融机构话语研究。前者是当前研究的热点，例如企业年报中的致股东信研究（Hyland 1998；黄莹 2012；胡春雨、李旭妍 2018）、商务合同研究（胡春雨 2015）、企业使命陈述研究（Sun & Jiang 2014）等等。商务媒体话语也是当前的热点话题，其中包括商务媒体话语中的隐喻（Koller 2004；胡春雨 2014a）。

商务翻译研究涉及英汉翻译和汉英翻译（高新华、刘白玉 2010；何家宁 2014；曾利沙 2017；胡春雨、谭金琳 2017）。与此紧密相连的是汉英商务语言的对比研究，包括汉英经济隐喻对比研究等（任朝旺、曾利沙 2016；胡春雨、徐玉婷 2017）。

商务英语教育研究涉及商务英语课堂教学（雷春林 2006；李丽 2010；朱文忠 2010；曾利沙 2011；徐珺、史兴松 2011；胡春雨 2011，2012）、商务英语专业人才培养模式（王艳艳 *et al.* 2014；严明 2015；刘法公 2015；王俊超 2018）、商务英语教师发展研究（鲍文 2013；郭桂杭、李丹 2015）等。本书也属于商务英语教育研究的范畴。

1.3.4　研究方法

商务英语的研究方法与要研究的内容紧密相连。仅以商务话语研究为例，就涉及会话分析、批评语类分析、批评话语分析、多模态话语分析、基于语料库的话语分析等（Bhatia 2017）。近年来，这些方法相互融合的趋势在增强，比如语类分析与语料库研究的结合，多模态话语分析与批评话语分析的结合等。本书在教改层面的研究则主要采取商务英语教育领域中的行动研究（详见本书第4章）。

1.4 短语研究

短语单位（phraseological unit）是本书研究的核心词。它源自斯拉夫、德国语言学中的一个术语，是对所有多词序列的总称（Moon 1998：5）。语言中存在大量频繁共现的、可预测的、约定俗成的短语单位，它们是本族语者自然、流利地使用语言的关键（Pawley & Syder 1983）。这些短语单位在口语、笔语中都普遍存在。比如，Altenberg（1998）研究了LLC（London-Lund Corpus）后发现，约80%的词语以短语的形式存在。而词汇短语既容易记忆，也容易整体提取，可以让学生在外语学习的初期阶段就让外语变得流畅，从而给学生一种成就感，激励他们继续学习（Porto 1998）。可见，词汇短语是教学的理想单位。

然而由于短语单位通常被当作一个整体看待，其语法和词汇/语义之间并非界限分明，它所引起的关注侧重于词语间的组合结构而不是聚合结构，因此在西方的语言研究中曾一度被忽略（Sinclair 2008：xv）。随着语料库逐步成为语言分析的主要数据来源，这些短语单位已成为语料库和语言描写的理想结合点，得到了极大的关注（ibid.：xvi）。

近年来语料库语言学在运用现代计算机技术处理巨量语料中发现了大量各种各样被传统研究忽视的短语现象，并且使这种现象变得可观察、可计量甚至可预测，由此形成了以频数驱动为特色的语料库短语研究。Sinclair更是在此基础上建立了自己的短语理论。他认为，语言交际中，形式选择不是单一进行的；词汇与词汇、词汇与语法、词汇和语法结合而成的型式与意义之间，都形成了紧密的共选关系；各种共选必然产生各式多样的短语序列，跨越语义–句法、语义–语用等界面，是典型的型式–意义–功能复合体（Sinclair 1991, 2004）。认知语言学家也有类似的观察，通过对习语构式的分析，Fillmore et al.（1988：501）总结道，"语言中存在大量高产且高度结构化的习语类表达，值得对之开展语法调查"。

纵观过去的半个世纪，短语研究方兴未艾，涉及词典编纂、语言习得、外语教学、认知语言学、心理语言学、语料库语言学等多个学科。可以毫不夸张地说，"短语研究已成为西方语言学界一个重要的理论和应用研究领域"（Cowie 1998：1），并逐步走向语言学舞台的中心。

1.4.1　术语与界定

由于分析视角或测量方法的不同，学界对语言使用中重复共现的多词现象采用了不同的术语或名称进行描述和分析，导致目前这一领域的术语缺乏统一规范，有些相同的术语被用来指称不同的研究对象，而有些相同的研究对象却使用不同的术语。

Wray（2002：9）给出了56个术语：amalgams – automatic – chunks – clichés – co-ordinate constructions – collocations – complex lexemes – composites – conventionalized forms – F[ixed] E[xpressions] including I[dioms] – fixed expressions – formulaic language – formulaic speech – formulas/formulae – fossilized forms – frozen metaphors – frozen phrases – gambits – gestalt – holistic – holophrases – idiomatic – idioms – irregular – lexical simplex – lexical（ized）phrases – lexicalized sentence stems – listemes – multiword items/units – multiword lexical phenomena – noncompositional – noncomputational – nonproductive – nonpropositional – petrifications – phrasemes – praxons – preassembled speech – precoded conventionalized routines – prefabricated routines and patterns – ready-made expressions – ready-made utterances – recurring utterances – rote – routine formulae – schemata – semipreconstructed phrases that constitute single choices – sentence builders – set phrases – stable and familiar expressions with specialized subsenses – stereotyped phrases – stereotypes – stock utterances – synthetic – unanalyzed chunks of speech – unanalyzed multiword chunks – units。

我们注意到，这些术语中还不包括语料库语言学中常用的"扩展意义单位"（Sinclair 1996）、型式语法（Hunston & Francis 2000）、语义序列（Hunston 2008）、词串（Biber *et al*. 1999；Cortes 2004，2006，2008；Hyland 2008）、N元组（Gries 2008）、词丛（Scott & Tribble 2006）等，以及认知语言学所谈的"构式"（Fillmore *et al*. 1988；Lakoff 1987；Goldberg 1995，2003，2006）。

术语的混乱既说明了短语研究的重要性及复杂，也暗示了学科之间缺乏有效对话，限制了短语研究向纵深发展。其实，即便phraseology一词也有两层含义，一用来指代属概念，指包括两个词以上的搭配、组合单位，简称短语；二是用来指该领域的研究，即短语研究。有些学者，为了避开phraseology的一词两义，使用了不同的术语。比如，Wood（2015：2）把"程式语系列"（formulaic sequence）界定为单个的多词单位，把"程式语"（formulaic language）界定为所有formulaic sequence的统称，而把"短语研究"（phraseology）界定为对formulaic language的研究。在本研究中，我们用phrase统指所有形态的短语单位（phraseological unit）或多词单位，无论这些短语单位是连续的（如demand and supply），还是非连续式的（如a * of）搭配框架（Renouf & Sinclair 1991）。

尽管术语纷繁复杂，但绝大多数学者对何为短语，还是有着较大的趋同性。这些观点可概括如下：短语"包容了一切人们偏好使用的语言序列以及所谓的固定习语"（Hunston 2002：138），具有预制件或半预制件式的特点（Skandera 2007：v），具有多层共选性（Stubbs 2009），并"将词、句法、语义和社会应用融于一身"（Ellis 2008：5），形式被整体记忆储存，并在即时交际中被整体提取，而不需要使用语法规则来加工分析（Wray 2002：213-231）。

另外一些学者给出了参数类的指标。比如，Wood（2015：3）指出，程式语具有三个特征：（1）多词单位；（2）意义或功能单一；（3）具有预制性特点，如同单词一样被整体储存和提取。Gries（2008：4）则归纳了六种定义参数：

（1）看短语内部成分的性质（单纯由词构成还是由词和语法构成）；
（2）看短语内部成分的数量（有两个还是多个成分）；
（3）看短语的使用频数；
（4）看短语内部成分的间隔程度（中间可否插入其他词或者句子）；
（5）看短语的可变性程度（可否有同一词根的词型变化或语法变化）；
（6）看短语的语义整体性、非整全性或可预测性。

1.4.2 短语研究的两大范式

Granger & Paquot（2008：28-29）曾归纳了短语研究的两大范式：一是以语言学理论为导向的传统研究、二是以频数驱动为导向的语料库研究[1]。前者多指前苏联及东欧学者在20世纪初开创的短语研究传统（Cowie 1981，1998；Howarth 1996；Moon 1998；Granger & Paquot 2008）。这些学者采用自上而下的研究路径，即以语言学理论为指导，其重要的方法特征是对短语单位的内部结构、语义特征等语言学性质进行精密

---

1 Wood（2015：4）也认为短语研究有两大路径：（1）自上而下的短语学家的研究；（2）分布研究，即语料库研究。他所说的短语学家，即指东欧传统的从事短语研究的学者。

的分析，由此产生了诸如合成性与非合成性（compositionality vs non-compositionality）、理据性与非理据性（motivation vs non-motivation）、透明性与非透明性（transparency vs opacity）、字面意义与比喻意义（literal meaning vs figurative meaning）等一系列区别标准。由此范畴化出自由组合（如blow a trumpet）、受限搭配（如blow a fuse）、修辞类习语（如blow your own trumpet）、纯粹习语（如blow the gaff）等短语单位，参见表1.1：

表1.1 搭配连续统（Howarth 1998：28）

	自由组合	受限搭配	修辞类习语	纯粹习语
词汇动词+名词	blow a trumpet	blow a fuse	blow your own trumpet	blow the gaff
语法动词+名词	under the table	under attack	under the microscope	under the weather

Cowie给出了更为宏大的分类，如下图：

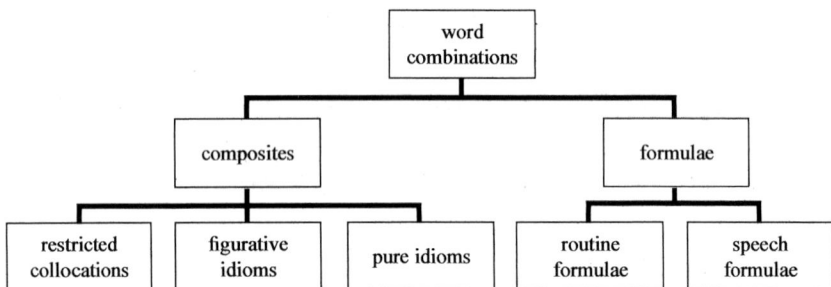

图1.5 Cowie（2001）的短语分类图（引自Granger & Paquot 2008：36）

除了早期分类中的自由组合（free combination）没有包含在组合（composites）中，其他三类保持不变。但他同时增加了程式语（formulae），包含两类：常规程式语（routine formulae），如Good morning这样的招呼语；话语程式语（speech formulae），如you know what I mean，are you with me类的组织话语或传递说话者态度的短语。

以频数驱动为导向的语料库短语研究则采用自下而上的研究路径，即从语料库提取有关语言现象的数据，凭借工具自动或半自动地处理原始数据，获得必要的量化数据分布信息；然后对数据的总体特征和趋势进行观察和描述；在进一步检查具体语言形式的环境信息、意义和功能特征之后，对研究对象作出适当的概括和解释（卫乃兴 2009）。之所以采用这种方法，是因为频数或概率信息反映了语言系统和语言使用的重要的内在属性。语料库研究者深信，高频出现的形式、意义和功能往往揭示了语言使用的核心和典型要素，揭示了交际过程中最经常使用的形式、最经常实现的意义和功能，与句法、语义和语用研究的许多问题密切相关；频数信息的变化还揭示出语言的动态变化信息，与惯用语化或词汇化、语法化等概念相关。这种自下而上的方法本质上是归纳的方法。

短语的语料库研究又可分为两种方法（见图1.6）：N元分析和共现分析。N元分析（又称词丛分析）旨在提取大于等于2个词的持续性的短语系列，以频数阈值为判断依据，包含词丛（或称词串、N元组）及搭配框架。共现分析指二词之间不连续的组合，其判断标准为统计检验。这两类方法在商务短语研究中的应用将在本书的第二和第三章进一步展开。

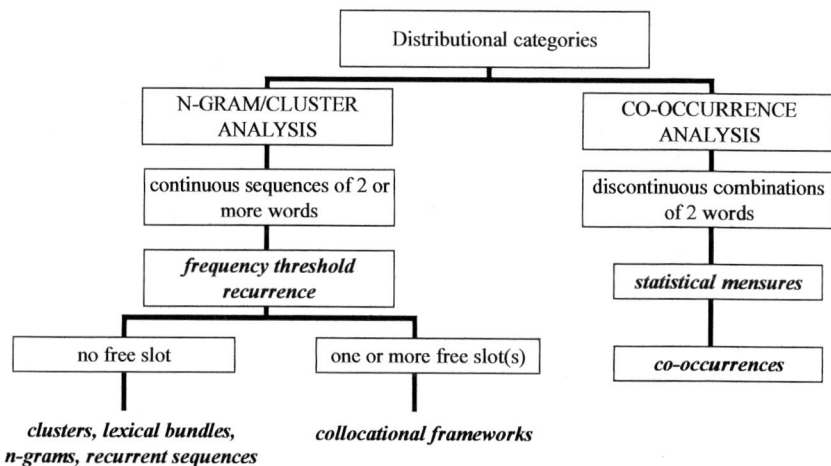

图1.6 短语分布分析示意图（Granger & Paquot 2008：39）

何安平（2013）总结了语料库短语研究的四大特征：（1）从词入手，无论是哪一种短语形态都至少有一个实实在在可观察的词，所以研究伊始就具有实证性；（2）关注词的共选模式，即词在语篇的局部语境（co-text）内多层语言特征的组合模式；（3）关注频数，通过频数驱动方式来归纳词在批量语境中反复出现的词汇、语法、语义和语用的显性或隐性特征；（4）任何形态的短语研究都最终指向意义的表述，指向语言意义的基本单位和构建模式。这是语料库短语研究的目的所在，它反映了该学派的宗旨：一是研究语言在真实语境中使用的倾向性规律；二是研究语言的意义单位如何构建话语意义。

1.4.3　Sinclair的短语理论

Sinclair几十年间所开展的以语料库驱动为特色的短语研究，硕果累累，引人注目，然而他本人并未给出一个确切的名称来概括其理论成果。其他学者尝试为之命名，将其称为"词汇语法理论""共选（co-selection）理论"等；Stubbs（2009）则把该理论命名为"短语理论"（Theory of Phraseology）。联系到Sincliar 2005年参加在比利时鲁汶大学召开的短语学国际会议时所投摘要的标题名称"Phrase, the Whole Phrase, Nothing but Phrase"［该摘要被收录到Granger & Meunier（2008）主编的*Phraselogy*一书中］，笔者认为，"短语理论"是最能概括Sinclair学术思想的名称。

Sinclair短语理论的基本观点是：（1）单词并非最基本的表意单位，意义体现于多个词及语法结构共选构成的短语中；（2）共选关系主要包括两个必选参数及三个可选参数（Sinclair 2004：141-142）：必选参数为节点词（node word）及语义韵，节点词为研究者的观察中心，是不变的量；语义韵是抽象概念，体现说话人/作者的态度、意图或感情取向，决定词项的其余四个参数选择；三个可选参数包括搭配、类联接及语义趋向。其中，搭配指与节点词共现的词，类联接指与节点词共现的语法结构，语义趋向指与节点词共现的、具有相同语义特征的一组词；（3）短语具有词语共选、持续复现、意义单位三大基本属性（Sinclair 2008：410），是本族语者语言知识的核心组成部分。

Stubbs（2009）在Sinclair的基础上进一步指出，意义单位的内部结构包含围绕节点词展开的搭配、类联接、语义倾向和语义韵四个参数，分别体现了词语、句法、语义和语用层面的关系。搭配涉及形符（tokens），指共现的词形（word-forms）；类联接涉及词类（classes），指共现的语法类别（grammatical classes）；语义倾向涉及话题（topics），指语篇连贯（textual coherence）；语义韵涉及动机（motivation），指交际目的（communicative purposes）。以上4个参数按具体到抽象的顺序排列，依次取各自的值，将意义单位结合为一个整体。

Sinclair的短语理论与传统词汇、语法理论有着极大的区别。传统的语言描写认为，词汇是词汇，语法是语法，把语言看作是词库和语法规则，强调基于语法规则的创造性。而Sinclair却强调：语言使用具有短语倾向，人们在多数情况下是一次性选择一串词来表达意义，因而语言的基本表意单位应该是短语而非孤立的单个词（Sinclair 2004）；型式（pattern）与意义不可分（Francis & Hunston 2000），词汇与语法不可分；语言使用既遵循生成语法学家所强调的自由选择原则（open-choice principle），也遵循习语原则（idiom principle），而习语原则在自然对话中比自由选择原则更重要。所谓习语原则，也就是说话者在使用语言时，会根据交际意图和谈话语境从心理词库中提取各种各样的预制短语（Sinclair 1991）。

Sinclai及其追随者的研究打破了词汇与语法之间的隔阂，将两者视为一体，既涵盖具体的词汇与句法搭配，也包括抽象的说话人意图及交际功能，是一个形式—意义—功能复合体。该理论为词汇大纲、教学中的词汇法奠定了基础（详见本章1.5.1），也为我们开展商务英语短语研究及语料库辅助的商务英语短语教学提供了强大的理论支撑。

1.5 语料库辅助商务英语教学研究

语料库作为20世纪80年代才崭露头角的一门交叉学科，它研究自然语言文本的采集、存储、加工和统计分析，目的是凭借大规模语料库提供客观翔实的语言证据。语料库提供了极其丰富的语言客观事实，我们应当充分利用语料库给我们提供的语言客观事实，避免前辈语言学家根据"内省"的研究方法做出的可能有片面性的结论，从而推动语言学的发展。与此同时，我们还应当使用文本数据挖掘技术和信息自动抽取技术，从语料库中挖掘和抽取非语言学的知识。基于语料库的商务英语短语研究能够对商务英语的语言特色进行客观描写，是探讨商务英语学科和教学的前提（详见第3章）。

语料库语言学是语言学与计算机科学相结合的产物。如果从1964年第一个机读语料库（Brown corpus）问世算起，它已经历了半个多世纪的发展。语料库不但"能强化、反驳或者修正研究人员的直觉"（Partington 2003：12），展示出预期不到的语言型式，而且还能帮助研究人员挖掘非语言信息（冯志伟 2010：1），故而被应用于与语言相关的诸多领域。

随着计算机的普及、互联网的兴起，语料库的用户已经由原来的少数语言学家、词典编纂者、人工智能研究者扩展到广大语言工作者、教师与学生。语料库能提供丰富的教学资源，这已是一个不争的事实。当前，"语料库应用于教学的研究已跨出了宣传和介绍其可能性与潜在价值的阶段，而落实到了探究如何与其他学科的理论和方法相结合，以解决在应用过程中的理论困惑和实施问题"（何安平 2009：214）。

在*Teaching and Language Corpora*（Wichmann *et al.* 1997）一书的第一章里，Leech 指出教学与语料库研究之间显然已经达成了一种学科共进（convergence）。这种共进有三个重点：第一是直接将语料用于教学（即"教语料库语言学"，"教如何利用语料库"以及"用语料库来教"）；其二是语料间接用于教学（如工具书的出版、教材开发和语言测试等）。另外，还有一些面向教学的语料库建设（专门用途语言语料库、母语习得语料库及二语学习者语料库）。目前，语料库在语言教学中的应用主要表现为间接应用，而直接应用一般局限于较高层次的学习者。然而，只要语料库语言学完成当前所面临的两大任务，那么，语料库必将在语言教学中决定"教什么"和"如何教"时发挥更为根本的作用。

如何把语料库语言学的理念、方法和成果有效地应于普通英语（general English）教学，是近些年来国内外学者较为关注的问题（Johns 1991a，1991b；Flowerdew 1993；Leech 1997；Widdowson 2000；Sinclair 2004；Scott & Tribble 2006；李文中、濮建忠 2001；何安平 2004；梁茂成 2009；桂诗春 *et al.* 2010），但对如何把语料库的理念和技术应用到商务英语教学的研究尚不多见。本节拟探讨语料库应用于商务英语课堂教学的理论基础、具体步骤，从而使语料库能在商务英语教学课堂上发挥其积极的教育功能，培养学生自主型与探究式的学习模式。

1.5.1　语料库应用于商务英语课堂教学的优势

Hunston（2002：137）认为，语料库对语言教师的职业生涯有两大影响：一是语料库会导致对语言的新描写，从而使教师对教什么的看法产生根本性的转变；二是语料库本身能被用来开发新的教学材料，并为新的大纲设计、教学方法奠定基础。以下将从三个角度探讨语料库应用于课堂教学的优势。

（一）语料库语言学带来了语言描写的新模式

语料库语言学的重要贡献之一就在于它把短语作为语言描写的基本单位。在语料库语言学家看来，所有出现频率较高、形式和意义较固定的、大于单个词的结构都可称为短语。短语结构的稳定性和语义的可预测性使得短语容易习得和应用，而短语结构中的离散性（即可变成分）正是创造性使用语言的空间。短语是语法、语义和语境的统一体，充分提升学习者的短语意识，建立以短语教学为纽带的教学法是学习商务英语切实可行的新路子，将有可能扭转目前商务英语教学投入多效益少的僵局，把商务英语教学带入一个崭新的世界。

商务英语短语有稳定的搭配意义，较固定的语法结构限制和特定的语用环境，因此，在学习和应用时快捷方便、准确流利，有着许多其他教学法所没有的优势（胡春雨 2011）。在教学中，我们应改变以往对词汇的简单认识，充分发挥短语在各个语言层面中的作用，培养学生的短语意识，以较小的投入获得较好的效果。

（二）语料库语言学的理念有助于设计更有效的教学大纲及教学法

语料库的使用会引发新的大纲设计思路，其中最有名的就是Sinclair & Renouf（1988）提出并在Willis（1990）书中得到全面阐释的"词汇大纲"（lexical syllabus）。Sinclair & Renouf（1988）指出，以往的词汇教学仅仅是语法教学的附属品，词的选择没有代表性和科学性，教科书中普遍存在着脱离词的实际用法而孤立谈词汇的现象。他们认为，以词汇为纲的外语教学就是首先从大型语料库中选择最常见的词型，然后学习这些词的最基本的使用模式（pattern），再接着学习与这些词最常见的搭配词。因此，英语教学的重点应放在：语言中最常见的词形；这些词形的核心用法模式；它们的典型组合（Sinclair & Renouf 1988：148）。

Lewis（1993，1997）在词汇大纲的基础上提出了"词汇法"（Lexical Approach）这种颇有影响的语言教学法。词汇法的基本理念可以概括为以下三点：（1）预制短语（而非生成学派所提出的句法）才是语言使用者内化知识的基础；（2）语言习得的一个重要方面在于理解和产出未经分析的、整体性的预制短语；这些短语是语言学习者领会语言模式、词法和那些传统上一贯被认为是"语法"的原始数据；（3）相应地，外语学习中应注重对短语的掌握，教师在课堂上不应对目的语作过多的分析，而应把学习者的注意力引导到短语上，以达到熟练使用目标语言的目的（Lewis 1993：95）。

（三）语料驱动的学习模式可以提高学习者的自主性和积极性

现代教育的理念是以人为本，强调学生要参与知识建构的全过程，以激发学生的创新思维，培养学生分析问题和解决问题的能力。把语料库应用于课堂教学的一个重要方法是Tim Johns提出来的数据驱动学习（data-driven learning）。在他看来，"研究……不能只留给研究人员去做"（Johns 1991b：2），因此，他主张应由学生自己积极主动地从真实语料中去发现语言事实，让学习者成为"研究者"，"其学习需要通过接触语料来驱动"。为适应不同层面学习者的学习需求，数据驱动学习可以是教师指导的，也可以是由学生主导的（即发现式学习），但基本上来说，数据驱动学习是以学习者为中心的。Johns（1991a）将数据驱动学习中借助语料库进行的归纳式推理过程分为三个阶段：（对检索结果的）观察，（对显著特征的）分类，以及（对规则的）概括。DDL能从三个方面促进学生的学习：首先，学生对自己努力发现的东西能更主动地去记忆；其次，学生通过语料库能发现原来被教师或教科书忽视的语言型式；最后，学生能提高通过语境获取意义的技能（参见Hunston 2002），而且利用语料库观察和分析语言信息有利于发展学习者的智能（何安平 2004：57）。

1.5.2　语料库应用于商务英语课堂教学的可行性

上节探讨了语料库应用于课堂教学的优势，但如何设计基于语料库的系列学习任务，从而使学习者能够充分理解、欣赏乃至运用地道的商务英语，则值得进一步的推敲。结合相关研究成果和笔者的教学经验，我们提出以下几个步骤。

（一）建立相关语料库

Sinclair（2004：2）指出，"语料库无论其大小，被很多教师看作有用的工具，而且被越来越多地用在每天的教学中"。我们认为，应用到课堂教学的语料库至少要有以下两类：教学型语料库和研究型语料库。前者包括学生使用的商务英语教材，目的是让学生看到自己已经熟悉了内容的语料，通常规模较小。后者指教学领域之外的汇集了大量真实自然语言的语料，通常规模较大，其作用是为教学语料库提供常见词汇表和语例参照，也可供教师设计任务和学生进行拓展式学习时使用。

（二）选定目标项

课堂时间非常宝贵，而通过语料库检索发现或学会某一语言规律和所消耗的时间相比，有可能得不偿"时"（胡春雨 2004：324）。所以，如果教师要在有限的课堂时间内使用DDL的方法，那么他们就一定要集中到那些对某个群体的学生来说比较困难的语言项目，或者是那些出现频率较高而学生并没有很好掌握的语言项目。

（三）设计学习任务

学习任务的指令要有明确的目标和具体步骤提示。制作语境共现要适合学生的当前水平和学科知识的要求。调解学习任务的难易度可以表现在：控制每次设定的目标词数量和要检索的课文的数量。

（四）组织实施

教师组织课堂活动，使学生通过实践活动学习所选定的语言项目。组织实施时，首要考虑的是该类活动与其他教学活动的时间分配。其次，教师对讨论要进行解释、评价，使学生了解讨论的成果和存在的问题等。具体的方式则多种多样：教师可以对某个教学项目做检索或对某个词项做搭配统计，把活页（handout）发给学生，让学生自己验证、自我发现商务词汇的典型用法；在有条件的学校，可以在教师的指导下，让学生自己上机，选择语料库和语料库索引软件，独立研究自己感兴趣的语言点；或是让学生利用语料库在线索引，直接访问和索引在线大型语料库。

（五）后续学习活动

重复是记忆之母，语言学习要重复多次才能被习得。教师可以通过布置作业，使学生知道下一步做什么，如何巩固成果。

1.5.3　语料库应用于商务英语课堂教学示例

把语料库应用到商务英语课堂教学的案例比比皆是，限于篇幅，这里仅举一例来说明如何把上述步骤融入到课堂实践中。

（一）建立相关语料库

由于笔者正在从事*Principles of Economics*教学，故而所建教学语料库由该教材的语料构成（详见第3章表2.1），而研究型语料库则由Nelson（2000）所建的百万词的"商务英语语料库"（Business English Corpus）以及通用语料库（如British National Corpus）等构成。

（二）选定目标项

在学完 *Principles of Economy* 的第六章后，笔者选择了IMPOSE这个频率很高、搭配非常丰富的动词作为学习目标。

（三）设计学习任务

在设计学习任务时，首先给出两个完整的例句让学生寻找合适的词项：

(1) If the Ice Cream Eaters are successful in their lobbying, the government _____ a legal maximum on the price at which ice cream can be sold.

(2) When the government, moved by the complaints of the Ice Cream Eaters, _____ a price ceiling on the market for ice cream, two outcomes are possible.

（四）组织实施

然后让学生分组讨论，找出目标项。讨论结束后，笔者使用 WordSmith Tools 5.0把该教材语料库中含IMPOSE[1]的所有索引行提取出来（共有106行），然后让学生观察IMPOSE的右搭配特征。下文给出该词的部分索引行：

```
1     ts use of gasoline. They impose a $0.50 tax for each gall.
2     ll back imports, only to impose a 20% tariff (declining o.
3     n-kind transfer does not impose a binding constraint, and.
4     Volcker disinflation did impose a cost of temporarily hig.
5        D), the tax is said to impose a deadweight loss (area C.
6     r mobile phones, clearly impose a negative externality on.
7     peal the price floor and impose a price ceiling $1 below .
8     sic persuade Congress to impose a price ceiling of $40 pe.
9     cerned Congress votes to impose a price floor $2 above th.
10    s the U.S. government to impose a quota on the number of .
11    soland might threaten to impose a tariff on steel unless .
12     of Tradeland decides to impose an import quota on foreig.
```

图1.7　经济学教材语料库中IMPOSE的部分索引行

---

1 本书中的英文检索词若全部字母为大写，表明检索时会包括其下的所有屈折变化形式，如 IMPOSE包括impose, imposing, imposed, imposes等。下同。

学生从索引行中找到了诸如tax，tariff，constraint，cost，loss，quota等众多的搭配词。有的学生表示，虽然对IMPOSE的用法不算陌生，但当看到上述索引行时，感到非常惊奇，觉得"impose的搭配不可思议地多"。这时笔者使用WordSmith软件自动呈现IMPOSE的搭配词表，并和学生的观察进行对比。课堂气氛变得非常活跃。

有的学生对the tax is said to impose a deadweight loss这句话中也使用impose感到惊奇，并认为如果要自己表达，就会使用lead to而不是impose。这种基于真实语料的、以学生为中心的发现式学习，比传统的基于生造例子的、单靠教师讲解灌输语言知识的学习，更有利于增加学生对词汇共选的感性认识，强化其搭配意识。

（五）后续学习活动

在后续活动中，笔者让学生使用免费软件去调查自己作文中IMPOSE的用法，找出差距。并在后续的课上，花费几分钟时间让学生使用该词口头造句。同时，让学生思考这一问题：TAX是IMPOSE的重要搭配词之一，而TAX也可以和LEVY一起使用（如下例），那么这两个动词有什么区别呢？

(3) When the government **levies** the **tax** on buyers, the buyer is required to place $0.50 in the bowl every time a cone is bought.

(4) In either case, when the tax is enacted, the price paid by buyers rises, and the price received by sellers falls. In the end, buyers and sellers share the burden of the **tax**, regardless of how it is **levied**.

(5) In some circumstances, however, selling pollution permits may be better than **levying** a Pigovian **tax**.

(6) State and local governments also **levy** individual and corporate income **taxes**.

(7) The division of the burden in Figure 6-8 is not necessarily fifty-fifty, and the same outcome would prevail if the law **levied** the entire **tax** on workers or if it levied the entire tax on firms.

在总共47例LEVY中，其搭配名词都只有TAX，可见在经济学文本中，LEVY的搭配力远不如IMPOSE。

以上个案研究说明，语料库辅助的商务英语词汇教学，可以提升学生的词汇搭配意识，让他们从语料库语言学的视角重新审视貌似熟悉的内容，进而廓清近义词之间的细微区别。

1.6 小结

　　本章首先对商务英语教学与研究的起点Business English进行界定，并在此基础上梳理了商务英语专业与学科的内涵与外延；同时指出短语研究正从语言学的边缘走向语言学舞台的中央。本章还梳理了与短语相关的术语以及短语研究的两大范式，即短语的传统研究范式和短语的语料库研究范式。后一种范式将在接下来的第2和第3章进一步拓展为商务英语词汇的N元分析与搭配分析，并同时吸纳前一种传统研究范式的精华。本章最后探讨了语料库辅助商务英语教学的优势和可行性。这些前导性研究将在本书的第4至第6章转化为更具系统性和操作性的语料库短语辅助商务英语主题式教学方案和评估手段。

第 2 章
商务英语短语的N元分析

传统的短语研究多关注语言中一小部分形式固定的多词序列，例如习语、惯用语、动词搭配、复合词等多个类别。以频数驱动为特色的N元分析法，依赖计算机处理巨量语料的能力，可发现远超越于上述短语概念的大量多词现象，并且使这种现象变得可观察、可计量甚至可预测，这是研究商务英语短语的良好起点。本章着重阐述N元分析法的相关概念及操作方法，并以自建的商科课程教材语料库（BTC-1）为例，展示商英N元短语的特征。

2.1 相关概念

N元组（N-gram），也称为词丛（word cluster）或词串（lexical bundles），是由计算机自动切分的，高频复现的、长度不同的连续词语片段（Biber *et al.* 1999；Scott & Tribble 2006）。这些连续性的词语片段是"一气呵成的、连贯的、有词汇和语法范式的、可表达语义和语用功能的话语序列"（O'Keeffe *et al.* 2007：63）。它们是"形式与功能高度相关的语篇基本构件"，起着"启动和发展语篇的框架功能"（Biber *et al.* 2004：399），可作为研究话语的基石（ibid.：371）。

N元分析的实质是：让软件按照一定的物理长度标准对文本切分，得到不同长度的短语序列。这种方法是典型频数驱动的，往往设定频数阈值（threshold frequency）。比如Biber等强调，频繁出现在同一语域若干文本中的词语系列方为词串，而不考虑所提取词语序列的结构形式，也不管其是否为习语（Biber *et al.* 1999：990）。

如果按照Gries所界定的短语六参数，N元组具有以下特征（参见Gries 2008：16）：

1）看短语内部成分的性质；N元组由词构成；

2）看短语内部成分的数量；N元组的内部成分大于2，但一般不超过5；

3）看短语的使用频数；通常只有达到某一频数值，才被界定为N元组；

4）看短语内部成分的间隔程度：N元组中间是连续的，没有任何间隔；

5）看短语的可变性程度：N元组通常不具备可变性；

6）看短语的语义整体性：N元组不一定具备完整的语义性。

N元分析采用计算机自动提取的方法，尽管相当一部分词语系列在句法结构和语义方面不完整，但这种方法能提升量化研究的准确性，而且其结果能凸现规律性的特征，"能够更穷尽地勾勒出整个语言的词汇相貌"（Sinclair 2008：410），故而受到众多学者的热捧。

2.2 研究方法

任何语料库研究都离不开相关语料库、语料库检索工具及研究者在该领域的专业知识。本书的研究语料来自我们正在建设的商科课程教材语料库（Business Textbook Corpus-1；以下简称BCT-1）。语料分别取自经济学、管理学、营销学、金融学、人力资源管理五个学科入门的权威英文版教材各一本，作为我校国际商务英语学院本科生2–3年级多门商科课程的教材（详见表2.1）。

表2.1　广东外语外贸大学国际商务英语学院
商科课程教材语料库（BTC-1）概览

名称	来源	大小
人力资源管理教材子语库	*Human Resource Management*. US: South-Western College Pub. 2010	21万词次
经济学教材子语库	*Principles* of *Economics* (6th ed.) US: South-Western College Pub. 2012	36万词次
管理学教材子语库	*Principles of Management*. US: McGraw Hill Higher Education. 2008	23万词次

续表

名称	来源	大小
金融学教材子语库	*Principles of Managerial Finance* (13th ed) US：Prentice Hall. 2011	28万词次
营销学教材子语库	*Principles of Marketing* (15th ed.) US: Prentice Hall.2013	32万词次
合计：140万词次		

本章使用WordSmith[1]的WordList功能，开展N元分析。从图2.1可看出，WordSmith具有三大核心功能：Concord，KeyWords和WordList。Concord程序主要具有索引和计算搭配词两种功能，WordList可以生出词表及词丛表，KeyWords则可生出主题词表及核心主题词表。

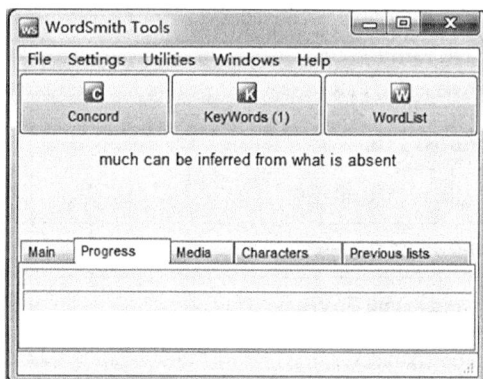

图2.1　WordSmith Tools 5.0的主界面

语料库分析方法的一个重要方面是词频分析。词频涉及词次（token）和词型（types）两个概念（也有分别称作型符和类符）。词次是一个文本中所有词的数目，比如在The book is the most interesting one I have ever read. 这句话有11个词，其词次为11，但因the一词出现过2次，故其词型为10。WordSmith Tools在统计词次时，把包含数字等符号在内

---

[1] 这是Michael Scott研发的WordSmith Tools 5.0。该软件是第三代语料库工具的代表，特别适合在PC机上开展研究。

的统计结果称为tokens（running words）in text（见表2.2序号1），把排除这些符号的统计结果称为tokens used for word list，因而后者总是要少于前者（见表2.2序号2）。型/次比（type/token ratio，简称TTR见表2.2序号4）是计算文本词汇密度（lexical density）的一种方法。TTR和文本大小关系密切，通常文本越短，TTR值越高。为了使TTR具有较强的可比性，WordSmith作了标准化处理，对文本每1000个词的TTR都依次重新计算，最后计算出的各个1000词的平均TTR被称作标准型/次比（standardized TTR，见表2.2序号5）。

表2.2　BCT-1的词汇统计数据

序号	Basic Statistics	BCT-1
1	tokens (running words) in text	1,401,335
2	tokens used for word list	1,367,734
3	types (distinct words)	26,171
4	type/token ratio (TTR)	1.91
5	standardized TTR	1.87
6	standardized TTR std.dev.	96.57
7	standardized TTR basis	1,000
8	mean word length (in characters)	5.87
9	word length std.dev.	2.80
10	sentences	73,044
11	mean (in words)	32.29
12	std.dev.	1,497.92

语料库的N元数据处理与分析按照以下四个步骤进行：

首先，使用Wordsmith Tools的WordList功能，分数次计算、提取商英上述五个学科教科书的词频信息，设定Wordlist的词丛长度为2-4词，提取BCT-1五个子库的二至四词词丛表。以探究商务学科英语短语序列的理想长度。

第二步，根据界定频数提取其中的高频词块。高频标准的设定可因语料库的大小而定。比如，Biber *et al.*（1999）曾界定的频数阈值为每百万词10次以上；Biber *et al.*（2004）则把标准提高到每百万词40次以上；而Corts（2004）及Hyland（2008）的界定标准均为20次/每百万词以上。考虑到本研究的库容为1.4百万词，我们把频数阈值设定到50次，对于每个子库（即每本书）则设定为5次。

第三步，提取、对比分析五个学科共用词丛，统计共用词丛在各子库所占比例，以回答：（1）商英学术文本中是否存在"核心词丛"的问题？（2）商务学科英语中词丛的语篇功能与语法结构有何种共选关系？

2.3 商务英语词丛的频数特征

采用N元分析的学者多仿效Biber *et al.*（1999）的研究范式，以四词词丛作为研究的对象，原因有二：（1）相当一部分四词词丛结构上包含三词词丛，且比五词词丛的使用频率高出好几倍；（2）四词词丛的数量较为合理，属于手动检查索引行、分类可操作的范围（Chen & Baker 2010：32）。本节通过分析二至四词词丛，侧重寻找研究商务英语课程教材（即BCT-1语料库）短语序列的理想长度。

2.3.1　二词词丛

二词词丛（或称二元序列）是最短的多词序列。本研究结果显示，其中频数不低于5次的有40,183个，频数不低于50次的有2,725个。表2.3列出了其中前50个二词词丛（#代表数字）。不难看出，除了# percent外，其他词丛都出现在所有五本教科书中。频数最高的前10位（如of the，in the）似乎都是没有具体意义的序列。排序第11和第14的for example，such as则表明商科课程教材的话语倾向于举例进行论证。排序第27位的more than则说明"比较"是商务英语的另一显著特征。

从排序第18位的the firm开始，我们发现了多很能体现商务英语具体内容的二词词丛，它们大概可分为以下三类：（1）包含the firm，the company，the price，the market（若拓展至前100位，则包含the world，the economy，the organization等）；（2）cost of，value of，price of等；（3）另外一种规律是：the firm's，company's。

表2.3　商务英语中的二词词丛

排序	词丛	频数	文本数	排序	词丛	频数	文本数
1	# #	9564	5	26	by the	1171	5
2	of the	8043	5	27	more than	1171	5
3	in the	6626	5	28	cost of	1145	5
4	to the	3092	5	29	from the	1100	5
5	and the	2770	5	30	the same	1081	5
6	on the	2415	5	31	# and	1046	5
7	for the	1916	5	32	value of	1040	5
8	of #	1909	5	33	number of	1036	5
9	is the	1904	5	34	the firm's	1006	5
10	that the	1806	5	35	to #	1001	5
11	for example	1801	5	36	the market	997	5
12	of a	1788	5	37	if the	994	5
13	# percent	1777	4	38	in #	989	5
14	such as	1709	5	39	as the	963	5
15	in a	1624	5	40	# the	922	5
16	can be	1608	5	41	the #	918	5
17	as a	1548	5	42	figure #	863	5
18	the firm	1416	5	43	a #	862	5
19	to be	1413	5	44	in this	847	5
20	at the	1411	5	45	for a	845	5
21	the company	1348	5	46	to a	826	5
22	it is	1336	5	47	and other	821	5
23	is a	1324	5	48	# to	801	5
24	with the	1259	5	49	with a	774	5
25	the price	1216	5	50	the united	764	5

2.3.2　三词词丛

三词词丛频数不低于5次的有22,821个，约为二词词丛频数的一半；频数不低于50次的有591个，不到二词词丛频数的三分之一。表2.4列出了其中的前50个三词词丛。与表2.3对比，频数最高的前50位三词词丛中，不能全部出现在五本教材中的个数明显增多（共有9位），其中排第49位的the money supply只出现在经济学教科书中。

表2.4　商务英语中的三词词丛

排序	词丛	频数	文本数	排序	词丛	频数	文本数
1	# # #	1955	5	26	the long run	311	5
2	of # #	873	5	27	each of the	298	5
3	the united states	722	5	28	from # to	288	5
4	# percent of	579	4	29	table # #	285	3
5	more than #	555	5	30	a number of	283	5
6	figure # #	552	4	31	to # #	276	5
7	goods and services	552	5	32	at the end	275	5
8	# to #	534	5	33	# # per	273	5
9	the cost of	484	5	34	# # in	270	5
10	the price of	468	5	35	the short run	268	5
11	the number of	464	5	36	of goods and	259	5
12	in the united	455	5	37	supply and demand	259	5
13	as a result	433	5	38	cost of capital	237	4
14	the value of	430	5	39	# # percent	236	4
15	the quantity of	417	4	40	some of the	234	5
16	one of the	414	5	41	in other words	231	5
17	# # and	400	5	42	is # #	231	5
18	# and #	385	5	43	the use of	231	5
19	value of the	360	5	44	example # #	229	2
20	the end of	350	5	45	the interest rate	223	2
21	as well as	323	5	46	# # the	219	5
22	the amount of	321	5	47	part of the	216	5
23	in figure #	318	5	48	# per share	215	2
24	in chapter #	315	5	49	the money supply	214	1
25	what is the	315	5	50	in this case	213	5

对比前50位二词和三词词丛还发现，很多高频的二词词丛镶嵌在三词词丛中，如 the united →the united states；# percent →# percent of；more than →more than #；cost of →the cost of；price of →the price of；value of →the value of；number of →the number of 等。也有一些不在前50位甚至不在前一百位的二词词丛，镶嵌在前50位的三词词丛中，如：amont of排在第120位，但the amount of却在三词词丛中排在第22位。

另外，一些明显带有学科意义的短语，如goods and services，the long run，the short run，supply and demand，the interest rae，the money supply，都出现在前50位中。

2.3.3　四词词丛

四词词丛频数不低于5次的有7,939个，约为三词词丛频数的三分之一；频数不低于50次的有116个，不到二词词丛频数的20%。表2.5列出了其中前50个四词词丛。

表2.5　商务英语中的四词词丛

序	词丛	频数	文本数	序	词丛	频数	文本数
1	# # # #	1244	4	26	on the basis of	101	5
2	in the united states	439	5	27	can be used to	100	5
3	from # to #	276	5	28	you need to understand	100	2
4	at the end of	270	5	29	more than # million	98	5
5	of goods and services	254	5	30	shown in figure #	97	5
6	in figure # #	207	4	31	the next # years	96	5
7	the value of the	189	4	32	# # per share	95	2
8	in the long run	175	5	33	the end of #	95	4
9	# percent of the	170	4	34	# and # #	94	5
10	in table # #	154	3	35	the end of the	94	5
11	more than # #	154	5	36	of # # #	92	3
12	the present value of	151	2	37	the quantity of money	92	1
13	at the same time	148	5	38	the size of the	89	5
14	as a result of	139	5	39	in the form of	88	5
15	in the short run	137	5	40	in this case the	88	5
16	# # and #	136	5	41	# # to #	87	5
17	in the following table	131	2	42	finance problem # #	87	1
18	# to # #	116	5	43	personal finance problem #	87	1
19	for each of the	115	5	44	one of the most	86	5
20	figure # # shows	113	4	45	are more likely to	85	5
21	run aggregate supply curve	109	1	46	of # # and	85	3
22	the united states and	108	5	47	# # per year	83	5
23	quantity of goods and	103	1	48	an increase in the	83	5
24	shown in the following	102	2	49	the price of a	82	3
25	the aggregate demand curve	102	1	50	each of the following	80	3

第一眼看四词词丛似乎较为理想，相当一部分都是我们所熟悉的固定用法，如at the end of, at the same time, as a result of, in the long run, in the short run, on the basis of等。但是，商务类短语似乎不如三词词丛的多。比如：of goods and services排名第5，频数254；goods and services在三词词丛单位中排名第7，频数552，其中有相当数量出现在四词词丛provide goods and services中。同样，the short run虽然在笔者感觉中不如in the short run更像短语，但其频数为268，排名第24；而in the short run虽排名第9，但其频数仅为137。也就是说，还有近一半的the short run没有出现在in the short run中。观察the short run的索引行，竟然发现有50例the short run aggregate-supply curve，而没有1例... demand curve；此外，还发现有11例the short run trade-off，其中9例出现在the short run trade-off between inflation and unemployment；另外一种使用为the short-run and long-run。

以上表明，尽管很多学者认为在研究学术英语时，四词词丛是最为理想的长度（参照Biber *et al.* 1999；Biber *et al.* 2004；Corts 2004，2006，2008；Hyland 2008；Chen & Baker 2010；Shin & Kim 2017；高霞2017），但如果我们考虑具有学科重要性的短语序列，三词词丛也许是更为理想的长度。当然，这一结论还有待于进一步验证。总之，商英短语的N元结构既应重视四词词丛，也不应忽视三词词丛。

2.4 商务英语词丛的结构特征

鉴于本研究的目的重在服务于不同商科课程的英语教学，故而不能停留在词丛的频数特征调查上。本节分析商务教科书中词丛的结构。关于词丛的结构分类，在早期研究中，已有Biber *et al.*（1999：1014-1015）把口语中的词丛分为14类，而把学术话语中的词丛分为12类。后来，Biber *et al.*（2004）进一步把学术语篇中的四词词丛归为3大类，即：（1）含有动词结构的词丛，（2）含有从属小句结构的词丛，（3）含有名词短语和介词短语的词丛。每个大类又再分出若干个小类，详见表2.6。

表2.6　学术语篇中四词词丛的结构分类（Biber *et al.* 2004）

大类	小类
Lexical bundles that incorporate *verb phrase* fragments	1a.　(connector +) 1st/2nd person pronoun + VP fragment 1b.　(connector +) 3rd person pronoun + VP fragment 1c.　Verb phrase (with non-passive verb) 1d.　Verb phrase with passive verb 1e.　yes-no question fragments 1f.　WH-question fragments 1g.　discourse marker + VP fragment
Lexical bundles that incorporate *dependent clause* fragments	2a.　1st/2nd person pronoun + dependent clause fragment 2b.　WH-clause fragments 2c.　*If*-clause fragments 2d.　(verb/adjective) to-clause fragment 2e.　*That*-clause fragments
Lexical bundles that incorporate *noun phrase* and *prepositional* phrase	3a.　(connector +) Noun phrase with of-phrase fragment 3b.　Noun phrase with other post-modifier fragment 3c.　Other noun phrase expressions 3d.　Prepositional expressions 3e.　Comparative expressions

　　参照表2.6中Biber等的词丛结构分类框架，我们对BTC-1商科课程教材语料库中频数不低于30的309个词丛进行了结构分析，结果见表2.7。

表2.7　BTC-1中四词词丛的结构分类

大类	小类	频数	举例
含有动词短语的词丛（13.9%）	1a. 第一二人称＋动词短语	0	
	1b. 第三人称＋动词短语	6	figure # # shows
	1c. 动词短语（非被动式）	16	you need to understand
	1d. 动词短语（被动式）	8	can be used to
	1e. "是否类"短语	0	
	1f. WH- 疑问类短语	0	
	1g. 话语标记语+动词短语	13	when it comes to

续表

大类	小类	频数	举例
含有从属小句结构的词丛（0.6%）	2a. 第一二人称＋非独立从句	0	
	2b. WH疑问类从句	0	
	2c. *If* 从句	1	to be # #
	2d.（动词/形容词）＋ to 不定式	1	if the price of
	2e. *That* 从句	0	
含有名词短语和介词短语的词丛（85.4%）	3a. 含有of 的名词短语	109	the value of the
	3b. 有后置语修饰的名词短语	17	goods and services demanded
	3c. 其他类型的名词短语	59	the United States and
	3d. 介词短语	79	in the United States
	3e. 表比较的短语	0	

　　表2.7显示，不同结构类型词丛的使用频数存在巨大差异：含有名词短语和介词短语的词丛比例最高（85.4%），其中又以the N of N的名词短语居多，显示出商科教材这类学术类话语语篇的名词化短语倾向。因为含有动词短语的词丛（13.9%）和含有从属小句结构的词丛（0.6%）合计比例还不到15%。

2.5 商务英语词丛的功能特征

　　Hyland（2008）曾在Biber *et al.*（2004）及Hyland（2005）等研究的基础上，把学术类语篇词丛的功能分为研究型（research-oriented）、语篇型（text-oriented）、参与型（participant-oriented）三大类和11小类，详见表2.8。

表2.8　四词词丛语篇功能分类（Hyland 2008：13-14）

类别比例	功能	举例
研究型	定位（location）	at the beginning of, at the same time, in the present study
	过程（procedure）	the use of the, the role of the, the purpose of the
	量化（quantification）	the magnitude of, a wide range of, one of the most
	描述（description）	the structure of the, the size of the, the surface of the
	话题（topic）	in Hong Kong, the currency board system
语篇型	过渡（transition signals）	on the other hand, in addition to the, in contrast to the
	结果（resultative signals）	as a result of, it was found that, these results suggest that
	结构（structuring signals）	in the next section, as shown in figure, as shown in table
	框架（framing signals）	in the case of, with respect to the, on the basis of
参与型	立场（stance features）	are likely to be, may be due to, it is possible that
	融入（engagement features）	it should be noted, as can be seen

参照表2.8的词丛功能分类框架，我们又对BTC-1商科课程教材语料库中的309个高频词丛（即频数不低于30）进行了功能识别和分类，结果见以下表2.9。

表2.9　BTC-1四词词丛的功能分类

类别	功能	频数	举例
研究型 74%	定位（location）	26	at the end of；in the long run
	过程（procedure）	0	
	量化（quantification）	57	## and #；# percent of the
	描述（description）	52	the value of the；the present value of
	话题（topic）	94	run aggregate supply；the United States of

续表

类别	功能	频数	举例
语篇型 20%	过渡（transition signals）	4	on the other hand；in other words the
	结果（resultative signals）	3	as a result of；as a result the
	结构（structuring signals）	38	in the following table；in this chapter we
	框架（framing signals）	17	for each of the；on the basis of
参与型 6%	立场（stance features）	4	can be used to；are more likely to；
	融入（engagement features）	4	you need to understand；as we will see

表2.9显示，BTC-1的高频四词词丛中属研究型的比例高达74%，远远超过另外两种类型。研究型词丛与研究者所谈话题相关，涉及学科知识、事件发生的地点、时间等，主要用以帮助作者建构自己外部世界的真实行为和经历。表2.9显示在这类词丛下属的五个小类中，其中涉及学科话题的使用最为频繁（94个），其次是量化类（57个）和描述类（52个）。显示出商科教材侧重话题知识描述和注重量化信息的学科话语特点。

BTC-1的高频语篇型词丛比例为20%，其中主要为结构类词丛（38）和框架类词丛（17）。它们与语篇的起承转合相关，主要用于语篇组织及信息或论证的组织，对于篇章连贯性举足轻重。而参与型词丛涉及作者与（潜在）读者的互动，属于人际功能层面。在BTC-1中仅占6%的比例。

2.6 四词词丛的功能与结构内在关联

进一步考察上述BTC-1高频四词词丛各个子功能类型所使用的语言结构，还发现两者之间一些有意义的内在关联，如表2.10所示。

表2.10   BTC-1四词词丛的功能与结构内在关联

功能类别	频数	结构类别特征	举例
话题类	94	80%为名词类短语,尤其是N of N式	the aggregate demand curve; shares of common stock
量化类	57	40%为名词类短语,多带数字类词	# percent of the; more than # million
描述类	52	70%为名词类短语	the value of the; quantity of goods and
结构类	38	依次为动词词丛、介词词丛和名词词丛	see figure # #; in the following table
定位类	26	60%是介词类词丛	see figure # #、at the end of
框架类	17	60%是介词类词丛	for each of the、on the basis of
融入类	4	多带第一或第二人称代词	you need to understand; as we will see
立场类	4	多带情态类词	can be used to; are more likely to
过渡类	4	多为介词类词丛	on the other hand; in other words the
结果类	3	多为介词类词丛	as a result of; as a result the

　　表2.10所展示的四词词丛的功能与结构关系表明了语言形式与语用功能的统一,有助于我们在商务英语教学中将短语的形式结构与其表述的语用功能类倾向相结合。

2.7 小结

　　N元分析法是一种简易而高效的短语研究方法。其本质是根据词形的外在物理毗邻位置对序列进行不同长度的人为切分,统计共现频数,设定频数阈值,从而自动提取对研究有价值的词语序列。本章通过由经济学、管理学、金融学、营销学、人力资源管理五门学科教科书构成的小型语料库,旨在发现商务英语教材中较为理想的短语单位。研究显示,尽管大部分学者认为四词词丛是研究短语的理想长度，本研究却发现二至四词词丛各有其研究价值，尤其不应忽视三词词丛，因为这些短语单位往往包含重要的商务学科信息。另外，本章的研究也显示了 N 元分析存在一些问题，比如，提取的 N 元组含有大量结构不完整、语义不清晰的强干扰序列。更重要的是，N 元分析的起点不是单个的词，而在学科英语表达中有很多重要概念的术语是以单词的形式出现。这一缺点，有望通过下一章开展的基于主题词搭配分析得以化解。下一章聚焦从主题词入手，侧重单个主题词和主题词搭配研究如何揭示学科知识的问题。

第 3 章
商务英语短语的搭配分析

　　使用语料库研究短语，除了上一章所用的N元分析较为常用外，搭配分析也是非常经典的研究方法。搭配分析的起点可以是任何研究者感兴趣的语言单位，似带有某种随意性；但以语料库主题词作为研究的起点，则能使研究更具客观性。本章将从主题词入手，聚焦单个主题词及其拓展研究。包括使用WordSmith的KeyWords功能提取商务学科英语主题词，并使用Concord功能开展主题词搭配分析及与之紧密相关的索引分析。

3.1 相关概念

　　语料库对词语搭配的研究成果主要体现在Sinclair及其同事的研究中。早在1966年，Sinclair（1966：415）就指出："我们使用节点（node）这一术语来称呼进行搭配研究的对象，并可以将跨距（span）定义为节点两侧与其相关的词语数量，由跨度确立的范围内所有词项均成为搭配词（collocates）"。Jones & Sinclair（1974）发表第一份基于语料库的词语搭配研究报告，该研究在Sinclair（1966）的基础上确立了一系列重要原则和基本方法，包括跨距界定、统计方法、搭配词与节点词相互吸引力的测量、显著搭配的确定等等。之后，Sinclair（1991：170）把搭配定义为"两个或两个以上的词在文本中短距离内的共现"。但是，这个短距离到底在什么位置最佳呢？经过多年的实证研究，Sinclair认为4：4的跨度（即节点词两侧各4个单词）最为理想，并给予搭配一个新的定义："搭配是两个词同时出现，而中间间隔不超过四个单词。这是横组合方向最简单、最明显的关系"（Sinclair 2004：114）。在计算语言学领域，一般把跨度5：5，即节点词两侧各5个单词。比如，在第三代语料库检索工具WordSmith Tools和第四代语料库检索工具Sketch Engine中，缺省跨度都是5：5。

搭配词提取涉及搭配强度（strength of collocability）的计算。用来计算搭配强度（strength of collocability）的方法有两类。一类是通过计算在跨距内每个词位的频数分布，根据峰值的显著性来确定搭配强度。但是，仅凭搭配词的频数并不能确定该搭配词是否与搜索词具有真正意义上的搭配关系。一些高频搭配词的出现可能是由于该词本身在语料库中频数就很高，另外一些搭配词的出现很可能纯属偶然。

在语料库语言学中，还有几个和词语搭配紧密相连的概念，如类连接（colligation）、语义倾向（semantic preference）、语义韵（semantic prosody）。其中的类联接指语法范畴（如词性）之间或词语与语法范畴之间的组合。比如cases 一词经常与数量词some，many，most，more，both，several共现，构成了"determiner + cases"这样的语法共选关系。又如bubble，这个反映近年经济活动的高频词就有一组类联接模式，如下：adj +bubble：speculative，unsustainable；n + bubble：doctom，housing，internet，property，stock，market；bubble + v：burst，collapse等等（参见胡春雨 2014a）。

语义偏好指词项与周边词在语义上的频繁共选倾向，它关注惯常搭配词的语义特征或类别。语义韵指由上述这些语义倾向所带出的语言使用者的立场、态度或感情取向特征，它散布于多个词的范围内，是形成整个词项意义的决定因素（Louw 1993：157）。例如，set in常和winter, bad weather, gloom, decline, rot等表示不好的词或词组共现（Sinclair 1991）。语义韵被认为"语料库研究迄今最为重要的贡献"（Sinclair 2003：178），因为前计算机时代无法将语言使用的延伸语境如此大批量地凸显出来。比如，前面提到的bubble, set in都具有明显的消极语义韵。

下节将借鉴Michael Nelson在其博士论文中的主题词搭配研究路径来揭示商务学科英语主题词的特征。

3.2 研究方法

Nelson（2000）曾将自建百万词的商务英语语料库（简称BEC）和BNC Sampler参照语料库相比照生成了主题词表，并对前1,000主题词进行直观辨识，将其分为5个语义范畴，然后从每个范畴各选取10个词（合计

50个主题词）作为样品来研究其语义偏好，最后归纳出这5类主题词倾向与10类具有明显语义偏好的搭配词共选，由此从词汇搭配的语义层面凸现了商务英语词汇更深层面的特征。

　　本研究也从提取商务英语的主题词作为切入点，并在此基础上对商务英语主题词进行分类研究，然后从每类词汇中选择有代表性的词语开展商务英语主题词的搭配分析。

　　在语料库语言学中，主题词（keywords）指那些通过"观察语料库"（observed corpus）与"参照语料库"（reference corpus）进行对比，使用频率达到统计显著性的词（Baker 2004；Scott & Tribble 2006；Bondi 2010）。统计主题词时一般要遵循以下标准：统计主题词时一般要遵循以下标准：（1）需根据研究目的事前考虑参照语料库的大小、体裁、时间跨度等；（2）主题词在语料库中的出现率必须达到使用者设定的次数；（3）两个语料库的词次不可能完全一样，所以比较的是它们的百分比。然后再看百分比的差别有无显著性意义。在与参照语料库作比较时，主题词在语料库中的频率通过卡方检验或对数似然率检验等概率统计后获得。Wordsmith提供了两种检验p值的统计手段供用户使用，一种是卡方检验，另一种是Dunning（1993）的对数似然性检验（Log likelihood test）。后者较适合于体积较大的语料库。

　　主题词的语料库提取一般要遵循以下几个步骤：（1）根据研究目的，建立"观察语料库"（或"观察文本"），并选择合适的"参照语料库"。参照语料库一般为通用语料库，其规模一般应大于观察语料库。（2）使用语料库软件生成两个分别基于观察语料库和参照语料库的词表。由于同一个单词可能具有多种形式，如动词rise具有rises，rose，risen，rising等屈折形式，而名词rise也有rises这种屈折形式。这时候，就需要考虑使用语料库的词形还原（lemmatization）功能，将语料库中词汇的屈折形式进行归并。譬如，把rises，rose，risen，rising都归并到RISE这个lemma中。第三代语料库分析工具（如AntConc，WordSmith Tools等）内嵌了词形还原程序，但需要用户提供一个用于词形还原的词表。（3）通过对比观察语料库和参照语料库中词语各自的频数及两个语料库各自的规模（参照表4.1），就可以把差异显著的词语提取出来；其中，差异的显著性通过卡方（chi-square或X^2）检验或对数似然比（Log-likelihood ratio，简称LL）检验来确定。X^2（或LL）值越高，主题性越强。有时候，我们只需报道X^2（或LL）值对应的显著水平的p值即可。P值越低，显著性水平越高，判断该词是主题词的把握就越大。

在本研究中，我们仍然使用WordSmithTools 5.0提取主题词。观察语料库为上章所介绍的商务英语课程教材语料库（BCT-1），参照语料库为百万词次的AmE06和Crown语料库。两者都源于Brown家族语料库，属于普通英语语料库。BCT-1主要选自2008年至2013年出版的教材语料，与参照语料库中的语料来源年份较为接近。我们选择使用对数似然性检验，并把p的最大值设定为0.000001，主题词的最低频数不小于10，主题词的上限数量为5000，如以下图3.1所示：

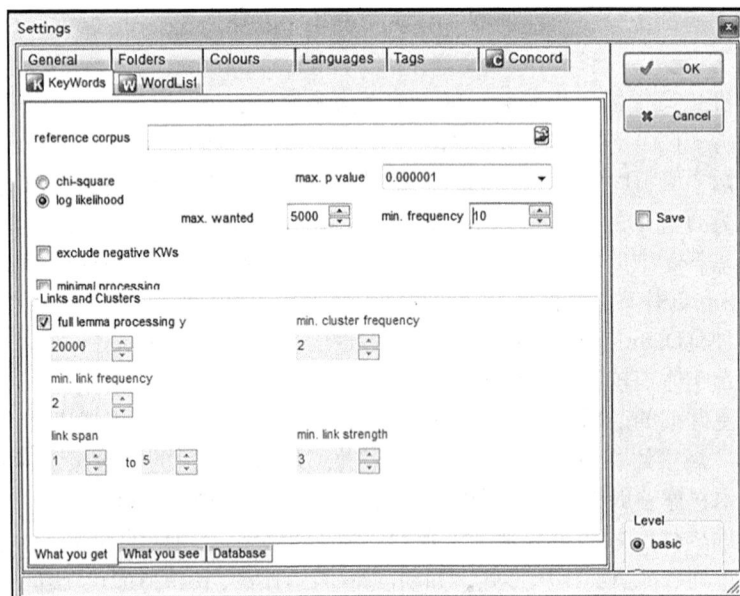

图3.1 主题词设置

在以上的设定条件下共产生了2,328个主题词，其中1,336个为正主题词，其余的为负主题词。图3.2是主题词表的截图。从左到右看，分别为：N代表主题性排序的高低（如MAREKET的主题性最高）；第二栏Keyword列出BCT-1的主题词；第三栏Freq.列出每一个主题词在BCT-1中的频数；第四栏%列出每一个主题词的频数在BCT-1总库中的百分比；第五栏RC.Freq.和第六栏RC.%分别列出主题词在参照语料库中的频数及占比[1]；第

---

[1] 两个语料库的词次不可能完全一样，所以比较它们的百分比，然后再看百分比的差别有无显著意义。

七栏Keyness列出主题词的主题性高低（以LL值表示）；第八栏P列出统计概率值。

N	Key word	Freq.	%	RC. Freq.	RC. %	Keyness	P.	Lemmas	Set
1	MARKET	7,138	0.51	806	0.04	8,441.14	0.0000000000		
2	PRICE	5,898	0.42	499	0.02	7,603.24	0.0000000000		
3	FIRM	4,475	0.32	284	0.01	6,174.14	0.0000000000		
4	EMPLOYEE	4,293	0.31	397	0.02	5,397.38	0.0000000000		
5	#	33,601	2.40	26,983	1.33	5,360.17	0.0000000000		
6	CUSTOMER	3,485	0.25	219	0.01	4,816.89	0.0000000000		
7	COMPANY	4,943	0.35	969	0.05	4,608.72	0.0000000000		
8	VALUE	4,021	0.29	566	0.03	4,378.23	0.0000000000		
9	COST	4,532	0.32	868	0.04	4,277.83	0.0000000000		
10	PRODUCT	3,517	0.25	479	0.02	3,879.68	0.0000000000		
11	MANAGER	2,687	0.19	182		3,653.43	0.0000000000		
12	CONSUMER	2,540	0.18	227	0.01	3,222.71	0.0000000000		
13	RATE	3,460	0.25	764	0.04	3,012.76	0.0000000000		
14	CASH	2,006	0.14	135		2,730.88	0.0000000000		
15	STOCK	2,044	0.15	178		2,611.60	0.0000000000		
16	SALE	2,111	0.15	314	0.02	2,245.10	0.0000000000		
17	DEMAND	2,199	0.16	364	0.02	2,230.01	0.0000000000		
18	CAPITAL	1,756	0.13	165		2,195.96	0.0000000000		
19	SUPPLY	1,884	0.13	223	0.01	2,188.60	0.0000000000		
20	BRAND	1,597	0.11	111		2,158.15	0.0000000000		
21	FIRM'S	1,273	0.09	13		2,150.51	0.0000000000		
22	EXAMPLE	2,886	0.21	829	0.04	2,099.96	0.0000000000		
23	TAX	2,563	0.18	631	0.03	2,082.52	0.0000000000		
24	ORGANIZATION	2,281	0.16	500	0.02	1,994.05	0.0000000000		
25	PAY	2,751	0.20	803	0.04	1,976.85	0.0000000000		
26	HR	1,196	0.09	20		1,961.12	0.0000000000		
27	CAN	6,127	0.44	3,597	0.18	1,945.52	0.0000000000		
28	CURVE	1,352	0.10	106		1,775.16	0.0000000000		
29	SELL	1,885	0.13	401	0.02	1,677.01	0.0000000000		
30	EMPLOYER	1,487	0.11	196		1,660.32	0.0000000000		
31	QUANTITY	1,115	0.08	47		1,654.54	0.0000000000		
32	JOB	2,731		981	0.06	1,538.22	0.0000000000		

KWs | plot | links | clusters | filenames | notes | source text

图3.2　BCT–1主题词截图

接着，我们参照Nelson（2000）等的分类，将主题词按语义分成五个词汇群（lexical fields），并开展词语搭配分析。比如，把CUSTOMER归入商务相关人员。之后，再从上述5类词中每类选择5个代表的主题词，借助于WordSmith软件，计算出各自的搭配词，并将搭配词归入不同的语义群（semantic group）。

由于搭配词是计算机根据所设定的参数自动提取，难免会出现个别错误判断，因而研究者还有必要看看索引行，通过搭配词的上下文语境（co-text）进行判断。比如，mounting inflation和inflation and mounting evidence中的mounting很不同；同样，inflation fight crippled economy 中的crippled在修饰economy而不是inflation，因而不能计算在内。此外，一个词的用法在不同的语境中也可能存在很大不同。比如在inflation raises federal borrowing costs中inflation被拟人化而属于"隐喻"，也不同于…raises inflation的用法。

3.3 商务英语主题词的特征分析

本节从自建的140万词的商科课程教材语料库（BCT-1）提取商务英语主题词，先做主题词的对比分析，然后探究主题词之间的内在学科知识关联。

3.3.1　商务英语主题词的对比分析

商科主题词的对比分析包括两个方面：一方面将BTC-1的前100个主题词与Nelson（2000）基于百万词的商务英语语料库（BEC）所获得的前100位商务英语词表进行对比；另一方面在BCT-1内部的5本学科教材子语库之间进行频数分布对比。

表3.1是从BCT-1提取的商务学科英语前100主题词，表3.2是Nelson（2000）基于百万词的商务英语语料库（BEC）所获得的前100位主题词。二者对比发现的相似点至少有二。首先，两者都含有MAREKET，PRICE，FIRM，EMPLOYESS，BUSINESS，PRODUCT，MANAGER，FINANCIAL，PER，PROFIT等典型商务英语词汇，尽管这些词的排序不尽相同（如BUSINESS在Nelson的BEC主题词表排第一位，在商科教材语料库BCT-1中排序第61位）。其次，两者都含有共同的功能词ITS。而二者的差异至少有三：（1）BCT-1中的前100主题词中有体现教科书特色的CHAPTER，EXAMPLE，DISCUSS等词，BEC则没有；（2）BCT-1中的情态词包含CAN，MUST，而BEC中的情态词为SHALL，WILL；（3）BEC中有FAX，MAIL，DATE等反映商务信函特色的词。

表3.1　商务英语（BCT-1）前100个主题词

序	主题词	序	主题词	序	主题词
1	MARKET	7	COMPANY	13	RATE
2	PRICE	8	VALUE	14	CASH
3	FIRM	9	COST	15	STOCK
4	EMPLOYEE	10	PRODUCT	16	SALE
5	#	11	MANAGER	17	DEMAND
6	CUSTOMER	12	CONSUMER	18	CAPITAL

续表

序	主题词	序	主题词	序	主题词
19	SUPPLY	47	INTEREST	75	CHANGE
20	BRAND	48	DECISION	76	ORGANIZATIONAL
21	FIRM'S	49	SHARE	77	COMPANY'S
22	EXAMPLE	50	BUYER	78	OPERATE
23	TAX	51	PURCHASE	79	LABOR
24	ORGANIZATION	52	BUY	80	LEVEL
25	PAY	53	PER	81	ACCOUNT
26	HR	54	FINANCIAL	82	FLOW
27	CAN	55	B	83	GOOD
28	CURVE	56	EARNINGS	84	REVENUE
29	SELL	57	EACH	85	DEBT
30	EMPLOYER	58	CHAPTER	86	DISCUSS
31	QUANTITY	59	AGGREGATE	87	INVENTORY
32	JOB	60	BENEFIT	88	NET
33	DIVIDEND	61	BUSINESS	89	AMOUNT
34	ASSET	62	RISK	90	PLAN
35	MANAGEMENT	63	WAGE	91	AFFECT
36	INVESTMENT	64	CALCULATE	92	OBJECTIVE
37	PERFORMANCE	65	MARKETERS	93	RETAILER
38	PROFIT	66	MARGINAL	94	REDUCE
39	INFLATION	67	ADVERTISE	95	COMMON
40	ITS	68	MUST	96	EQUILIBRIUM
41	INCOME	69	COMPETITIVE	97	PROMOTION
42	INCREASE	70	ECONOMY	98	FINANCE
43	STRATEGY	71	COMPETITOR	99	SELLER
44	SERVICE	72	BOND	100	POLICY
45	USE	73	WORKERS		
46	TOTAL	74	RETURN		

注：表中的#代表数目字。表中包含FIRM，FIRM'S，是因为本研究所用的词形还原词表
（lemmalist）没有把firm's纳入FIRM中。

表3.2 商务英语语料库（BEC）前100个主题词（Nelson 2000）

序	主题词	序	主题词	序	主题词	序	主题词
1	BUSINESS	26	INVESTMENT	51	COPY	76	PC
2	COMPANY	27	SHARE	52	ACCOUNT	77	INCREASE
3	MARKET	28	INTERNET	53	OUR	78	INVOICE
4	CUSTOMER	29	COST	54	DISTRIBUTOR	79	COM
5	OK	30	TO	55	DELIVERY	80	INCLUDE
6	PRODUCT	31	DATE	56	CASH	81	REGARD
7	SALE	32	GLOBAL	57	WE	82	PAYMENT
8	FAX	33	PROFIT	58	COMPANY'S	83	TAX
9	MANAGEMENT	34	SELL	59	AGREEMENT	84	TRADE
10	PRICE	35	REGISTER	60	GROUP	85	OR
11	FINANCIAL	36	PROJECT	61	OFFER	86	OFFICE
12	BANK	37	PERFORMANCE	62	GROWTH	87	TELEPHONE
13	BILLION	38	YEAR	63	DIRECTOR	88	ENGINEER
14	SERVICE	39	INTERNATIONAL	64	INFORMATION	89	MEETING
15	STOCK	40	ITS	65	PROPERTY	90	FIRM
16	ORDER	41	MILLION	66	NETWORK	91	FINANCE
17	EXECUTIVE	42	CORPORATE	67	DIGITAL	92	NEW
18	CONTRACT	43	RATE	68	SHAREHOLDER	93	SYSTEM
19	CLIENT	44	BUYER	69	TEL	94	FOCUS
20	MAIL	45	CREDIT	70	FOR	95	RECEIVE
21	CONTRACTOR	46	INDUSTRY	71	TERM	96	PURCHASE
22	WILL	47	SUPPLIER	72	INVESTOR	97	EXPENSE
23	MANAGER	48	TECHNOLOGY	73	REVIEW	98	TEAM
24	PER	49	BUDGET	74	EMPLOYEE	99	STRATEGY
25	SELLER	50	SHALL	75	TARGET	100	STRATEGIC

　　进一步对比BCT-1内部5个子库的主题词表，发现主题词在不同学科子语库中的使用频数是不一样的。比如，FIRM在五个子库共出现5746次，但在教科书*Principles of Economics*和*Principles of Managerial Finance*中的频数远高于其他三个子库（见以下用检索软件中"Plotting"工具展示的图3.3），分别约占总数约23%和50%。显示其在则两个学科子库中的话题特征。

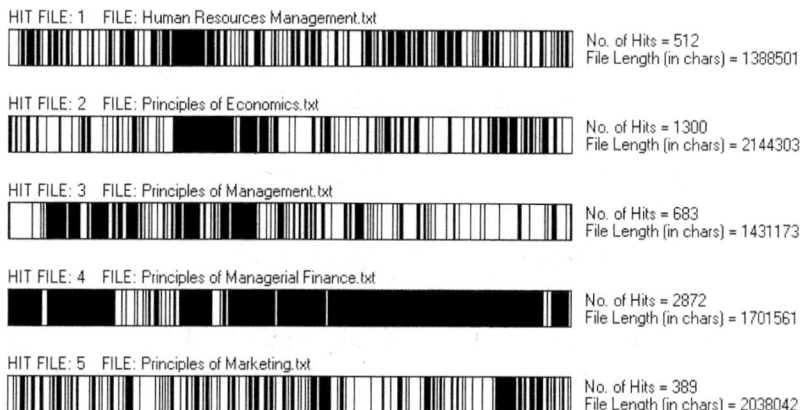

HIT FILE: 1　FILE: Human Resources Management.txt

No. of Hits = 512
File Length (in chars) = 1388501

HIT FILE: 2　FILE: Principles of Economics.txt

No. of Hits = 1300
File Length (in chars) = 2144303

HIT FILE: 3　FILE: Principles of Management.txt

No. of Hits = 683
File Length (in chars) = 1431173

HIT FILE: 4　FILE: Principles of Managerial Finance.txt

No. of Hits = 2872
File Length (in chars) = 1701561

HIT FILE: 5　FILE: Principles of Marketing.txt

No. of Hits = 389
File Length (in chars) = 2038042

图3.3　FIRM在5个子语库的频数分布图

　　若使用"Plotting"工具展示主题词firm's在5本教科书子库的频数分布，则发现有更大的差异，如图3.4所示：

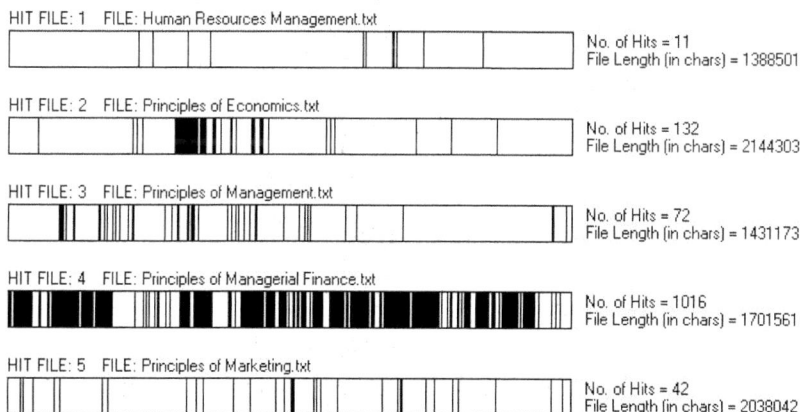

HIT FILE: 1　FILE: Human Resources Management.txt

No. of Hits = 11
File Length (in chars) = 1388501

HIT FILE: 2　FILE: Principles of Economics.txt

No. of Hits = 132
File Length (in chars) = 2144303

HIT FILE: 3　FILE: Principles of Management.txt

No. of Hits = 72
File Length (in chars) = 1431173

HIT FILE: 4　FILE: Principles of Managerial Finance.txt

No. of Hits = 1016
File Length (in chars) = 1701561

HIT FILE: 5　FILE: Principles of Marketing.txt

No. of Hits = 42
File Length (in chars) = 2038042

图3.4　firm's在5个子语库的频数分布图

N	File	Words	Hits	per 1,000	Dispersion	Plot
1	firm's (Overall)	1,374,666	1,273	0.93	0.856	
2	firm's Human Resources Management	208,356	11	0.05	0.413	
3	firm's Principles of Economics	357,726	132	0.37	0.264	
4	firm's Principles of Management	220,931	72	0.33	0.696	
5	firm's Principles of Managerial Finance	277,208	1,016	3.67	0.846	
6	firm's Principles of Marketing	310,445	42	0.14	0.812	

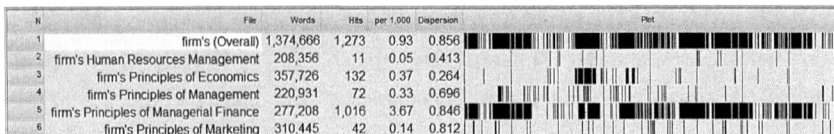

图3.5　firm's的频数分布对比统计

图3.4和3.5均显示firm's在金融学教材子语库（Principles of Managerial Finance.txt）中有超高密度的呈现，这些高度可视性解图直观地提醒我们去关注该学科的知识和话语特征，具体在这个案例来说就是"企业"在金融学话语中是一核心概念，很值得在教学中多角度多层面地探讨其带出的与金融相关的话题及其在语言表述方面的规律性特征。

3.3.2　商务英语主题词间的内在关系

我们认为，在学科英语研究中，研究者不能满足于把所提取的主题词进行语义分类，还应按照学科知识的内在逻辑，揭示主题词之间的语义内涵和关联，如图3.6所示：

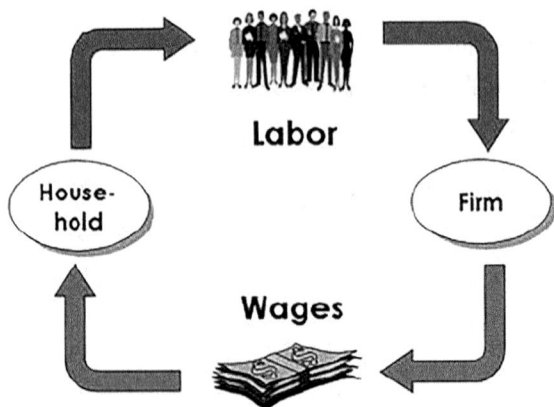

图3.6　四个主题词之间的内在关系

上图展示了两大经济参与者"家庭"（household）与"企业"（firm）之间的内在关系，即家庭通过提供"劳力"（labor）给"企业"，获取"工资"（wages）。

为了更好地阐释主题词之间内在的关系，我们在下节进一步展示如何通过选择重要的学科主题词开展搭配研究，以此提升师生的短语意识，并同时建构学科知识。

3.4 商务英语主题词FIRM的搭配研究示例

本节以之前从BCT-1提取的高频主题词FIRM为例，展示商科主题词与商科基础知识的关系。选择FIRM这一名词是因为它的主题凸现性。首先，即便firm's没有被归入到FIRM中，其主题性排序仍仅仅次于MARKET，PRICE（见表3.1）。其次，在上一章所研究的二词词丛中，the firm排序第18位，是所有商务英语词汇中排序最高的，the firm's排序第34位，使用频数也高于排序第36位的the market。故而，我们选择FIRM来分析其搭配词，并且对比BUSINESS，COMPANY等语义相近词的搭配特征，以此揭示商务活动最为重要的主题概念：企业。

我们采用AntConc[1]提取FIRM的搭配词。首先，选择计算搭配强度的统计模型。我们选择传统的MI，见图3.7：

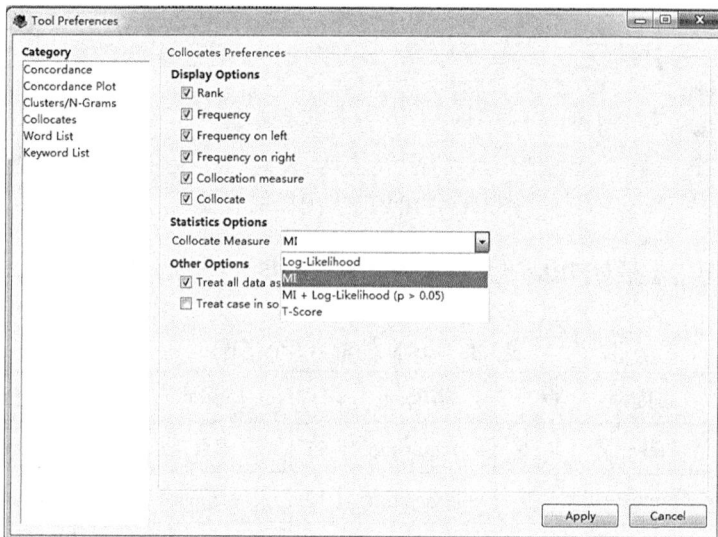

图3.7　AntConc搭配设定

---

1 源自Anthony, L. (2017). AntConc (Version 3.5.0) [Computer Software]. Tokyo, Japan: Waseda University. Available from http://www.antlab.sci.waseda.ac.jp/.

接着，在搭配界面中设定跨距为左4右4，最低频数为10，按照统计值排序。结果生成661个搭配词词型，搭配词的词次总数为37,402，如图3.8所示：

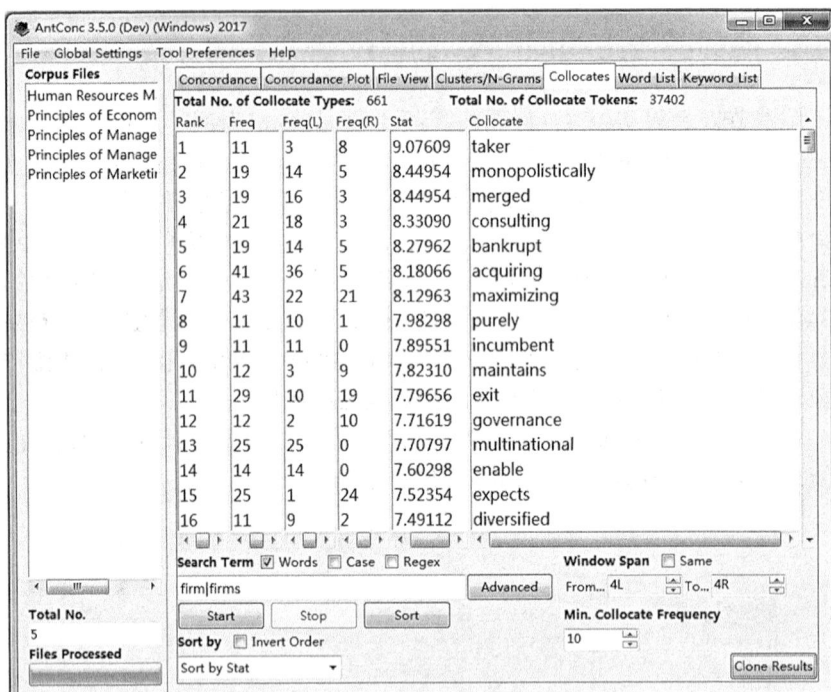

图3.8　FIRM的搭配提取界面

第三步是对FIRM的前100搭配词作进一步分析。详见表3.3。

表3.3　FIRM的前100个搭配词

序	搭配词	序	搭配词	序	搭配词	序	搭配词
1	taker	6	acquiring	11	exit	16	diversified
2	monopolistically	7	maximizing	12	governance	17	enables
3	merged	8	purely	13	multinational	18	unable
4	consulting	9	incumbent	14	enable	19	monopoly
5	bankrupt	10	maintains	15	expects	20	competitive

续表

序	搭配词	序	搭配词	序	搭配词	序	搭配词
21	owners	41	chooses	61	faces	81	operations
22	repurchase	42	wishes	62	leverage	82	retained
23	households	43	creditors	63	externality	83	raise
24	pays	44	weighted	64	shares	84	assets
25	payout	45	debts	65	financing	85	profitability
26	conversely	46	smaller	66	hire	86	attractive
27	prospects	47	subject	67	directors	87	affects
28	maximize	48	breakeven	68	establish	88	fixed
29	operate	49	hires	69	ratios	89	issued
30	borrow	50	dividend	70	entry	90	typical
31	differentiated	51	stockholders	71	currently	91	ability
32	enter	52	failed	72	portion	92	cannot
33	patent	53	compete	73	produce	93	sheet
34	condition	54	manufacturing	74	shareholders	94	assume
35	profit	55	dividends	75	analyze	95	operating
36	acquired	56	acquire	76	facing	96	target
37	liquidity	57	earnings	77	profits	97	consistent
38	profitable	58	capacity	78	assuming	98	liabilities
39	structure	59	decides	79	goal	99	considering
40	perfectly	60	s	80	capital	100	normally

　　打开 firm 的索引行还发现，往往会有多个搭配词同时与节点词一起共现。比如，表3.3排名第二的搭配词 monopolistically 和排名第20的搭配词 competitive，就有6次出现在这样的四词词丛中，由此揭示了"垄断企业、竞争公司"这样一个学科核心概念，如图3.9所示。

Concordance Hits 6		
Hit	KWIC	File
1	All this should seem familiar. A monopolistically competitive firm chooses its qu	Principles of Economics
2	competition. In other words, a monopolistically competitive firm, unlike a perf	Principles of Economics
3	ce equals marginal cost. For a monopolistically competitive firm, such as that	Principles of Economics
4	unit sold is zero. By contrast, a monopolistically competitive firm is always eage	Principles of Economics
5	a perfectly competitive firm, a monopolistically competitive firm, both, or neit	Principles of Economics
6	re hired as the consultant to a monopolistically competitive firm. The firm repo	Principles of Economics

图3.9 搭配词monopolistically及competitive与节点词firm的索引行

这种现象在词丛表中表现得更加明显，比如以firm's为首的四词词丛表（见表3.4）。

表3.4 以firm's为首的前30个四词词丛

排序	词丛	频数
1	firm's cost of capital	25
2	firm's goal of maximizing	12
3	firm's earnings per share	10
4	firm's ability to meet	7
5	firm's board of directors	7
6	firm's free cash flow	7
7	firm's weighted average cost	6
8	firm's cash conversion cycle	5
9	firm's common stock is	5
10	firm's operating breakeven point	5
11	firm's ability to pay	4
12	firm's assets were sold	4
13	firm's average collection period	4
14	firm's earnings before interest	4
15	firm's operating cash flow	4
16	firm's stock is currently	4
17	firm's ability to make	3
18	firm's capital structure and	3

续表

排序	词丛	频数
19	firm's cash flow. the	3
20	firm's corporate governance structure	3
21	firm's investment in accounts	3
22	firm's marginal-cost curve	3
23	firm's net cash flow	3
24	firm's net profit margin	3
25	firm's net working capital	3
26	firm's overall cost of	3
27	firm's profitability and its	3
28	firm's target capital structure	3
29	firm's total revenue minus	3
30	firm's value if cash	3

　　表3.4中的四词词丛也可称为主题词拓展词丛[1]（keyword-extended cluster），因为它们是"基于主题词的索引行提出的词丛）（Scott 2014：168）。该表基于firm's这一主题词提取的四词词丛明显带有firm's+N这一名词短语结构，由此带出了"企业目标""资金/资产运营""企业盈利"等一系列重要概念或话题。为了更加系统地考察FIRM与其搭配词之间的关系，我们提取了含有FIRM的三词词丛，结果见表3.5展示的前50个词丛：

---

[1] 这里将基于主题词的索引行分析产生的词丛称为"主题词拓展词丛"，为的是将其区别于"主题词词丛"（即KeyWords clusters，见Scott 2014: 236）。后者指的是预设跨距内重复同现的主题词与主题词共选。全书同。

表3.5　FIRM的三词词丛

排序	词丛	频数	文本数	排序	词丛	频数	文本数
1	the firm's	1006	4	26	firm's stock	41	2
2	of the firm	329	5	27	that a firm	41	5
3	a firm's	210	5	28	firm's value	39	3
4	that the firm	145	5	29	a competitive firm	37	1
5	the firm is	123	5	30	calculate the firm	35	1
6	if the firm	116	4	31	firm's cost	35	2
7	to the firm	97	4	32	a firm is	32	4
8	the firm has	93	5	33	u.s. firms	32	5
9	the firm to	88	4	34	firm has a	31	4
10	of a firm	83	3	35	a firm has	30	5
11	in the firm	73	5	36	firm's ability	30	5
12	on the firm	72	2	37	a firm to	28	5
13	for the firm	68	5	38	firm's capital	28	1
14	the firm can	67	5	39	firm's total	28	2
15	the firm will	59	5	40	the firm would	28	2
16	when a firm	53	5	41	firm's earnings	27	1
17	and the firm	50	2	42	for a firm	27	4
18	firms in the	50	5	43	a firm can	26	4
19	if a firm	49	5	44	households and firms	26	1
20	by the firm	48	4	45	the firm and	26	5
21	number of firms	43	1	46	firm's operating	24	1
22	firm's financial	42	5	47	the acquiring firm	24	2
23	the firm must	42	1	48	the firm may	24	3
24	a firm that	41	2	49	the firm should	24	5
25	firm's cash	41	1	50	when the firm	24	4

　　若将最高频的三词词丛of the firm拓展为索引行（见图3.10），则会显示该词丛通常出现在N（oun）+ of the firm这样的名词短语结构型式中，比如the value of the firm，the key account of the firm，the...activities of the firm等等，同样揭示了由"企业"这一概念带出的，与之前firm's+N结构相近似的话题。

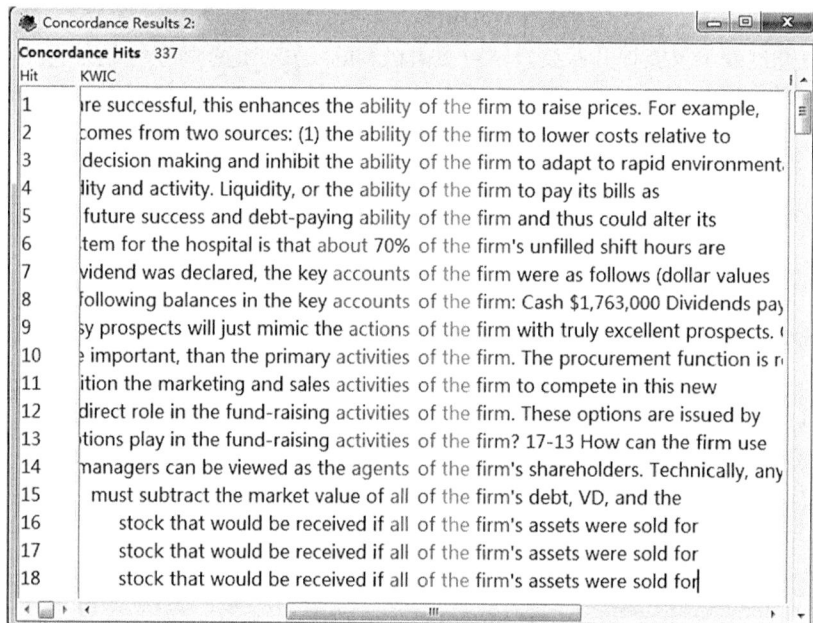

图3.10　从三词词丛of the firm拓展的索引行

　　由此可见，从高频的学科单个主题词出发，拓展其N元词丛，进而再拓展至更宽泛的词丛索引行，是透过语料库主题词构建学科基础概念和核心知识的有效途径，这种探究也体现了语料库短语研究的两大范式融会贯通。

3.5　小结

　　本章以商务英语教材语料库的主题词为抓手，开展主题词在各种长度词丛中的词语搭配研究，从短语视角揭示了商务英语的短语结构和意义功能特征。结合上一章的商务英语词丛研究结果，我们发现商务英语短语有以下特点：（1）大部分商务英语词汇来自普通英语词汇，但在不同的搭配语境中有不同的含义。比如principal在principal and interest中表示"本金"，在principal and agent中表示"委托人"，这类意义是在隐喻机制作用下、通过该词的本义"首要的"引申、转义而来；（2）商务英语主题词汇往往具有极强的搭配能力，比如raise可以和money，fund，finance，interest rate，standard of living等几十个商务名词（或词组）搭配；（3）商务英语短语具有名词型结构倾向，很多名词（词组）往往也是商务术语，具有较强的系统性。比如，business，economics，interest rate，exchange rate等。这种探究过程不仅能提升商英教师对短语机制的认知，还能将研究结果直接引入课堂教学。本书接下来的第四至第六章便是对短语研究结果进行教学加工的实证性探索。

第4章
语料库辅助的商务英语短语教学实施总略

在第1至第3章介绍本研究背景、相关理论、核心概念和范例演示的基础上，本章转入更为系统的实证研究部分。主要从整体上阐述语料库短语理念和技术应用于广东外语外贸大学国际商务英语学院本科"综合商务英语"课程的教学改革，创新商务英语主题式教学的行动研究。具体内容包括支持教研行动的核心理念和三轮实施方案，也包括在实施过程中遇到的具体问题及其解决方案。

4.1 教研行动背景和目标

正如本书前言所述，教研者作为多年从事商务英语教学的教师，一方面深感传统"文本细读"结合"语法–翻译"教学模式的局限性；另一方面也观察到商务英语本科生短语意识和使用能力薄弱的问题。此外，教师自身缺乏对"语言的短语机制"的认识，也导致他们不知如何教短语（Howarth 1998：186）。

基于上述问题，教研者尝试在商务英语专业本科"综合商务英语"课程中引入语料库语言学的短语理论及其技术，实施语料库辅助的主题式教学。通过自建商务英语教学资源库，运用语料库检索工具以及主题词表、搭配词表、词丛表及索引行的提取和分析技术将多种形态的商务英语短语引入多个商务主题教学。从微观教学目标看，此次教研旨在提高大学生商务英语短语意识和能力，帮助其建构主题相关的商科基础知识，并同时提高其使用语料库工具和在线语料库平台进行自主学习的能力。从宏观教研目标看，它还试图通过教学实验创新将语料库理念与技术融入商务英语类课程的教学设计及评测方式，以资推广。

4.2 教研行动核心理念

　　运用语料库短语理念和技术辅助商务英语主题式教学的思路有以下两个核心理念的支持。

4.2.1　以内容为依托的主题式语言教学理念

　　从20世纪80年代兴起的以内容为依托的教学（Content-based Instruction，以下简称CBI）是一种将目标语言与主题内容有机融合的教学理念（Content and Language Integrated Learning，以下简称CLIL）。它为外语教学提供了新视角。其目的是让"学生通过第二语言获取信息内容并同时发展技能"（Brinton *et al.* 1989），其理据是基于认知科学和二语习得理论，即人类的智力活动对内容知识和过程媒介具双重重要性，故作为过程媒介的语言，包括其形式、功能和意义，均需在教学中与内容融为一体。

　　Met（1999）曾将CBI按内容和语言的权重细分为六种具体教学模式的连续体（见表4.1）。

表4.1　融合内容和语言的教学理念连续体（Met 1999：9-10）

A CONTINUUM OF CONTENT AND LANGUAGE INTEGRATION					
Content-Driven			Language-Driven		
Total Immersion	Partial Immersion	Sheltered Courses	Adjunct Model	Theme-Based Courses	Language classes with frequent use of content for language practice

　　如表4.1所示，这六种模式从左到右呈内容权重递减而语言权重递增排序，即完全浸泡式教学→部分浸泡式教学→保护式教学→专业课加语言教学辅助模式→主题式教学模式→利用内容进行语言操练。其中基于主题的语言课程较多应用于外语教学，因为它有利于最大限度地基于专业内容来传授语言技能，又可在提高语言运用能力的同时帮助学生获得学科

知识，提高学生在某一学科背景中运用外语的能力。这完全符合《高等
学校商务英语专业本科教学质量国家标准》（王立非、张斐瑞 2015）中商
务英语专业建设的复合型人才培养目标。国内学者曾对CBI的理论基础与
教学模式进行过论证（雷春林 2006；蔡基刚 2011，2013；毛亚英、陈莉
萍 2013），亦有将CBI应用中国背景下商务英语教学的可行性探讨（李丽
2010；孙有中、李莉文 2011）。其中有实证研究表明CBI模式在商务英语
听力和阅读方面能显著提高学生的语言水平及有效改善学生的学习态度
（李丽 2010），也有提倡在计算机辅助教学普及和慕课背景下不断完善CBI
在大学英语ESP教学的应用模式的研究（王守宏 *et al.* 2015）。近年来，有
基于语料库自身优势而将其作为教学工具与资源嵌入"内容+语言"的双
重目标教学的探讨（Rizzo & Perez 2015；Carloni 2015），然而，如何针对
不同类型的商务英语课程选择上述CBI教学理念连续体中阶段模式、如何
实施及如何评测教学效果等相关研究成果仍不多见。

我国目前的商务英语教学课程设置中既有语言技能型课程，又有商
务知识实践类课程。既有一般商务用途英语（English for General Business
Purposes），也有特殊商务用途英语（English for Specific Business English）。
在CBI教学模式中对外语知识能力和商科知识能力的权衡选择则要依据每
一门商务英语课程的教学目标来决定。例如"综合商务英语""商务英语
听说"及"商务英语写作"等专业核心语言课程就具有语言技能型和一般
商务用途英语的双重属性，既要突出语言知识教学和语言技能的训练，又
要关注商科基础知识的学习。其目标和属性与CBI主题式教学的目标与特
征不谋而合。所以，将主题式教学模式应用于专业核心语言课程具有理论
依据。

4.2.2　语料库语言学的教学加工理念

语料库语言学的"教学加工"（corpus pedagogic processing）是指引教
师和学生将大型语料库的语料、调查结果、乃至语料库技术转化为利于实
现日常语言教学目标的资源以及教学手段的加工过程（Widdowson 2003；
Braun 2005；Flowerdew 2008；何安平 2008）。这是一个必须有语言教师
和语料库研究者共同参与、反复沟通与合作的协调过程（mediation）。

语料库的教学加工至少涵盖三个层面。首先是实现"教学资源富集"
（Braun 2005：55），即建设教学语料库。它包括"整合教科书语料库、学
生语料库以及其他一切与教学内容相关的语料资源，或就某个领域、某门

学科而建立的专业话语语料库，甚至是围绕某个主题或专门话题建设的专题语料库，由此汇集成一个对师生开放的教学平台。教学语料库的规模不一定很大，但是其内容必须与该课程的教学大纲和日常教学目标密切相关；同时除了文字版本还有相对应的或配套的录音或视频等多模态版本"（何安平 2013b：119）。

第二个层面是将语料库技术作为一种现代教育手段经过教学加工走进课堂。现代计算机技术在处理巨量语料的过程中发现了丰富的多词单位现象，并且使这种现象变得可观察、可计量，甚至可预测，由此形成以频数驱动为特色的、基于语篇或特定语域话语自下而上的短语意义模式，从而以一种更为细致、透彻的语言媒介渗透到学科英语教学中。这一层面的教学加工还包括语料库的信息检索技术与互联网、多媒体等其他现代教育信息技术的整合使用。

第三个层面是将上述语料库资源和教学手段转化为师生所能够接受的教学形式。因为"任何一种教学手段如果不能以便捷的方式融入师生的正常教学轨道，都算不上教学创新"（Mauranen 2004：99）。把语料库对学科英语短语的研究成果经过教学加工转化为日常教学活动或评测活动是一个师生共同参与创设的过程。其中包括自建与日常教学目标相匹配的"微型文本"设计练习活动并辅以教学指令语等等。这也是本次教研的亮点之一。

目前国外已有高校如意大利Urbino大学（Carloni 2015），将语料库的教学加工融入了上述的CLIL教学模式中。其创设的语料库辅助CLIL教学平台不仅为多个学科的教师提供CLIL教学方法咨询服务，也同时建设学科CLIL教学语料库和互联网资源，提供专业核心词汇分层分析、学术英语短语教学、乃至课堂观察评价等指引。本项目则从语料库辅助商务英语短语教学切入CLIL教学。

"商务英语中的短语有稳定的搭配意义、较固定的语法结构限制和特定的语用环境，在学习和应用时快捷方便、准确流利，因此，基于短语的教学法有着许多其他教学法所没有的优势"（胡春雨 2011）。近年来国内学者（王立非、黄湘琪 2011；张立茵 2012；杜海紫 2013；王冬梅2009；石静 2012；Jing 2013；郭云云 2016）对于语料库技术应用于商务英语写作及口语教学等已有初步探索，但关于商务英语短语教学的研究成果仍不多见，其中有学者（胡春雨 2011，2012，2014b）曾探讨语料库应用于商务英语短语教学的理论依据和具体措施。本研究正是基于此类探索性和开创性研究，将基于短语的语料库辅助教学嵌入到商务英语主题式教学中，力图通过实证研究来检验这一新的教学模式能否提升学生对商英短语的意识和使用能力，并同时增长商科知识以及强化自主学习能力。期待形成可操作、可测评的教学模式加以推广。

4.3 教研行动实施方案

本次教研行动称为"语料库短语辅助的商英主题式教学改革"，旨在解决"综合商务英语"课程教学的两大问题：（1）如何帮助学生识别、理解和产出商务英语话语中既富含商务知识和信息又具有商务英语文体特征的多种形态短语；（2）如何评估语料库辅助的商务英语短语教学的有效性。采用的是教师行动研究的路径，即由任课教师就上述问题开展实证研究，目的不仅是描述和解释课堂，更重要的是引起课堂教学的变化和改进。行动研究是一个呈螺旋状循环上升的过程，可归纳为计划、实施、观察和反思四个步骤（王蔷 2002）：首先由教师通过对教学实践中的感受并意识到的问题设计一个有针对性的解决办法；然后付诸教学实践；接着调查并收集数据对教学效果进行评估；最后在分析和评价的基础上重新调整教研问题以继续下一轮的研究（王蔷 2002；McNiff 1988）。据此，本研究设置了以下总体方案（见表4.2）。

表4.2　行动研究总体步骤及内容描述

总体步骤	步骤内容	具体描述
计划	意识问题、提出问题	学生短语意识薄弱、短语能力匮乏、商科内容与语言分离、自主学习能力有限
实施	提出办法、实施方案	语料库辅助的商务英语短语教学； 三轮行动、六个商科主题、历时一个学年
观察	调查、收集数据、评估效果	通过课堂观察、课后作业、测试、学习者反思日志和调查问卷等方式，评测学生主题相关的商科知识的建构和重要商务语言使用能力的提升，及评估商务英语短语教学活动形式的有效性
反思	调整问题、推进下轮行动	明确小结本轮行动研究已解决、未解决和待解决之问题； 廓清下一轮行动研究可改进之处

4.3.1 教研思路

按照表4.2的行动步骤，教研者在商务英语专业本科二年级的"综合商务英语"课堂教学中首先导入语料库短语理念及相关语料库技术，然后将语料库辅助的短语教学嵌入六个商科主题（包括市场营销、社会保障、领导力、商业伦理、货币银行学和投资学）的单元教学中，共计三轮，为期一学年。在三轮教研行动中，教研者始终以主题词为切入点，再经过拓展形成多种形态的短语单位，运用主题词表、词丛表、搭配词表及索引行的提取和分析技术，设计一系列教学活动并实践于日常教学，旨在引导和敦促学生在"观察-假设-验证"的教学过程中提高学生的商务英语短语能力，特别是商务主题词的深度知识，同时帮助学生构建与专门话题相关的商科基础知识，并提升其自主学习能力。

这一教研思路依据于Sinclair（1991，2004）提出的"词汇语法"理论，即语言使用具有短语倾向性；大多数时候，词必须组合起来才能产生意义。而词语在语境中反复呈现的共选模式（pattern of co-selection among words）直接关联其语境意义（详见第一章1.5）。词的选择受制于它的周边词，或者说它与周边词存在着多个层面和多个意义的关系，正是这些关系决定了词或词组在语境中的真正意义（何安平，2013a）。例如，market一词在短语market segmentation（市场细分）中表示"潜在的买家的集合"；在短语Europe market中market则表示"产品或劳务交易的潜在的地域"；在market share中该词却表示"每年交易产品或劳务的总量"。可见，语言使用的这种短语倾向于引导人们将构建语言意义的最基本单位落实到词项（lexical item）而非单词（word）。Sinclair（2004）称其为"拓展意义单位"（extended unit of meaning）；它成为语料库视角下短语的多种形态之一。其余的短语形态还包括"搭配框架"（collocational framework）、"组织框架"（structural framework）、"型式语法单位"（pattern grammar）、"语义序列单位"（semantic sequence）、"词串"（lexical bundle）等等（何安平 2013a，b）。这些短语形态在本研究的商务英语教学资源库中有丰富的体现（详见第五章的具体案例）。

从语料库短语理念的视角切入商务英语的主题式教学，突破了以往专业词汇教学中仅关注单个词的专业性或半专业性词汇的局限。更重要的是，从关注专题的主题词入手，通过构建其在批量化专题语境中的意义模式，包括主题词拓展词丛、短语框架（phrase-frame，参见Fletcher 2007）等，既可以链接专业基础知识的核心概念，又可以掌握专业短语在真实语境中的规律性特征，从而实现CBI中专业知识和外语能力同步提升的教学目标。目前对某些专业词汇使用规律的语料库研究成果比较丰富（胡春雨2011，2012，2014b；Jing 2013），但对于如何从主题词和词丛推及专业概念知识的研究成果仅见于Rizzo & Perez（2015）；该研究基于通信工程学术话语语料库的主题词分析，以探讨将语料库主题词理念应用于CLIL的优势，但并未证实该路径的有效性。

　　本教研行动尝试将主题词及词丛应用于商务英语主题式教学，形成相对稳定的活动和测评形式。每个商科单元的主题教学思路依次为"主题听说热身""主题阅读分析"和"语言知识巩固"三个环节；每个环节均渗入基于语料库的多形态商务英语短语课堂活动形式，每个单元学生以独立、结对或小组合作的形式完成基于语料库的课后自主学习任务，在句酷批改网（http://www.pigai.org/）上提交单元反思日志，并参加效果评测。

4.3.2　教学对象

　　本研究的对象为广东外语外贸大学商务英语（国际金融）专业的51名二年级本科生（包括2014级的23名和2015级的28名）。他们之前已经接受过一年本科教育，已修过"综合商务英语（1）""综合商务英语（2）""商务英语听说"和"当代商业概论"等课程，入学前的高考英语单科成绩在129分到142分之间。

4.3.3　教学资源

　　"综合商务英语"课程的指定教材是《商务英语综合教程3》和《商务英语综合教程4》（高等教育出版社，2011）。教研者先将这两册单系列课本自建成电子版的教材语料库，后来加入国内外同类同水平的其他商务英语教材语料，如《体验商务英语》，《职场英语》等，建成101万词次的综合商务英语课程教材语料库（以下简称BTC-2教材总库，见以下表4.3）。同时还拓展至更为丰富的互联网语料资源，如每隔1年半就与维基百科同步更新的维基在线语料库（Wikipedia Corpus，https://corpus.byu.edu/wiki/）、拥有4.5亿词次的COCA在线语料库（https://corpus.byu.edu/coca/）、嵌入BNC的一亿词次的Sketch Engine for Language Learning（SkELL，http://skell.sketchengine.co.uk/run.cgi/skell）以及香港理工大学730万词次的Hong Kong Financial Service Corpus（HKFSC，http://rcpce.engl.polyu.
edu.hk/HKFSC/）等等。在进行语料库教学加工和教学实施时，主要使用
AntConc语料库检索分析工具。

表4.3　广东外语外贸大学国际商务英语学院综合商务英语课程教材
语料库（BTC-2）概览

名称	来源	大小
《商务英语综合教程》教材子库	《商务英语综合教程（1-4）册》，高等教育出版社，2011	39万词次
《商业概论》教材子库	*Business Essentials* (9th Edition), Pearson Publications, 2013	23万词次
《体验商务英语》教材子库	《体验商务英语》（*Market Leader*，3th Edition），高等教育出版社 & Pearson Publications，2012	33万词
《商务短语动词》子库	*Business Phrasal Verbs*，Athelstan Publications，2007	3.3万词
《职场英语》教材子库	*Intelligent Business*，外语教学与研究出版社 & Pearson Publications，2016	2.7万词
合计：101万词次		

　　表4.3中的BTC-2教材语料库既含有商科入门教材《商业概论》，也有
融合商科重要概念与语言技能的商务英语类教材，如《商务英语综合教
程》、《体验商务英语》和《职场英语》，还有基于语料库编写、以搭配教
学为纲的《商务短语动词》（*Business Phrasal Verbs*）。它们在内容上相互
补充，基本涵盖了基础商务知识的重要话题。在建库过程中，保留了教材
中正文部分的文字（删除首页、前言、目录、正文图片、索引和尾页等），
并对教学指令语用"[ ]"进行标注。

4.4 教研行动实施过程

　　本节依据总体方案的4大步骤（见表4.2）报告三轮教研行动的实施
概貌。

4.4.1　发现和诊断问题

教研者凭借在教学过程中感觉和意识到传统"文本细读结合语法－翻译教学"教学模式中学生在商务英语短语输入和输出上存在诸多问题后，先对学生掌握商英短语的现状进行调查。方式是依据Nelson（2000）从语义范畴基于词频对商务英语主题词所作的五个分类框架，即商务活动中的人（people in business）、商务活动（business activities）、商务行为（business action）、商务描述（business description）、商务事件与实体（business events and entities），从BCT-2教材总库中提取并遴选每类2个、共计10个高频商务英语主题词（即为manager、employee、business、market、describe、access、raise、financial、sale、ownership），然后借鉴Paribakht & Wesche（1993）的词汇知识量表VKS设计"商务主题词知识量表"，考查学生对这10个词的知识层次：1 没见过、不认知；2 见过，但不知词义；3 见过，语义可能是（填写英文近义词或中文翻译）；4 认识，语义肯定是（填写英文近义词或中文翻译）；5 我能在商务语境/情境中使用这个词组成搭配结构（写短语）。其中，3、4和5三个层次可多选。详见附录3。

结果表明，100%的学生（2014级共23人）自述对这10个词的知识层级在3级以上；其中63.64%的学生（14人）自述为4级，即对这10个词均认识并能准确写出中文对应词或英文近义词；但仅有4.35%（3人）的学生能准确写出这10个词在商务语境中的任一个搭配结构；能准确写出7个目标词搭配结构的学生占比仅为56.52%（13人）。

上述诊断结果大致印证了之前（见本章4.1）提到的教学问题，即学生能识别这些商务英语高频主题词，但对其在商务语境中的搭配意义掌握不多，短语意识和能力薄弱。通过课堂师生交流及对有代表性学生（自述层级整体较低的学生）的访谈，教师得知，受访学生意识到自身短语意识的缺乏，且陈述原因为：以往的语言教学中并没有刻意关注、理解和使用商务英语短语；课外主要通过查证搜索引擎（如百度、爱问等）或是电子词典（如有道、金山词霸等）来了解词汇意义，此外无其他方式来进行自主学习。

4.4.2　导入语料库理念和工具

在第一轮教研行动启动前，教研者对学生进行教研理念导入和语料库工具实操训练。内容包括介绍语料库短语教学理念、教学大纲要求及课堂活动模式。例如，让学生了解词汇教学的组织原则是搭配，而非单个词汇或者语法规则。又如，每个单元的任务流程是：基于任务的学生课前发现式自主学习（discovery）→课堂主题听说读写活动的语言产出操练（production）→学生基于任务的个人或小组展示（presentation）。课堂进行的语料库辅助的商务英语短语教学活动的流程是"观察–假设–验证"，而不是"讲解–操练–复用"。此外，教师还教授了语料库检索分析工具AntConc、COCA在线语料库、维基在线语料库和句酷批改网的基本使用技巧。前三者供学生进行商务英语短语自主学习所用，句酷批改网则是供学生提交习作以备建学生习作语料库和提交学习者反思日志以作教学反馈。

4.4.3 第一轮教研行动概述

在该轮教研中，教研者在对教学问题调查诊断的基础上（见本章4.4.1）提出以下假设：

假设1：基于短语的语料库辅助的商务英语主题式教学短期内能促进学生的短语意识和能力的提升，及与主题相关的商科知识的建构。

假设2：基于短语的语料库辅助的商务英语主题式教学能提高学生的自主学习能力。

基于以上假设，教研者就"市场营销（marketing）"与"社会保障（social security）"两个主题单元的教学设计并实施了第一轮教研行动方案（见表4.4）。

表4.4 第一轮教研行动方案

主题／学时	教学内容、活动形式及预期目标
市场营销 共18学时	环节一：主题听说热身
	1）基于词丛的填词和口语活动：提升短语意识、建构主题知识框架 2）术语辨析：明晰主题相关的商务英语短语术语内涵

续表

主题 / 学时	教学内容、活动形式及预期目标
市场营销 共18学时	环节二：主题阅读分析 主题精读文选"中国超市呈现出口机遇"，在大意理解、结构分析、难点化解三步教学活动中嵌入： 1）基于选文主题词拓展词丛的语篇图示教学：提升短语意识和能力、理解语篇大意和结构 2）基于选文主题词的搭配和类连接分析的师生问答：提升短语意识、习得主题词深度知识 3）基于选文主题词索引行的词语填空与短语翻译练习：习得主题词深度知识
	环节三：语言知识巩固 1）基于重点短语的句子释义（paraphrase）练习：复习巩固商务英语短语 2）学生基于语料库的自主学习成果展示：提升使用语料库工具进行自主学习的能力
社会保障 共18学时	环节一：主题听说热身 1）嵌入主题词和主题词拓展词丛的填词和口语活动：提升短语意识、建构主题知识框架 2）基于主题词和主题词拓展词丛的语篇听力填空：提升短语意识、丰富次话题知识
	环节二：主题阅读分析 两篇精读选文"社会保障体系不再适用了吗？"和"社会福利"，在大意理解、结构分析、难点化解三步教学活动中嵌入： 1）基于选文主题词的搭配和类连接分析的师生问答：提升短语意识、习得主题词深度知识 2）基于选文中半技术性词汇的索引行对比分析：建构次话题知识、习得词汇深度知识
	环节三：语言知识巩固 1）学生课外阅读选文"社会保障体系的潜在问题"的自主学习成果小组汇报：分享语篇大意、难点点评、短语学习等成果和心得 2）学生展示维基百科主题微型语料库自主学习成果：通过在线建虚拟专题微型语料库并提取搭配结构进行展示分享

课堂观察： 学生整体上对本轮教学持接受态度，可能是由于教学实验前接受了短语教学理念的导入。但是，在第一个环节，即"主题听说热身"中学生发言不踊跃，可能与商科知识的匮乏或语言与学科知识脱节有关。在第二个环节，即嵌入"主题阅读分析"的语料库辅助多形态短语练习中学生回答踊跃，部分同学甚至能主动提出问题。在第三个环节，即"语言知识巩固"中，学生对于教师提前布置的自主学习任务反映不够积极，有的甚至对课后自主学习（如"通过COCA通用语料库进行主题词搭配学习和词汇辨析"）显示出抵触情绪。而当有学生在堂上展示基于维基百科建构的社会保障专题微型语料库自主学习成果时，其他学生都能聚精会神地听取汇报，包括之前有抵触情绪的学生。

教学反馈： 教研者在阅读第一轮学生反思日志时，发现的积极反馈包括：（1）学生大多意识到商英短语不仅仅是商务术语，更重要的、且更难以习得的可能是商务搭配结构的深度学习，而这一点过去常被忽视；（2）不少学生同时意识到自己欠缺商务知识；（3）绝大部分学生认为通过语料库辅助的方法学习商务英语短语是个有趣、新鲜的途径，愿意继续。消极反馈包括：（1）大部分学生认为所使用的《商务英语综合教程》教材子库中的语例不够充分，不易归纳词语使用典型型式，且长句和难词很多；（2）到COCA在线语料库检索费时费力，不如百度百科来得快和有效；（3）半数以上的学生对于布置的自主学习任务有抵触（包括撰写学习者反思日志）。

同时教研者通过对有代表性的学生访谈还了解到以上负面反馈的主要原因有二：一是在过去的教学中没有养成对定期反思学习的习惯；二是对语言学习中出现的问题已经习惯通过社会网络引擎搜索直接获得答案，这样来得便捷，不用"费神"。

此外，教研者还通过"商务英语短语教学调查问卷"（附录6，分析详见本书第六章6.1.2）收集并分析学生对于短语意识和能力及自主学习能力提升的自我认识的数据，结合学生在该轮教研行动始末进行的"商务英语短语能力前测"（附录4，分析详见本书第六章6.1.1）和"商务英语短语能力后测"（附录5，分析详见第六章6.1.1）中的成绩对此分析，再次印证从反思日志中得到的反馈。

阶段性小结： 综合以上教学反馈，教研者认为经过第一轮教研行动，大部分学生的短语意识有一定程度的提高，表现为能在各种学习场合有意识关注到单个词的语境来习得和理解短语，但是，问题有二：（1）单元主题教学伊始，学生使用语料库提取的主题词和词丛进行口述建构主题知识这一活动对学生而言有难度：学生尚未能有效地使用短语；对教师而言，点评时对主题相关的学科知识广度和深度要求较高，且课堂讲解的时间不易控制，太长会空洞乏味，太短无法陈述清楚。（2）学生不认为商科知识有明显提升，说明短语意识提升与学科知识学习依旧脱节，原教学设计的商科知识与语言能力同步提升这一目标未能完全实现。

4.4.4　第二轮教研行动概述

通过第一轮教研行动尝试，教研者重新调整研究问题如下：

问题1：如何降低第一环节中教学活动的难度使得学生更加积极有效地参与？

问题2：如何改进课堂活动促使学生提升短语能力的同时构建主题相关的商科知识？

问题3：如何丰富任务类型，促使学生更有机会输出/应用短语？

基于上述问题，教研者就"商业伦理（business ethics）"与"领导力（leadership）"两个主题单元设计并实施了第二轮教研行动方案（见表4.5）。

表4.5　第二轮教研行动方案

主题 / 学时	教学内容、活动形式及预期目标
商业伦理 共18学时	学生通过自由词汇联想构建"商业伦理"主题概念图：构建专题知识框架
	第一环节：主题听说热身
	1）基于主题词和主题词拓展词丛的专题语篇听力问答及口头概述：构建专题语篇基本信息及学习相关短语 2）基于核心主题词ethics的搭配词表分析的师生问答：习得短语搭配结构、细化主题知识
	第二环节：主题阅读分析
	在精读选文"商业伦理反思"的大意理解、结构分析、难点化解三步教学活动中嵌入： 聚焦选文主题词索引行分析的师生问答：关注主题词的语境语义，提升短语意识

续表

主题 / 学时	教学内容、活动形式及预期目标
商业伦理 共18学时	第三环节：语言+学科知识巩固 1）基于主题词搭配的词语游戏——构词游戏、术语界定（知识抢答）：学习并巩固主题相关的重要概念 2）阅读选文"BP污染事件之评论与反思"案例读后写作：提升专题语境下使用商务英语短语的能力
领导力 共18学时	学生通过自由词汇联想构建"领导力"主题概念图：构建主题知识框架
	第一环节：主题听说热身
	1）基于主题词拓展词丛的专题语篇听力问答及知识拓展：构建专题语篇重要信息及学习相关短语 2）基于核心主题词leadership的搭配词表分析的师生问答：习得短语搭配结构、细化主题知识
	第二环节：主题阅读分析
	在精读选文"诠释领导力"大意理解、结构分析、难点化解三步教学活动中嵌入： 1）基于选文商务英语短语术语的学生自主学习展示：习得重要商务概念的内涵 2）基于选文组织框架类短语形态的语料库教学加工：关注商务文体写作风格 3）基于选文中半技术性词汇的索引行分析：深度习得商务英语词汇 4）基于选文中的主题词索引行分析：提升短语意识、习得主题词深度知识
	第三环节：语言+学科知识巩固与应用
	1）基于关键术语的连线练习（知识抢答）：巩固主题词短语、复习该主题的重要概念 2）主题电影观后作文"乔布斯的企业家精神"：提升在专题语境下使用商务英语短语的能力

此轮方案的改进有三：（1）在第一环节开始前，学生先以书面方式构建主题概念图，再由教师演示该专题主题词和主题词拓展词丛，并以听力语篇作为教学输入支架，然后才让学生做口头输出，目的是降低第一环节教学活动的难度。（2）此方案中增加学生口头和笔语输出的任务形式（口

头概述、主题写作等），目的是增加学生应用短语的机会。（3）引入了具有简易阅读界面的SkELL的网络在线检索代替COCA在线，同时将原来的23万词次《商业概论》教材子库拓展至101万词次的BTC-2综合商务英语课程教材语料库。

课堂观察： 学生对第一环节前的"基于自由词汇联想的主题概念构图"活动饶有兴趣，因为均有词/短语可写，可见大脑中已有的主题词和主题词拓展词丛正被初步唤醒。在第一个环节的听说系列活动中，通过"听力理解问答"，学生对该专题的基础知识有初步认识，故在后续基于主题词/词丛进行口头概述、以及通过观察主题词搭配词表截图来细化主题知识时，学生的发言更为踊跃。第二个环节较上一轮增补了短语形式（如意义迁移单位、组织框架和搭配框架等），增加了对术语的自主学习展示和主题词拓展意义单位分析的活动形式，学生均回应积极，尤其在在术语自主学习展示活动时热情极高。第三个环节中增加的语言及学科知识竞赛气氛更热烈，争先抢答。

教学反馈：（1）学生对课前进行的主题概念构图和课末的主题写作任务持肯定态度，认为趣味性强且有利于商科知识的学习和应用；（2）学生认为语料库辅助的词项训练有助于词汇深度学习：他们比以前更关注不同词汇在商务语境中的搭配知识；（3）有学生对AntConc软件和SkELL在线语料库资源表现出认可和推崇；（4）少数学生从课始的主题概念构图与课末的主题写作这两项活动中认识到自己在知识与语言两方面的不足。

此外，教研者对比学生在第二轮行动研究始末的"商务概念词项测试"的结果（试题见附录7和8），发现学生对40个关键商务词项在认知和产出层面的能力均有显著提升（详见第六章6.2.1）。与此同时，教研者还邀请了语料库辅助教学专家何安平以观察者身份参与课堂教学，并在课后与个别学生交谈。专家一方面肯定语料库辅助商务英语短语教学的改革创新，另一方面提出三个问题：一是如何在单元教学三个环节中贯穿"主题引领"的理念？二是语料库理念与技术如何更有效地融合学科内容与语言教学？三是在第二个环节的短语练习活动中如何引导学生通过关注词语在使用语境中的共选特征来归纳其意义模式（meaningful pattern）？为此她建议：（1）可尝试专题微型语料库（topic-based mini-corpus）提取的主题词及主题词拓展词丛进行语义范畴分类，从而构建该主题的主要内容与核心知识，并将此纳入课堂活动；（2）教师对学生答案作点评时可侧重其语言表达的优点和思维组织方面的亮点。

　　阶段性小结：综合以上源自课堂观察、反思日志和专家观课的三角论证，教研者认为第二轮教研行动有效性表现在：（1）新增的主题概念构图使学生在第一环节"主题听说热身"中对基于重要短语构建学科知识的敏感意识明显提升；（2）通过展示专题主题词的搭配词表及索引行，学生能更为有效地建构并细化学科知识并习得表达知识的重要语言形式；（3）主概念构图和主题写作使学生明晰了重要短语与商科概念间的关联并促进其在作文中的应用。与此同时，教研者也面临了更为具体的新问题：如何测知学生的商科知识与短语能力均得到提升？如何收集短语产出能力提升的表征？

4.4.5　第三轮教研行动概述

　　通过第二轮教研行动，教研者再次重构以下两个研究问题，作为第三轮教研行动之起点：

　　问题1：如何在活动设计中更加有机地融入商务主题知识与商务英语短语的学习？

　　问题2：如何更全面地评估学生学科知识与语言知识的同步提升？

　　基于上述新问题，教研者就"货币银行学"（money and banking）与"投资"（investment）两个主题单元的教学设计并实施了第三轮教研行动方案（见表4.6）。

表4.6　第三轮教研行动方案

主题 / 学时	教学内容、活动形式及预期目标
货币银行 共18学时	课前学生通过自由词汇联想预构"货币银行学"专题的核心概念图：初建专题基本知识框架
	课前学生预写题为"如何花钱？存款还是买房？"的作文：激活已有的相关专题知识和语言知识
	第一环节：主题听说热身
	1）基于听力语篇主题词和短语的听力理解问答和口头复述：建立主题性词语与语言主旨内容的关联 2）基于主题词拓展词丛和语篇型词丛的听力理解问答和口头复述：融合主题知识与语篇结构教学 3）基于主题词拓展词丛分类和命题构建的专题知识板块图描述：构建专题核心知识框架

续表

主题 / 学时	教学内容、活动形式及预期目标
货币银行 共18学时	**第二环节：主题阅读分析** 在精读选文"通胀、银行业及经济增长"大意理解、结构分析、难点化解三步教学活动中嵌入： 1）基于选文关键术语的学生自主学习展示：透过关键术语了解专题基础知识 2）基于选文主题词拓展词丛的阅读图示教学：提升短语意识、把握文章主旨 3）基于选文主题词的拓展意义单位分析：提升短语意识、习得主题词深度知识 **第三环节：语言+学科知识巩固与应用** 1）高频主题词单项选择词汇练习：巩固主题词和商科核心概念的关联 2）高频主题词拓展词丛单项选择练习、中国银行体系基础知识短语填空练习（知识抢答）：巩固商务英语短语及相关的专题知识 学生基于所学的主题词及主题词拓展词丛再次构建"货币银行学"专题的核心概念图：重构该专题的基本知识框架 学生再次撰写同题作文"如何花钱？存款还是买房？"：提升专题知识和语言知识的产出能力
投资学 共18学时	课前学生通过自由词汇联想预构"投资学"主题概念图：初建专题基本知识框架 课前学生观看相关专题的新闻视频后预写题为"投资中国房市是否理性？"的作文：激活已有的相关专题知识和语言知识 **第一环节：主题听说热身** 1）基于主题词和短语的语篇听力理解问答和口头复述：建立主题性词语与语篇主旨内容的关联 2）基于主题词拓展词丛和语篇型词丛的听力理解问答和口头复述：融合主题知识与语篇结构教学 3）基于主题词拓展词丛分类和命题构建的专题知识板块图描述：构建专题核心知识框架

续表

主题/学时	教学内容、活动形式及预期目标
投资学 共18学时	第二环节：主题阅读分析
	在精读选文"投资概要"大意理解、结构分析、难点化解三步教学活动中嵌入： 1）基于选文关键术语的学生自主学习展示：透过关键术语了解专题基础知识 2）基于选文主题词的拓展意义单位分析：提升短语意识、习得主题词深度知识 3）基于选文中半技术性词汇的拓展意义单位分析：提升短语意识、习得半技术性词汇深度知识 4）基于选文中的商务短语动词的拓展意义单位分析：提升短语意识、习得短语动词深度知识
	第三环节：语言+学科知识巩固与应用
	1）债券主题对话连线、基于主题词和短语填词（知识抢答）：巩固专题核心概念 2）投资语篇读后系列语言活动（给定首字母填词、基金可投资性分析是非判断、术语界定连线、词语/短语填空）：巩固短语和学科知识的关联
	学生基于所学的主题词及主题词拓展词丛再次构建"投资学"主概念图：重构该专题的基本知识框架
	学生再次撰写同题作文"投资中国房市是否理性？"：提升专题知识和语言知识的产出能力

此轮方案的改进有二：（1）首先由教师自建了上述两个专题微型语料库并提取主题词与主题词丛，然后由师生分别对此进行语义范畴分类，并建构该话题的商科知识框架，并融入到听说和读写活动，以促进学生对其表达的重要商科概念的理解和产出；（2）在主题单元教学始末，均要求学生基于自由词汇联想构建主题概念图和同题主题写作，以此对比学生在知识掌握和语言提升上的变化。

课堂观察：学生在课堂上对三个环节的教学活动均反应积极。

教学反馈：学生的反思日志对本轮的语料库短语嵌入商务英语主题式教学的模式和评估手段给予一致的正面评价。前后构建的主题概念图和前后同题作文的对比分析显示其知识体系及主题词拓展词丛表述能力也均有明显提升（详见第六章6.3）。语料库学教学专家现场观察数节课之后也认为，此轮教学活动中语料库短语理念体现明显，学生能熟练运用语料库信息技术，师生之间的互动形式丰富多样。

4.5 小结

本章阐述的语料库辅助商务英语短语教学行动研究持续了一个学年，内容覆盖六个商科主题的英语教学，教学方案历经三轮调整更新呈滚动式发展，语料库短语理念辅助商务英语主题式教学的教学实验模式日臻成熟。表现为：

（1）从最初教研仅关注教师认为重要的商务英语短语进行语料库辅助教学，发展到后来运用语料库主题词理念和建设教学微型语料库进行专门话题的主题词和主题词拓展词丛的提取和语义范畴分类，以构建专题核心知识框架及开展短语知识深度学习；

（2）商务英语教学资源库逐步扩大。从23万词次的单部教材子库拓展至101词次的覆盖国内外多部/套综合商务英语课程教材语料库BTC-2，从单一教材库发展为聚焦各个主题的分列式子库；

（3）语料库辅助教学的技术手段日渐丰富。从开始的索引行展示，提升至目标词的搭配词表提取、主题听力和阅读语篇的主题词和主题词拓展词丛提取和分析等；

（4）学生短语能力和专业知识认知的评估方式也越来越深入和细致化。从开始仅基于数量有限的主题词的短语知识测试和较为主观的调查问卷的学生自述反馈，到后来开发兼测知识与语言的商务概念词项测试；再发展到对比学生前后构建的主题概念图、前后产出的主题写作文本、以及学习者反思日志语料。

综合三轮教研行动收集的来自师生和独立观察者多方的反馈信息，以及对学生的主题概念图、主题作文及反思日志的分析结果均表明，本次教改行动研究已经基本达到预期目标，在一定程度上化解了研究初始要解决的问题。具体的教学案例展示和教学效果分析见第5章和第6章。

第5章
语料库辅助的商务英语短语教学案例

本章展示教研者运用语料库短语理念和技术于商英主题式教学的实施案例[1]。通过陈述每个教学案例的教学资源（包括语料来源、检索工具及教学加工）、活动展示（包括实施步骤、教学指令和参考答案）、设计说明（包括教学目的和语料库辅助教学思路）和案例述评（包括语料库短语形态和分析技术在该案例中的使用和目的）。展示的案例主要实施于"主题听说热身"和"主题阅读分析"这两大教学环节，其中各案例与第四章行动方案实施的关系见表5.1。

表5.1　本章案例与第4章教学方案的对应表

类别	名称	对应		
		教学主题	教学环节	行动方案
5.1 语料库辅助的语篇内容和主题知识教学案例	5.1.1主题词及词丛辅助听力文本大意预测与复述	货币银行学	第一个环节：主题听说热身	第三轮
	5.1.2主题词拓展词丛和语篇型词丛辅助主题知识和语篇结构教学			
	5.1.3主题词拓展词丛分类辅助专题核心知识构建			

---

1 本章部分案例在实施之后作局部修改。

续表

类别	名称	对应		
		教学主题	教学环节	行动方案
	5.1.4 主题词辅助语篇深度阅读教学	市场营销		第一轮
5.2 语料库辅助的商务学术语言深度教学案例	5.2.1 基于短语结构N+that（clause）的学术文体教学	社会保障	第二个环节：主题阅读分析	第一轮
	5.2.2基于半技术性词汇premium的跨体裁对比教学	商业伦理		第二轮
	5.2.3商务英语高频短语动词DEAL with的深度知识教学	投资学		第三轮

5.1 语料库辅助的语篇内容和主题知识教学案例

本节前三个案例均选自"货币银行学（Money and Banking）"单元主题式教学（见第四章4.4.5）的第一个环节"主题听说热身"。每一例在任务难度和预期效果上都较之前例有拓展和提升。第四个案例则选自"市场营销（marketing）"单元的第二个环节"主题阅读分析"（见第4章4.4.3）。

5.1.1　主题词及词丛辅助听力文本大意预测和复述

语料加工：

本案例基于网络听力语篇[1]"What Is Money and What Are Its Functions"的文字版和音频版进行语料库教学加工。首先，教师将下载的听力文本转换为579词次的微型文本（以下简称"微本"），取名money.txt（见附录9）作为教学目标语料，并以27,921词次的英语儿童文学作品《爱丽丝仙境漫游记》作为参照语料[2]（以下简称Alice.txt），使

---

[1] 选自"大耳朵英语"网站的试听材料，详见http://www.bigear.cn/res-2276-7777700134664.html。

[2] 选Alice.txt作为参照语料是因为它的总词量要比目标语料money.txt大5倍以上，且话题内容不一致，可更有效凸显目标语料的主题词。

用网络免费语料库检索工具AntConc生成主题词表（见图5.1），经词形还原（lemmatization）处理后遴选出36个实义词类的主题词。听力语篇的36个实义词类主题词按频次降序排列分别为money，value，standard，exchange，serve，payment，medium，wants，store，measure，item，functions，deferred，services，purchasing，power，meat，future，converted，barter，accepted，vacation，unit，sells，seller，price，pay，level，inconvenience，goods，dollars，costs，car，buy，baker，assets。同时提取money.txt的2-4字词丛，截取频数为3次及以上，且表意完整的词丛[1]共6个，按首字母排序分别为generally accepted，medium of exchange，purchasing power，standard of deferred payment，standard of value，store of value。

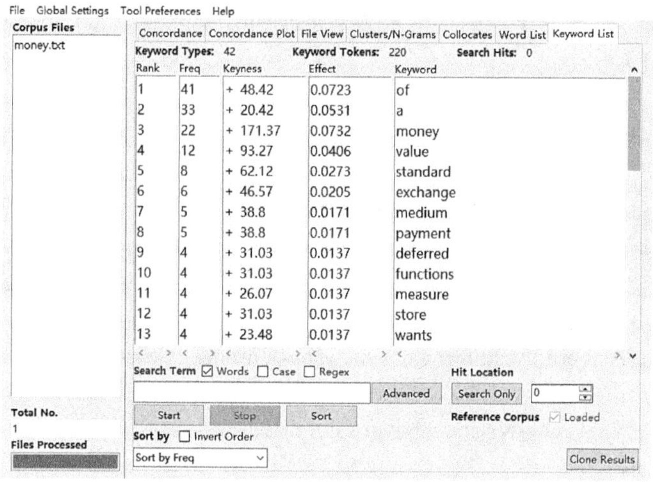

图5.1　money.txt的主题词表截图

教学实施：

步骤1： 教师在不提示听力语篇标题的情况下，展示AntConC界面下微本主题词表（见图5.1）及最高频实义词类的主题词money在微本的分布图（见图5.2），要求学生关注图中的实义词，结合之前修过的"当代商业概论"课程和正在学习的并列课程"货币银行学"来推测该听力语篇的主题与内容大意。

1　此处"表意完整的词丛"指内含N+N，ADJ+N，N and N，N of N，V+N等形式结构且能表达相对完整语义（如standard of deferred payment相较于deferred payment更为完整）的词丛，下同。

```
Plot: 1    FILE: money.txt
12  3    45 6 7    8          9 10112        13      14 115  17   18  1920 21      22
┌─┬────┬──┬─┬─┬──┬──────────┬──────┬─────────┬─┬─┬───┬────┬──┬┬──┬───────────┐       Hits: 22
│ │    │  │ │ │  │          │      │         │ │ │   │    │  ││  │           │       Chars: 3237
└─┴────┴──┴─┴─┴──┴──────────┴──────┴─────────┴─┴─┴───┴────┴──┴┴──┴───────────┘
```

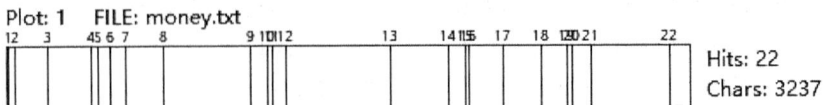

图5.2　主题词money在money.txt中的分布图

步骤2：教师在听取学生的答案之后，出示之前备好微本实义词类主题词表（见表5.2），指引学生将实义词类主题词作语义范畴归类。例如money，value等归入"货币描述"类，内含钱、价值等相关概念；standard，exchange，medium，payment，measure等归入"货币功能"类，内含标准、交换、媒介、支付、衡量等相关概念。

步骤3：学生在预测了语篇大意之后开始听录音，之后回答3个问题（见图5.3）。

Listening and speaking 1

What is money and what are its function?

Step 1: reading comprehension questions

● What are the four major functions of money? (Major idea)

● What is barter and what are the disadvantages of it? (Details)

● Can you show an example of deferred payment with money's role in it? As for this function, can you describe a very important constraint on money?
(Major specifics; RESTATEMENT/PARAPHRASE)

图5.3　听力理解问答

设计说明：

图5.3的问题1指向语篇的主话题，即货币四大主要功能。之前热身活动中接触过的主题词可帮助学生边听边速记表达四大功能的短语，如medium of exchange，standard of value，standard of deferred payment以及store of value。问题2和3分别指向货币四大功能的其中两个："交换媒

介（medium of exchange）"和"赊账延期支付标准（standard of deferred payment）"的具体内容。前者是通过比较"易货交易（barter）"来阐释此功能的涵义和优势；后者则通过贷款买车的案例来说明作为赊账延期支付手段的有效性会受到"物价水平"及"货币购买力"的制约。属于次话题层面的内容细听。

步骤4：在廓清语篇的主话题和次话题的内容之后，教师展示依据之前备好的主题词与高频2-4字词丛（见本小节"语料加工"部分）整合成表述主/次话题的关键性语言资源（见图5.4），要求学生使用这些主题词语口头复述"货币及其功能"这一语篇的大意。复述中要求涉及货币的定义及其四个功能，包括（1）交换媒介（medium of exchange）；（2）价值标准（standard of value）；（3）赊账延期支付标准（standard of deferred payment）；（4）价值储存（store of value）。

Listening and speaking 1

Step 2: oral summary

Definition: measure, value

Four major functions:

1. medium of exchange
   generally accepted, barter, buyer, seller, want, baker, meat, payment, purchase

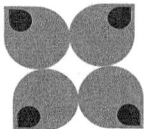

2. standard of value
   unit, measure, value, dollar, items, good, services, vacation

3. standard of deferred payment
   future, car, purchasing power, price, level

4. store of value
   converted, goods and services, inconvenience, cost, assets, generally accepted, medium of exchange

图5.4　基于主题词和词丛的口头复述任务设计

案例述评：

该案例依据语料库视角下的主题词能够揭示语篇的"主旨内容"这一主要功能（Scott & Tribble 2006：55-56），利用听力语篇"货币及其功能"中的实义词类的主题词及表意完整的高频词丛辅助学生把握语篇大意。其中步骤1是听前基于主题词"热身"。步骤2是引导学生通过对实义词类主题词进行语义归类以作内容大意预测。步骤3让学生在听的过程中验证之前的预测，同时使用主题词和高频词丛回答问题。步骤4是让学生通过口头复述中再次熟悉与语篇主题相关的关键性词语。这种从语篇主题词和高频词丛入手的思路可为每一步的活动实施提供教学支架。教师课前备好的主题词表和高频词丛表是支撑语篇重要内容和结构的关键性语言资源，它们不仅是该语篇的重要意义表述单位，同时也是学生在表述该话题时应知应会的词汇知识。学生在先听后说的四步活动中反复接触主题词和高频词丛，可从提升意识到促成使用两个层面来推进对语篇主题知识的理解和语言表述。

5.1.2 主题词拓展词丛和语篇型词丛辅助主题知识和语篇结构教学

语料加工：

本案例基于加拿大艺术家Paul Grignon在2006-2011年导演的金融记录片《钱就是债》（*Money as Debt*）三部曲之一的部分视频和录音文本进行教学加工。该作品展示的是现代银行体系及货币作为债务的本质，通过政府、企业和家庭惊人的负债来反映货币所体现的新形式"奴隶制"。教研者节选其中的第一和二章在堂上展示（以下简称视频1和视频2）。前者通过图片和画外音讲述货币创造的本质是通过信贷关系；后者则用一个通俗易懂的"金匠的故事"形象演绎现代银行体系的起源。

首先，教师将下载的两段视频脚本转换为1, 326词次的微型文本debt. txt（见附录10）作为目标语料，并以27, 921词次的《爱丽丝漫游记》作为参照语料，生成主题词表。从主题词表中选关键值最高的18个实义词，进行词形还原后制成一批检索项，分别为gold|money|goldsmith|depositor*|banker*|bank*|interest|claim*|vault|loan*|amount|borrower|coin*|credit|demand|banking|*check|create*|income|mint|silver|value。将检索词表整体导入AntConc的Clusters/N-Grams界面的高级检索中，提取含有这些主题词的2-4字词丛（结果见下图5.5）。从中遴选出表意完整的，如含"N+N""N *of* N""N *and* N""ADJ+NP""N+V"和"V+N"结构的主题词拓展词丛，共计16个。按照在语篇中出现顺序排列如下：gold and silver, casting coins, vault rental business, claim check, paper money, banks lend out, a low interest rate, at a higher interest, difference cover, cost of operation, remove their gold, silver to redeem, run on the bank, fictional loan money, central bank, emergency infusions of gold。

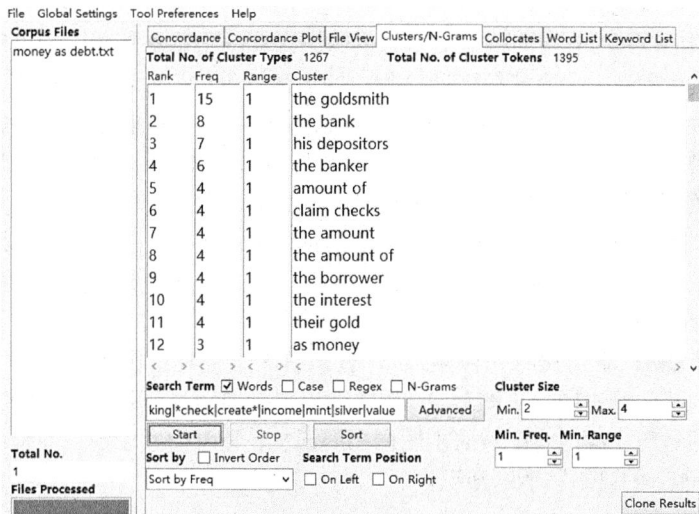

图5.5　由主题词拓展的2-4字词丛截图

教学实施：

　　步骤1：教师先展示图5.6的三个听力理解问题以及之前备好的主题词拓展词丛（见本小节"语料加工"部分），然后播放视频1，要求学生带着问题视听，并根据主题词拓展词丛的提示回答这三个问题。

Listening and speaking 2

Money as Debt

Step 1: Listening comprehension

Watch **Chapter 1 Introduction** in voiceover answer the following questions.

1. Who produced money and who created it?

2. How is money created?

3. Can you predict about theme of the simple story in Chapter 2?

图5.6　视听理解问答

设计说明：

图5.6的设问1指向视频的主旨内容，内含两个基本概念：货币印制发行和货币创造。前者指铸造印刷货币的主体铸币厂；后者指银行等金融机构的货币创造行为。设问2指向货币创造的机制，即商业银行或金融机构通过增加商业银行贷款而使经济体内流通货币量扩大。设问3要求学生根据视频1末尾的承上接下短语预测视频2的大致内容。

步骤2：教师确认学生了解了视频1的主要内容后，引导学生再回看主题词拓展词丛，教师解释其中cast，vault，redeem等生词，然后播放视频2"金匠的故事"。

步骤3：学生视听完视频2后，教师引导学生观察视频内容与主题词拓展词丛的配对图（见图5.7）。图的上半部是视频2故事内容发展的图示；下半部是与视频内容配对的主题词拓展词丛，请学生基于视频在脑中构建"货币创造的机制"话题知识。

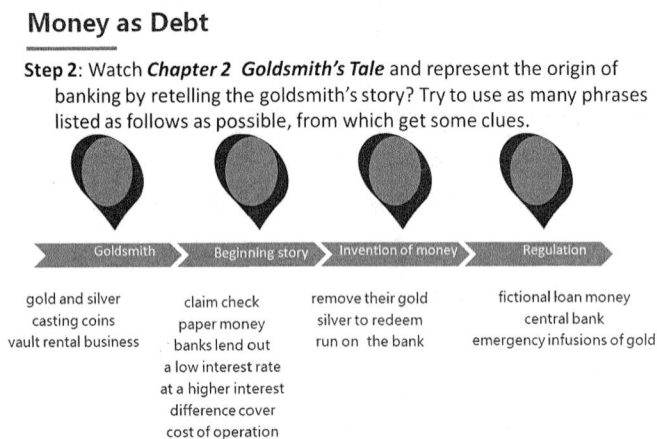

Money as Debt

Step 2: Watch *Chapter 2 Goldsmith's Tale* and represent the origin of banking by retelling the goldsmith's story? Try to use as many phrases listed as follows as possible, from which get some clues.

Goldsmith	Beginning story	Invention of money	Regulation
gold and silver casting coins vault rental business	claim check paper money banks lend out a low interest rate at a higher interest difference cover cost of operation	remove their gold silver to redeem run on the bank	fictional loan money central bank emergency infusions of gold

图5.7　主题词拓展词丛与视频内容的配对图

步骤4：教师进一步出示下图5.8，内含从debt.txt提取的叙事衔接类语言资源，主要是表示"过渡"的单词以及表示"过渡"和"框架"的语篇型词丛，详见本书第二章2.5小节）。包括时间与顺序（time and sequence）和让步与比较（comparison and concession）的表达方式等。要求学生借助这些词语，基于步骤3中已构建的内容框架复述"金匠的故事"。教师在必要时做内容提示。

Money as Debt

Step 2: At same time, you may use the following language resources on time and sequence and comparison and concession to connect events in your story.

Time and sequence	Comparison and concession
Once upon various time	Despite
Later	Contrary to
Soon	Rather than
Before long	Instead
Years went by	
Meanwhile	
For years	
In time	
In the event of	
Quite often	

图5.8　口头复述的语篇衔接资源提示

案例述评：

　　该案例与上一案例（见5.1.1）的不同在于教研者将debt.txt的主题词表中一批高频实义词拓展为2-4字词丛，经形式结构识别（详见本小节"语料加工"部分的说明），筛选出一批主题词拓展词丛，也可称为主题词短语（key phrases），专指那些"含有至少一个名词的三字或四字的词丛，它们要比单个主题词更准确地呈现语篇的主题大意"（Tyrkko 2010：88）。例如"复合性名词组合就能表述更为复杂的意念"（Bondi 2010：10）。本案例列举的主题词拓展词丛就呈现了比单个主题词更为完整或复杂的概念。其中从主题词bank（银行）拓展的词丛banks lend out（银行放出贷款），run on the bank（挤兑）和central bank（中央银行）就揭示了关于"银行行为"和"银行类型"的重要概念；而主题词拓展词丛claim check（取款单/取货单）也相对单个主题词claim（认领、索赔）更完整地展示了金融语境下"存放–支取"这一金融行为。从这个意义上说，基于语篇主题词拓展的词丛要比纯粹频数驱动的词丛/N元组更准确地指向语篇内容的主题特征。

　　本案例的步骤1和2反复引导学生关注主题词拓展词丛，是为了降低学生对视频1中重点术语理解的难度。其中步骤3的图5.8再次通过主题词拓展词丛将视频1的抽象专业知识与视频2的具体故事情节配对起来，更是为了帮助学生更深入地理解"货币创造的机制"这一抽象而复杂的次话题知识。综上所述，该教案设计的特点有三：（1）步骤3将语篇的主题词拓展词丛配对语篇知识内容（如图5.7），这是将主题内容和语言表达手段融为一体的"内容+语言"教学支架，有利于实现以内容为依托的主题式教学的双重目标。（2）在步骤4故事复述中呈现语言衔接手段提示（如图5.8）则是连接故事内容和语言资源的另一教学支架。（3）教师课前作了多种语料的教学加工，包括选择同一主题的教材之外的视频资源，制作微本，提取微本主题词表，再拓展至主题词拓展词丛表；运用了包括网络主题词搜索、截频、文字转换、语料库主题词和多字语提取等等现代教育信息技术。这些看似费时费力，但却可积少成多，由此逐步形成相关话题的视频、音频和文字的立体化专题教学资源库，可长期保留，反复使用。

5.1.3　主题词拓展词丛分类辅助专题核心知识构建

语料加工：

教研者从广东外语外贸大学国际商英学院自建的101万词次的BCT-2教材总库中提取有关"货币银行学（Money and Banking）"的所有文本，整合成1.96万词次的"货币银行专题教学子库"（以下简称"货币银行学子库"），作为课程教材《商务英语综合教程》第四册第五单元"货币银行学"的拓展资源。首先以100万词次的Crown语料库为参照语料库，生成货币银行学子库的主题词表（见下图5.9），选择头50个高频实义词，进行词形还原后制成一批检索项整体导入AntConc的高级检索界面中（见下图5.10）；然后用Clusters/N-Grams工具提取含有这些主题词的2-4字词丛（见下图5.12）；再从中遴选出频次为3次及以上的、表意完整（内含"N's N/NP""N + N""N *and* N""ADJ+N/NP""N + V"和"V + N"结构）的头50主题词拓展词丛，它们按照首字母排序分别为：banking and finance, banking sector, banking system, banks'assets, buyers and sellers, check clearing, commercial bank, credit card, credit markets, credit standards, credit union, currency exchange, currency values, deposit insurance, economic activity, economic commentary, economic conditions, economic growth, economic recovery, economic stability, electronic funds transfer, electronic money, electronic payments, exchange rates, financial advice, financial crisis, financial institution, financial institutions create money, financial intermediaries, financial system, financial transactions, government's bank, inflation rate, institutions create money, interest rate, international banking and finance, international monetary fund, international payments, international trade，loan associations，market operations，money and banking system，money market，nation's money supply，real economic activity，real estate，reserve requirements，savings accounts，savings and loan associations，savings institutions。

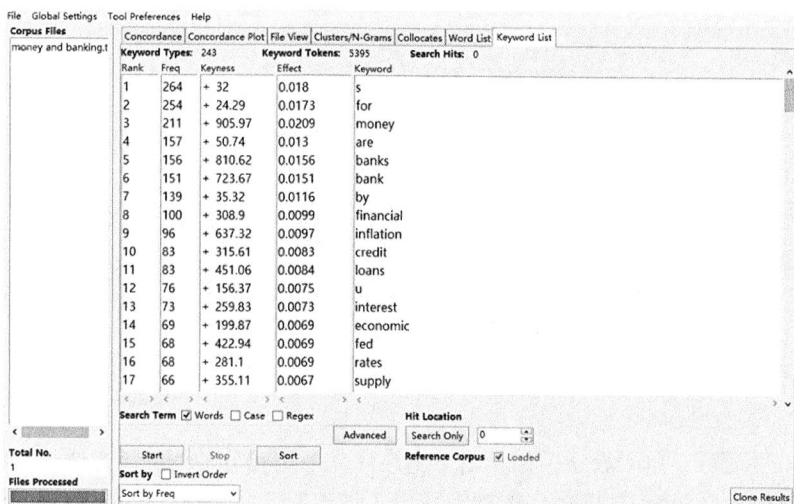

图5.9　货币银行学子库主题词表截图

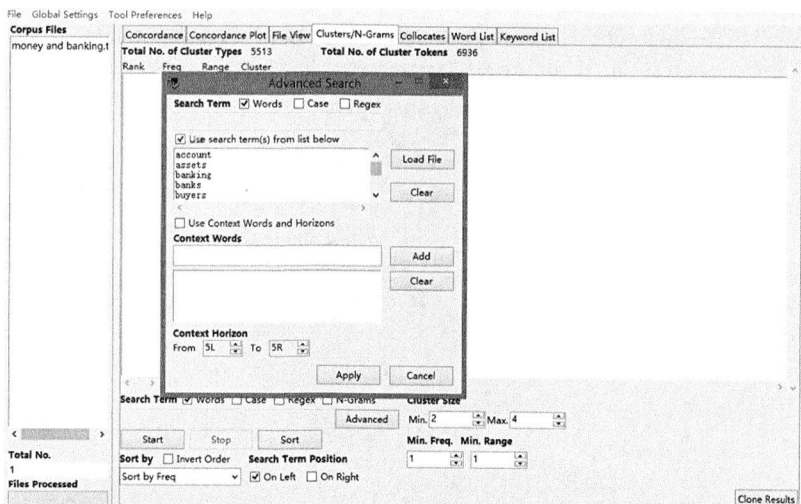

图5.10　批量检索头50个实义词类主题词拓展词丛高级检索界面

File　Global Settings　Tool Preferences　Help

| Corpus Files | | | | Concordance | Concordance Plot | File View | Clusters/N-Grams | Collocates | Word List | Keyword List |
| money and banking.t | | | | Total No. of Cluster Types　571 | | | Total No. of Cluster Tokens　3137 | | | |

Rank	Freq	Range	Cluster
1	66	1	the fed
2	47	1	money supply
3	41	1	the money
4	39	1	of money
5	32	1	the money supply
6	29	1	interest rates
7	29	1	the sellers
8	27	1	commercial banks
9	25	1	interest rate
10	25	1	nation's
11	25	1	the nation
12	24	1	federal reserve
13	24	1	financial institutions
14	24	1	for example
15	24	1	money and
16	24	1	the nation's

Search Term ☑ Words ☐ Case ☐ Regex ☐ N-Grams　　Cluster Size

Advanced　　Min. 2　　Max. 4

Start　　Stop　　Sort　　Min. Freq.　Min. Range

Total No.　　Sort by ☐ Invert Order　Search Term Position　　3　　1

1

Files Processed　Sort by Freq　☐ On Left ☐ On Right　　　Clone Results

图5.11　货币银行学子库主题词拓展词丛截图

教学实施：

步骤1： 单元教学伊始就请学生在课堂上用10分钟围绕该专题最高频主题词 "money" 进行自由词汇联想（见图5.12），预建一份主题概念图（学生初始的构图结果分析见本书第6章6.3.1）。

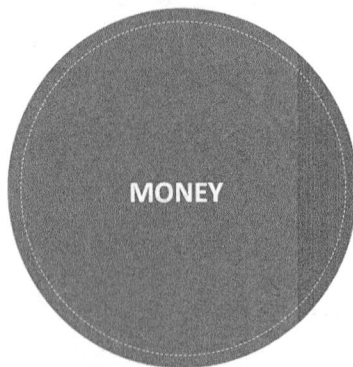

Try to map out all those associated words/phrases that pop into your mind when it comes to "money" within 10 minutes.

MONEY

Mapping by word association

图5.12　基于money的主题概念构图指令

步骤2：教师出示已备好的主题词拓展词丛（见本小节"语料加工"部分），要求学生以小组讨论的形式，结合之前学过的"当代商业概论"课程和正在同步学习的"货币银行学"课程的知识，将50个主题词拓展词丛按照图5.13的专题知识框架图进行语义内容归类，然后填写在相关的知识板块周边。

Corpus-aided CBI: phrase-based knowledge building

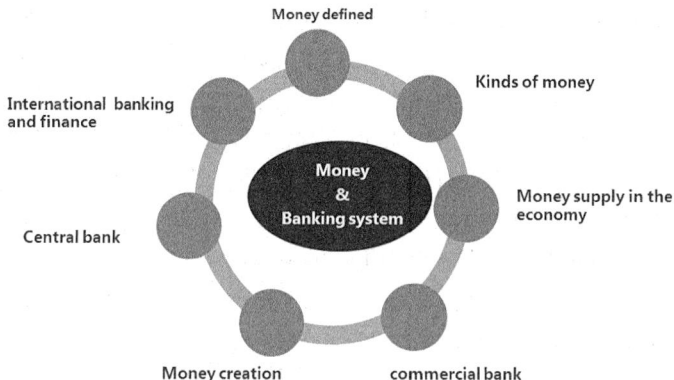

Money defined

Kinds of money

International banking
and finance

**Money
&
Banking system**

Money supply in the
economy

Central bank

Money creation

commercial bank

Try to categorize the listed key clusters based on this knowledge frame, based on your knowledge of monetary theory **in Macro economics and Money and Banking.**

图5.13 "货币及银行体系"专题知识板块图

步骤3：学生小组完成主题词拓展词丛的归类后，各小组派代表向全班展示加入归类词丛后的图5.13的细化版本，并对该版本涉及的各个知识板块作命题构建及拓展的口述。例如将词丛"electronic money"和"credit card"填入图中的"kinds of money"板块后，可构建"electronic money like credit card is a predominant type of money used nowadays"这一命题。又如，将"financial institutions create money"归入图中的"money creation"板块后，可将命题拓展为"financial institutions create money by expanding the money supply，taking in deposits and making much higher loans"。

步骤4：听完各小组陈述后，教师要求学生参照加入归类词丛后的知识板块图（见图5.13），重构或完善之前在步骤1构建的主题概念图（学生重构的结果分析见第6章6.3.1）。

案例述评：

本案例的特色有二。第一，教学的语料资源已经从单一本教材的某个单元语料拓展至BCT-2教材总库里相同或近似话题的专题子语料库，无论在专题知识和专题话语语言方面都实现了资源富集，从而更地有利于提取某个商务英语专题的核心知识和典型词语。第二，该案例虽然也融入了基于语篇主题词拓展词丛构建内容图示的元素，但上一例（见5.1.2）是由教师构建的完整主题知识图式，目的是帮助学生更好地理解语篇大意和核心知识；而本案例则是由学生先行基于标题主题词通过发散思维、自由联想构建主题概念图，而后在教师提供的主题词拓展词丛表和专题知识板块图提示下，先小组后个人，再构专题板块化知识。目的是让学生更多地参与到学科知识的构建过程之中，尤其是细化核心知识的语言表述资源。之前案例5.1.1和案例5.1.2中关于"货币定义""货币功能""货币形式""银行体系的由来"和"现代银行体系中货币的创造"等次话题的知识输入，再加上本案例提供的知识框架和基于专题子库的高频主题词拓展词丛表，都成为本案例构建更加充实、更加细化的专题知识体系的重要支撑。可以期待，学生单元教学末重构的主题概念图一定比之前的概念图有明显改善（详见第6章6.3.1的教学效果分析）。

5.1.4　主题词辅助语篇深度阅读教学

语料加工：

本教学案例基于课程教材《商务英语综合教程》第三册第十单元市场营销（Marketing）的主题阅读选文"中国超市呈现出口机遇"进行语料加工。教研者先将课文制作成1，382词次的微本（marketing.txt，见附录11）作为教学目标语料；以《爱丽丝仙境漫游记》作为参照语料，提取主题词共65个。词形还原处理后遴选出52个高频实义词类的主题词，再进行语义内容分类。按频数降序排列分别为：supermarket, market, China, food, Chinese, product, chain, store, retail, sell, system, consumer, sector, convenience, sales, small, wet, exporter, imported, marketing, multinational, shanghai, supplier, billion, city, distribution, estimated, Europe, fresh, government, local, produce, quality, traditional, class, company, competitive, development, domestic, foreign, formats, fragmented, fruit, major, packaged, price, procurement, rural, trade, urban, Walmart, wholesale。

　　教师凭借学科专业知识将上述主题词将大致分为三类。第一类是表述营销活动的对象的词汇，如company，consumer，（middle）class，exporter，government，supplier。他们之间有着千丝万缕的联系，例如"中产阶级（middle class）"是零售"公司（company）"的产品"消费者（consumer）"的重要组成部分；若以"政府（government）"/国家为行为主体，"公司（company）"的国际市场营销过程就是国际贸易，而"出口商（exporter）"或者"供应商（supplier）"就是其间的重要角色。第二类是修饰或限制商业实体或商务活动的词汇，如domestic，China，Chinese，Shanghai，city，traditional，foreign，multinational，imported，Europe，urban，rural，small，major，fragmented，competitive，fresh，packaged，wet。它们还可进行次范畴分类。例如前12个词可归为地域文化类，后7个可归为本质属性特征类。这些主题词还可互为上下义关系（如city与Shanghai）、部分与整体关系（如China与Shanghai）、或者对应关系（如domestic与foreign、local与imported、urban与rural）等等。第三类是与主题市场营销（marketing）密切关联的术语，如product，quality，price，distribution，format，wholesale，retail，chain，store，supermarket，Walmart，procurement，sales，trade，market，development等名词和produce，sell等动词。这些术语构建成市场营销专题核心知识：产品（product）、价格（price）、渠道（distribution）是市场营销组合（Marketing Mix：4Ps）中的三个维度。渠道（distribution）（也称place）中又有批发（wholesale）和零售（retail）两种基本销售形式；零售的形式（format）再进一步具体化为超市（supermarket）、连锁店（chain）和商铺（store）等。零售业两个最重要的商业活动则是采购（procurement）和销售（sales）。两个关键动词（produce和sell）则分别展示了商业活动中的两个最重要的行为"生产"与"销售"。经过上述的层层分类分析，可逐步廓清主题词与学科知识框架的层层语义关联。

表5.2　市场营销主题词语义范畴分类

商务语义范畴/次范畴	主题词
营销活动中的对象	company, consumer, (middle) class, exporter, government, supplier
营销活动中的实体	market, food, fruit

续表

商务语义范畴 / 次范畴		主题词
营销活动或实体描述	地域文化类	domestic, China, Chinese, Shanghai, city, traditional, foreign, multinational, imported, Europe, urban, rural
	本质特征类	small, major, fragmented, competitive, fresh, packaged, wet
营销组合		product (quality), distribution, price
营销体系基本形式		wholesale, retail
零售商形式		supermarket, chain, store
零售过程中的重要概念		procurement, sales
营销相关的商业行为		produce, sell

上述主题词及其分析技术嵌入到"大意理解""结构分析"及"难点化解"三个教学环节中，还需做进一步语料库加工。

例如，提取主题词marketing, market, supermarket和store的2-4字词丛（见图5.14），遴选出主题词拓展词丛作为市场营销体系中的零售/批发实体的具体描述形式，它们分别是：wet market, convenience store, Chinese/China's supermarket, marketing system, supermarket chain, department store, marketing bureau, supermarket sector, fragmented market, foreign market, mom-and-pop store, chain store, express store。

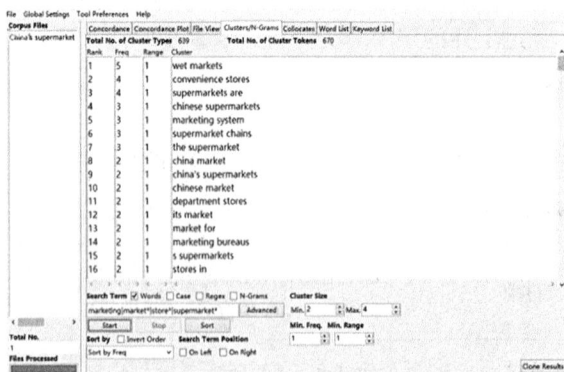

图5.14　含有marketing, market, supermarket和store的2-4词词丛截图

又例如，提取主题词拓展词丛marketing system的索引行，获取对市场营销体系的详细描述（见图5.15）。

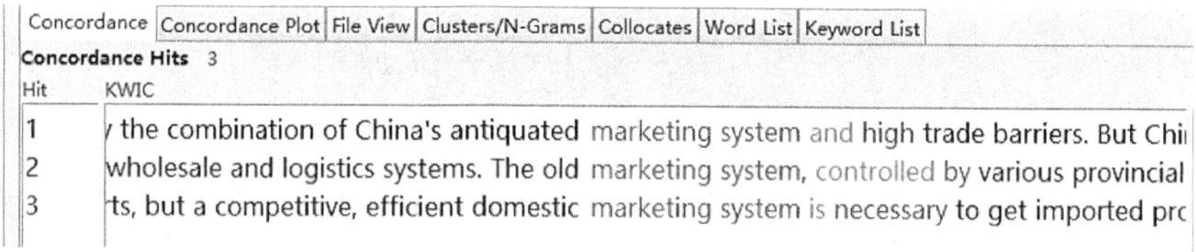

| Concordance | Concordance Plot | File View | Clusters/N-Grams | Collocates | Word List | Keyword List |

Concordance Hits　3

Hit	KWIC
1	/ the combination of China's antiquated marketing system and high trade barriers. But Chi
2	wholesale and logistics systems. The old marketing system, controlled by various provincial
3	ts, but a competitive, efficient domestic marketing system is necessary to get imported pro

图5.15　marketing system的索引行

教学实施：

步骤1： 在学生已预习课文的前提下，教师在主题阅读分析讨论部分的"大意理解"环节中要求学生自行列出选文的内容大纲，然后参照教师已分好类的主题词表（见表5.2），复述语篇大意。

步骤2： 在针对选文各部分信息内容作"重难点理解"的教学环节中，教师用图5.16展示选文第一段到第四段的重点内容提问。要求学生当堂细读文本；同时用AntConc展示某些主题词拓展词丛的索引行，还可点击任何一例索引行以呈现拓展语境的原文语段。例如图5.17展示了图5.15中marketing system的第2例索引行的拓展语境，细读后学生即可廓清了图5.16中问题1的中国传统市场营销体系的主要特征。

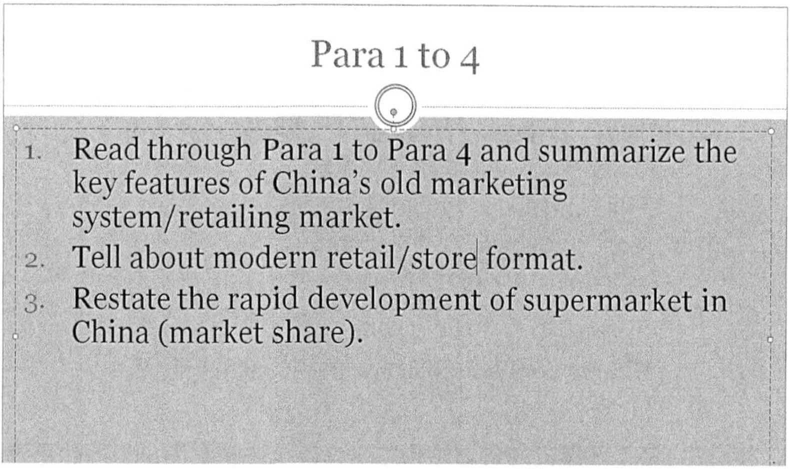

Para 1 to 4

1. Read through Para 1 to Para 4 and summarize the key features of China's old marketing system/retailing market.
2. Tell about modern retail/store format.
3. Restate the rapid development of supermarket in China (market share).

图5.16　选文第一部分重难点内容提问

and logistics systems. The old **marketing system**, controlled by various provincial and city marketing bureaus, consisted of small, fragmented wholesale and retail segments selling local produce; multiple layers of small brokers, wholesalers, distributors and government-licensed importers; and government-run retail outlets.

图5.17　图5.15索引行2的拓展原文

　　针对问题2，教师展示以format*为检索项，并且设定左1语境词为retail和store的局部语境（见图5.18，结果见图5.19）。提示学生关注零售形式。

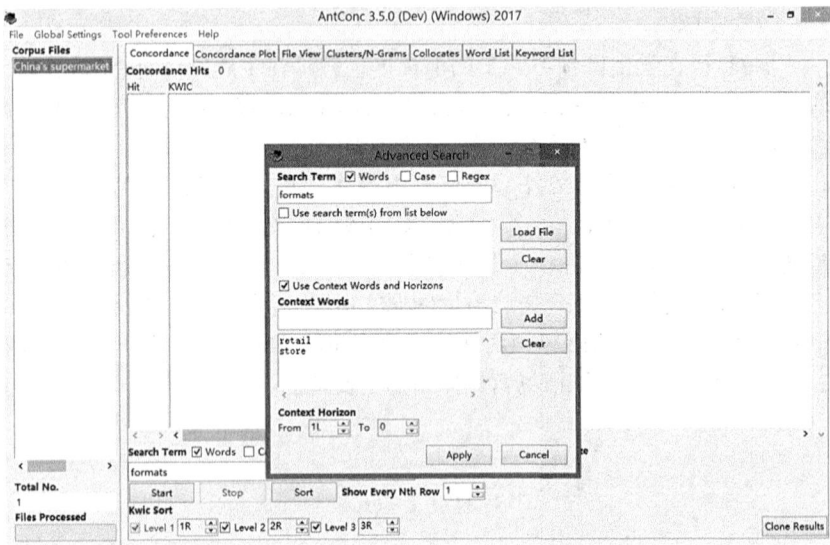

图5.18　retail/store和format*共选的高级检索界面

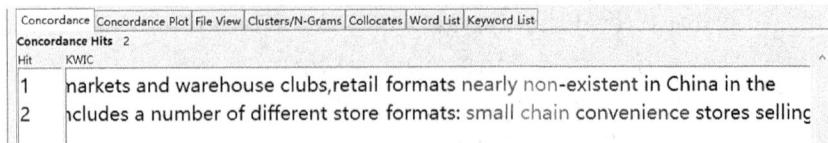

图5.19　retail/store和format*共选的索引行截图

　　步骤3： 鉴于该选文的语篇结构隐含一条"中国食品销售的超市化进程"时间轴线，教师设计图5.20的"超市化"进程图示，并再次展示"语料加工"部分提取的主题词拓展词丛作为提示，要求学生参照已提供的再次阅读的选文并填充图5.20的信息，即图中下划线的文字（而图中的黑粗体字部分是教师预先提供但选文中未提及的零售商形式）。之后请学生简述中国食品零售行业的超市化进程。

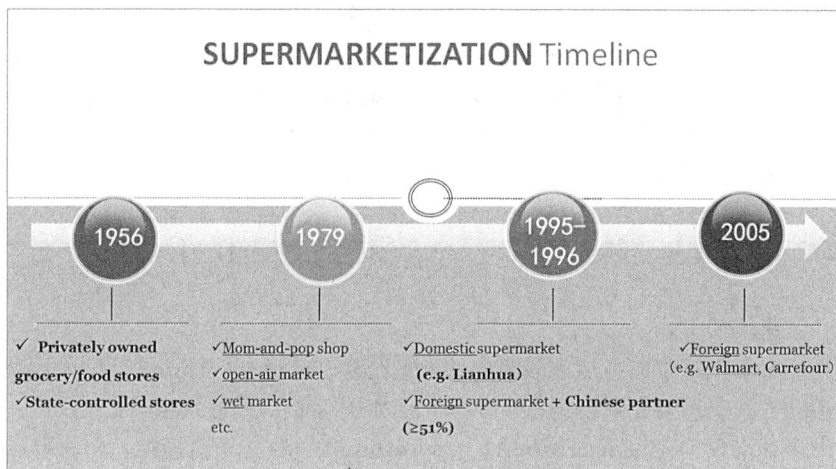

SUPERMARKETIZATION Timeline

| 1956 | 1979 | 1995–1996 | 2005 |

✓ **Privately owned grocery/food stores**
✓ State-controlled stores

✓ Mom-and-pop shop
✓ open-air market
✓ wet market
etc.

✓ Domestic supermarket
(e.g. Lianhua)
✓ Foreign supermarket + **Chinese partner**
(≥51%)

✓ Foreign supermarket
(e.g. Walmart, Carrefour)

图5.20　中国食品销售行业超市化进程时间线图

案例述评：

本案例的特点是利用选文的主题词、主题词拓展词丛及其语境分析实施了精读课文的"大意理解""结构分析"及"难点化解"三步主题阅读教学。其深度教学体现在语篇分析的三个层面。首先是语篇的核心内容，也是学科的基础知识。教师在课前对主题词的分类分析表明：从专题微型语料库中提取的主题词语义内容层层分类对于廓清专题学科的知识体系有重要意义，因为"主题词具有语篇的本质属性"（Scott & Tribble 2006：55-56）。它们是选文核心内容的重要载体，也应成学生主题阅读中关注的重点。第二是语篇各段的重难点解读，教师通过展示部分主题词的索引行（如步骤2），引导学生聚焦对重点内容的细读。第三是语篇结构的发展路向，教师通过"中国食品销售行业超市化进程时间线图"与主题词拓展词丛的匹配练习（如步骤3），帮助学生在掌握选文语篇结构特点的同时反复操练核心内容的短语表达方式。由此可见，如同听力教学一样，阅读教学中的主题词与主题词拓展词丛既可充当主旨内容和语篇思路的重要指针；

又能建构专题核心知识，两者融合用于选文阅读的大意理解、重难点信息提取以及语篇结构凸显，以这样一种简约、清晰和可视化的辅助方式来实现深入理解语篇和表述语篇的双重目标。

5.2 语料库辅助的商务学术语言深度教学案例

本节的三个案例主要在主题式教学的"主题阅读分析讨论"环节实施。第一例是将语料库短语结构教学嵌入阅读活动中以揭示语篇文体风格等特征；后两例则是使用拓展语料库资源辅助语篇中具有商务话语特色的短语深度知识教学。

5.2.1　基于短语结构"N+that（clause）"的学术文体教学

语料加工：

本案例基于商务学术话语中的常见结构"N+that（clause）"设计教学活动。教研者首先观察到在主题单元（如Business Ethics和Social Security）中多处出现"issue/fear/belief + that（clause）"这一短语模式，但语例有限。于是将教学资源扩展到学院自建的101万词次综合商务英语课程教材语料库BTC-2逾千例索引行，并作以下加工处理：（1）用网上免费下载的文本整理器（http://www.downcc.com/soft/280849.html）批量清除文本"杂音"（如处理段落首尾空格、段首跳格、段落间空行及全角标点变半角标点）；（2）用网上免费下载的Treetagger软件（http://www.cis.uni-muenchen.de/~schmid/tools/TreeTagger/）对所有语例进行词性自动附码。（3）用AntConc提取检索项为"NN* that_IN"的索引行共计1,120例（见图5.21），建成微型本N+that.txt（见附录12）。（4）用AntConc的搭配词表功能（Collocates）提取检索项L1位置的搭配词表（见图5.22），遴选其中最高频的30个抽象名词，按照频数降序排列分别为：fact, way, idea, principle, assumption, belief, option, claim, risk, reason, problem, evidence, notion, feeling, decision, argument, value, question, possibility, rumor, remark, information, fear, view, system, strategy, premise, message, likelihood, influence。（5）通过AntConc在BCT-2教材语料库提取以belief* that为检索项的所有语例（见图5.23）。

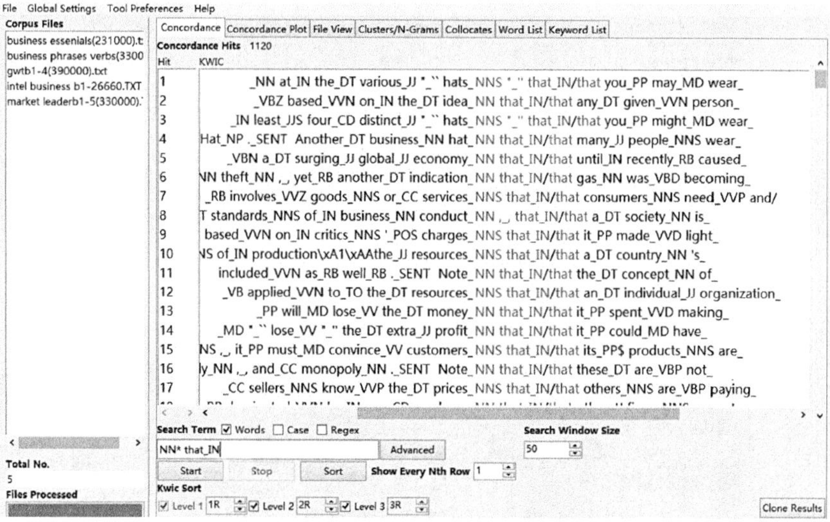

图5.21　NN* that_IN索引行截图

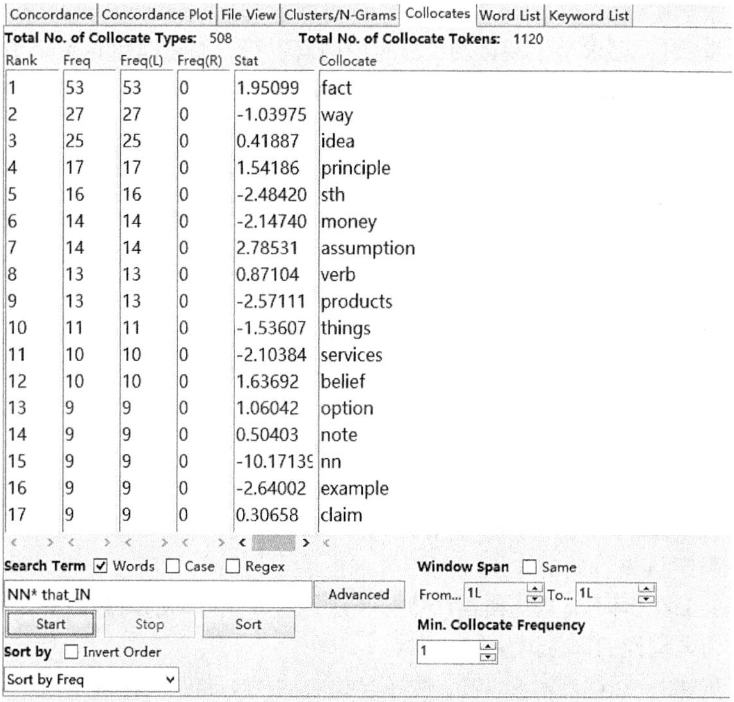

图5.22　NN* that_IN的L1搭配词表截图

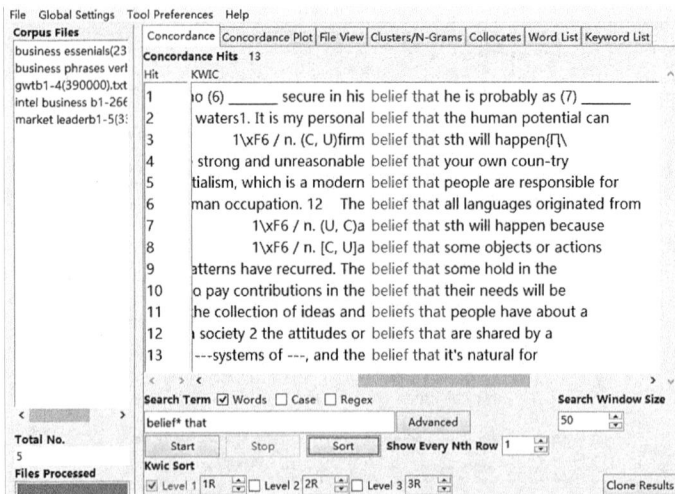

图5.23　belief* that的索引行截图

教学实施：

步骤1：要求学生阅读图5.23的13例索引行，必要时可拓宽语境以展示完整例句（如图中序号2和11扩展为例句1和2）；然后请学生按belief that的两种语法和语义模式进行分类。一类是"belief that+同位语从句"，即从句为belief的具体内容（如索引行2，详见例句1）；另一类是"belief that+定语从句"，即从句内容与belief无关而仅起着修饰限定的作用（如索引行11，详见例句2）。

例句1 It is my personal belief that the human potential can only be realized by the globalization of ideas.

例句2 ...the collection of ideas and beliefs that people have about a brand

步骤2：教师在听取学生的答案之后（如图5.23序号1-8、10和13均为"belief that+同位语从句"结构，而序号9、11和12为"belief that +定语从句"），进一步引导学生细察这两种结构在其用词或语法结构上有何不同。例如belief在图5.23序号9、11和12的从句语境中充当宾语或主语，从句起修饰限定该先行词的作用，为形容词性的定语从句；而在其他从句语境中，belief一词不充当任何语法成分，从句对该先行词的内涵做扩充说明，故称为名词性的同位语从句。

步骤3：教师展示图5.22，要求学生关注"N+that（clause）"中N位置的名词特点，引导学生分析"N+that+同位语从句"的语用意义或语篇功能。比如该结构中的N通常是抽象名词，或称"外壳名词"（shell noun），目的是聚焦信息点，而后用从句细述其内涵，可以使表达更为简洁而连贯，甚至抽象名词自身还会暗示笔者的认知和态度立场。

　　步骤4：教师展示上述"语料加工"部分提取的30个抽象名词并说明来源，要求学生对它们进行语义分类。例如将idea，assumption，belief，premise，view等归为思想观点类，而将problem，question等归为问题/话题类，而将 claim，argument，rumor，remark等归入言语论点类，risk，possibility，likelihood等则归入认知情态类。从而进一步认识该短语结构还可以揭示说话者对同位语从句中命题内容的认知和立场态度。因为有的抽象名词本身就有态度含义，例如观点类中的belief会比assumption传递更为肯定的态度；而rumor暗指从句中的具体内容不实的态度。

　　步骤5：教师请学生完成中译英句子翻译练习（如图5.24，图中的英文是后出的参考答案），要求分别使用和不使用"抽象名词+that+同位语从句"这个短语结构，然后对比两者各有什么文体效果（如第一句如译成"Microsoft believes that..."，可能会传递一种比较直白的、非正式的语气）。

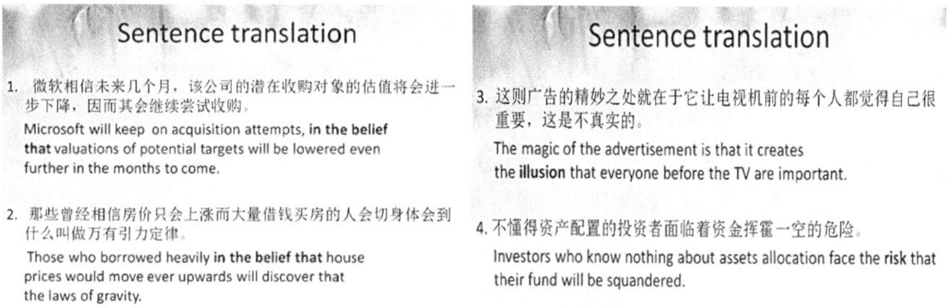

图5.24　"抽象名词+that+同位语从句"结构句子翻译练习

案例述评：

　　该案例依据语料库的短语理念，即语言研究应该给予来自语境中的那些典型的、反复出现的以及可重复观察到的完整话语事实。作为语境一个组成部分的话语语篇以及词语在该语篇中形成的语境模式（contextual patterning）都共同对该词语的意义起决定性作用（Firth 1957）。该例"N+that（clause）"可视为语料库语言学视角的一种短语形态，又可称为"型式语法"单位。简单地说就是与一个词高频关联使用的短语结构，通常以该词后接介词、词组和从句的形式出现（Hunston & Francis 2000：3）。将它作为"主题阅读分析"环节中"语言点分析"的一个教学点，旨在凸显商务英语学术话语的文体特征。其中步骤1通过展示某一个含有具体词的型式（BELIEF[1]+that）的一批语例引导学生观察和分类，以初步确定两种意义模式。步骤2通过师生互动，引导学生基于已有语言知识，将一个词的型式（a word and its patterns）拓展到一类词的型式（a pattern and its words），并尝试分析其话语风格和语用特征。步骤3通过事前提取的搭配词表，引导学生做语义归纳与分类。步骤4基于提取商务话语进行翻译训练及对比分析，以强化学生对这类短语单位的理解与使用能力。层层深入的设计涵盖了短语结构的形式、意义和功能，同时也是"观察–假设–验证"等系列思维活动的提升过程。

5.2.2　基于半技术性词premium的跨体裁对比教学

语料加工：

教研者留意到半技术性词汇在商务教材语篇中高频出现，比如premium在Business Ethics，Social Security和Leadership等单元的主题阅读选文中反复出现。教研者先在39万词次的《商务英语综合教程》教材子库获得8例premium，发现有at a premium price和place/put a premium on两个短语结构。因实例太少，又从101万词次的BCT-2教材语料库中提取32例，剔除重复和无关语例后留下19例完整例句，保存为premium.txt（见附录13），然后按照商务话题分作五类（见表5.3）。

表5.3　按商务次话题分类后19个premium的完整例句

商务次话题	完整例句
股票 价格	1. In April 2000, the Anglo-Dutch Unilever NV announced it would buy flagging Ben and Jerry's stocks for 43.50 a share, *a large **premium** over* the previous day's closing price of 434.93. 2. CSN, one of Latin America's large fully integrated steelmakers, is offering €5.75 a share for 100 percent of Cimpor's capital, *a **premium** of 5 percent* on Thursday's closing price.

---

1 本书用全大写字母表示的英语单词表示一个词簇（lemma）内含其各种形式变体。

续表

商务次话题		完整例句
市场营销	产品定位 / 品牌创立	1．The eau-de-cologne is positioned as *a premium fragrance*. It is priced at the top end of the market. 2．For loyal buyers of *Godiva premium chocolates*, performance includes such sensory delights as aroma, flavor, color, and texture. 3．Mmm, I suppose we could offer some free content. Then make readers pay a subscription for *premium content*—extra materials like DVD workout programmes—that sort of thing. 4．When Citibank introduced its credit card in the Asia-Pacific region, it launched it sequentially and tailored the product features for each country which *maintaining its premium positioning*. 5．For lovers of upscale coffee products, Starbucks has long been the standout brand *with a premium image* as the "home of affordable luxury." 6．Can Starbucks reposition the brand so it appeals to the convenience market without tarnishing *the company's premium image*?
	产品定价	1．"Often fair trade is sold *at a premium*," he charges, "but the entire premium goes to the middlemen." 2．The other assistant manager, meanwhile, has urged just the opposite approach: raise room rates by at least 20 percent and sell food to rescue workers and hospitals *at a premium price*. 3．One will always find a Rolex in an upmarket distribution outlet and *at a premium price*. 4．They get the right to promote their chocolate products not only as "fair-trade" but, often, as "organic" products as well—categories that typically command *premium retail prices*. 5．Historically, building a brand was rather simple. For that, consumers were prepared to *pay a premium*. 6．It's definitely "no frills", but I'm always willing to *pay a premium for* business class, so long as it isn't exorbitant. 7．In fact, FLO *pays an even higher premium on* organically certified cocoa—$200 instead of $150 per ton—and the extra cost, of course, shows up in retail prices. 8．Ask for two *premium economy tickets* to New York on 4th June, returning on 9th June. 9．*Premium sales*-promotion technique in which offers of free or reduced-price items are used to stimulate purchases.

续表

商务次话题	完整例句
保险	1. If insurance for additional amount and/or for other insurance terms is required by the Buyers, prior notice to this effect must reach the Sellers before shipment and is subject to the Sellers' agreement, and the extra *insurance premium* shall be for the Buyers' account.
其他	1. The hotels *place a premium on* customer satisfaction.

教学实施：

步骤1：教师展示图5.25，要求学生依据索引行的局部语境猜测"at a premium price"，"place/put a premium"和"insurance premium"这三个短语的语义。教师可拓展相关语例的上下文引导学生关注其中的语境提示词。如图5.26显示Rolex（劳力士手表）周边有"elegant high achiever"和"upmarket"等修饰词，所以"at a premium price"表示这一奢侈品牌定价高昂。图5.27的语境中"more concerned with making important decisions that may break with tradition but are humane"，"moral"，"right"和"rather than"等提示"put a premium on"表示"更关心/重视"之意。图5.28的语境词"insurance for additional amount"和该结构修饰词"extra"相互参照，提示"insurance premium"意为"保险费"。

Hit	KWIC
1	I\xA1\xAFm always willing to pay a premium for business class, so long as it isn\
2	. The eau-de-cologne is positioned as a premium fragrance. It is priced atthe top end of
3	has long been the standout brand with a premium image as the \xA1\xB0home of affordable
4	. For that, consumers were prepared to pay a premium. It\xA1\xAFs definitely \xA1\xB0no frills\
5	100 per cent of Cimpor\xA1\xAFs capital, a premium of 5 pecent on Thursday\xA1\xAFs closing p
6	isn\xA1\xAFt exorbitant. The hotels place a premium on customer satisfaction. Premium sales-pr
7	in an upmarket distribution outlet and at a premium price. Can Starbucks reposition the brand
8	food to rescue workers and hospitals at a premium price. One will always find a Rolex in
9	1\xB0Often fair trade is sold at a premium,\xA1\xB1 he charges, \xA1\xB0but the
10	as well\xA1\xAAcategories that typically command premium retail prices. In fact, FLO pays an even
11	1\xB1 he charges, \xA1\xB0but the entire premium goes to the middlemen.\xA1\xB1 For lovers
12	content. Then make readers pay a subscription for premium content\xA3\xADextra materials like DVD wo
13	s premium positioning. For loyal buyers of Godiva premium chocolates, performance includes such sens
14	prices. In fact, FLO pays an even higher premium on organically certified cocoa\xA1\xAA$200
15	ellers\xA1\xAF agreement, and the extra insurance premium shall be for the Buyers\xA1\xAF account.
16	t features for each country which maintaining its premium positioning. For loyal buyers of Godiva pr
17	\xA1\xAFs stocks for 43.50 a share, a large premium over the previous day\xA1\xAFs closing pri
18	hotels place a premium on customer satisfaction. Premium sales-promotion technique in which offers
19	the Buyers\xA1\xAF account. Ask for two premium economy tickets to New York on 4th June,
20	market without tarnishing the company\xA1\xAFs premium image? They get the right to promote their

图5.25　premium.txt微型语料库中premium的索引行截图

9 As a contrast, consider Rolex. The genuine Rolex watch is the same certified chronometer anywhere in the world; its positioning—as the timepiece for the elegant high achiever—is the same around the world, as is the advertising message. One will always find a Rolex in an upmarket distribution outlet and at a `premium` price. Or consider Unilever's Lifebuoy soap, which has different ingredients in India compared to East Africa. However, Unilever positions the soap in the same way in both markets—as an inexpensive everyday soap that has antibacterial properties and protects health.

图5.26　at a premium的拓展语境截图

And whereas many managers are overly concerned with "fitting in" and not rocking the boat, those who emerge as leaders are more concerned with making important decisions that may break with tradition but are humane, moral, and right. The leader puts a `premium` on substance rather than on style.

图5.27　put a premium on的拓展语境截图

4) Except in cases where the insurance is covered by the Buyers as arranged, insurance is to be covered by the Sellers with a Chinese insurance company. If insurance for additional amount and/or for other insurance terms is required by the Buyers, prior notice to this effect must reach the Sellers before shipment and is subject to the Sellers' agreement, and the extra insurance `premium` shall be for the Buyers' account.

图5.28　insurance premium的拓展语境截图

　　步骤2： 学生在了解了premium几个涵义后，教师展示之前按次话题归纳的19个语例（见表5.3）。遮盖表1左栏的次话题名称，要求学生阅读右栏的各组例句并说出分别指向哪一种商务次话题语境。然后进一步引导学生关注不同含义的premium的语境搭配词及结构型式。以市场营销中的产品定位（product positioning）和品牌创立（branding）次话题语境的活动指引为例（见图5.29和图5.30）。

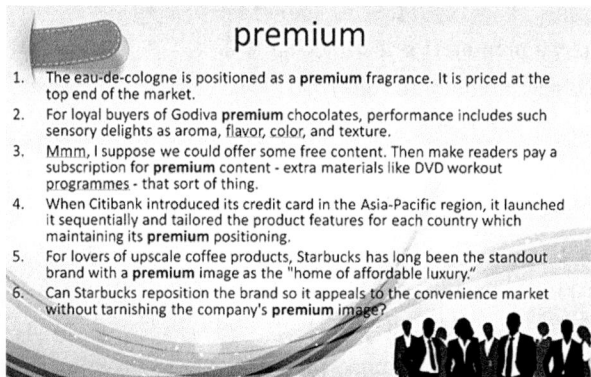

premium

1. The eau-de-cologne is positioned as a **premium** fragrance. It is priced at the top end of the market.
2. For loyal buyers of Godiva **premium** chocolates, performance includes such sensory delights as aroma, flavor, color, and texture.
3. Mmm, I suppose we could offer some free content. Then make readers pay a subscription for **premium** content - extra materials like DVD workout programmes - that sort of thing.
4. When Citibank introduced its credit card in the Asia-Pacific region, it launched it sequentially and tailored the product features for each country which maintaining its **premium** positioning.
5. For lovers of upscale coffee products, Starbucks has long been the standout brand with a **premium** image as the "home of affordable luxury."
6. Can Starbucks reposition the brand so it appeals to the convenience market without tarnishing the company's **premium** image?

图5.29　用于产品定位和品牌创立语境的premium短语结构分析指引（1）

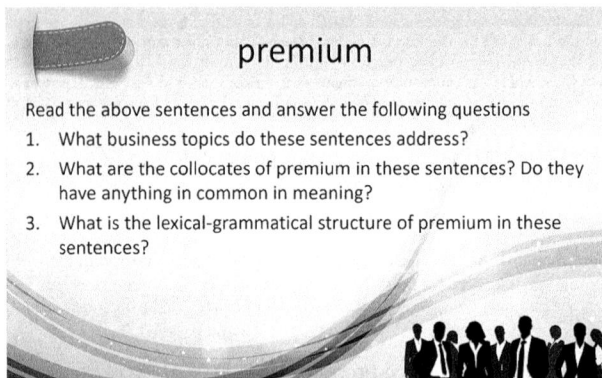

图5.30　用于产品定位和品牌创立语境的premium短语结构分析指引（2）

设计说明：

图5.30中问题1指向premium使用的商务次话题语境：即用于表述产品定位和公司品牌创立。问题2和3分别指向该词在这类语境中的词汇共选和语法共选特征。例如图5.29中6例premium右1搭配词中，前三句的fragrance，chocolates和content与"产品类"有关；后三句的positioning和image与"定位类"有关；而premium均作为名词修饰语与它们构成"premium+N"结构这一短语型式，表示"高端品牌"和"高价定位"。采用类似的方法还可分别归纳premium在三类商务次话题语境中各自的搭配词的语义偏好及短语型式，包括：

（1）股票类搭配词（股票溢价话题）：premium of+溢价幅度（比例）
+on/over+基数

（2）产品类/买卖类搭配词（产品高位定价话题）：

sell at/pay a premium（price）+产品名称

pay a（high）premium for/on+产品名称

premium＋产品名称

（3）保险类搭配词（保险费话题）：insurance premium

步骤3：教师继续展示从在线语料库COCA的General book和General Journal体裁中检索premium索引行及其搭配词表（分别见图5.31和5.32），请学生课后自行对比分析该词在一般语境和商务语境中的搭配结构和搭配词有何异同。例如，从图5.31中的18个索引行可见，premium在一般语境中的短语型式除了at a premium、premium+产品和insurance premium和商务语境相同之外，还高频出现了premium+notice结构；继续考察COCA中

premium的搭配词发现（见图5.32）验证了notice确是其高频搭配词，且泛指"缴费通知"。

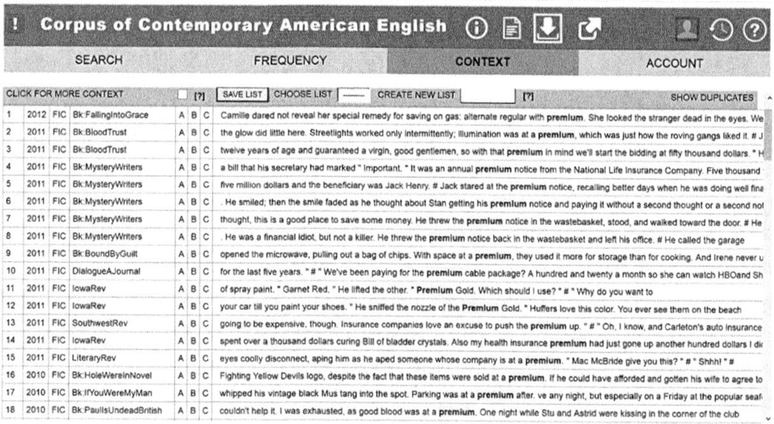

图5.31　COCA综合类体裁语料中的premium索引行截图

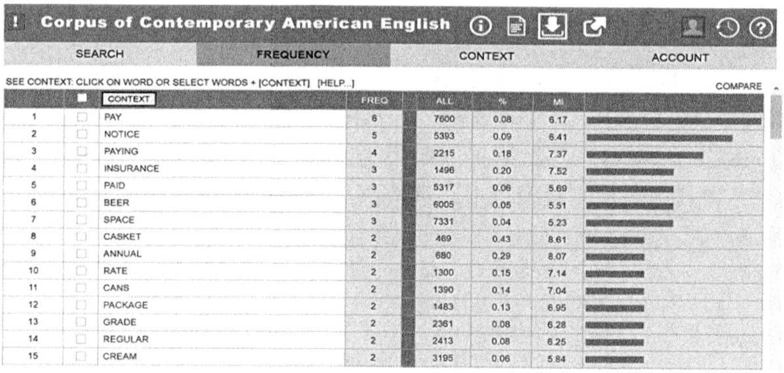

图5.32　COCA综合类体裁语料中的premium搭配词表截图

案例述评：

　　本案例旨在提升学生对半技术词汇（semi-technical vocabulary）在商务英语中应用特点的敏感意识。专业的半技术性词汇是"在普通语言中也有使用，但在专门话语语境使用频数更高且语义高度依赖语境的词汇"（Farrell 1990：11）。与专业技术词汇不用的是，半技术词汇由普通词汇转化而来，往往一词多义，且高度依赖语境，导致在特定语境下产生不同于普通英语语境下的意义，在其语境意义型式中具抽象性、多样性和灵活性，故成为商务英语词汇学习的难点（顿官刚 2002；陈琦、高云 2010；王卉 2012）。本案例瞄准BTC-2教材总库中反复出现的半技术性词汇premium（类似的还有principal、capital、depress等），凸显其在不同商务语境中的不同含义（见步骤1）。同时，深入探讨各种含义的premium的词汇语法共选特征，引导学生对其搭配、类连接、语义偏好三个层面最终形成各种不同的premium短语型式（见步骤2）。此外，还将课堂教学延伸到课后自主学习，指引学生通过对比分析该词在通用英语和商务英语中意义建构的异同（见步骤3）。还有，本案例经过从数十万词的《商务英语综合教程》教材子库到百余万词的BCT-2教材总库，再到数亿词的网络通用语料库COCA的层层拓展，体现了语料库资源富集的教学加工理念，切实解决了单本教材语例偏少的问题。教研者课前的语料库加工准备，尤其是基于商务次话题分类量化语例，表现出商英教师应具备的学科知识、语言学知识和现代教育信息技术等多重学科素养。

5.2.3 商务英语高频短语动词DEAL with的深度知识教学

语料加工：

本案例以《商务英语综合教程》第四册第十一单元主题阅读选文高频出现的短语动词DEAL with为例，先从BTC-2教材总库中提取DEAL with共366例（见图5.33）。然后提取跨距为2-4个词的右侧搭配词词表（见图5.34），将其中出现三次及以上名词按语义范畴大致归为三类（见表5.4）。

```
                    you're going to be dealing with a company overseas, you'
     on 91 cut back on spending 91 deal with a complaint 8 deal with
                    boss for a pay rise dealing with a customer who has
                    boss for a pay rise dealing with a customer who has
      , all agents are expected to deal with a customer's booking
                  had plans in place to deal with a flu pandemic. Management
          2010 as the firm sought to deal with a global recession and
                   said we may have to deal with a lawsuit. 4. The company
                 the sentence we had to deal with a lot of complaints.
               a big department, and we deal with a lot of employees.
             with A.1. 2 2. 3 3. 1 B. 1.The bank deals with a number of US
       spending 91 deal with a complaint 8 deal with a problem 7, 20 deals with 7, 13,32, 96,
                   find a successful way to deal with a problem My job
                        life? deal v. If you deal with a problem, you do
                  the skills to recognise and deal with a range of challenges.
```

图5.33　DEAL with在BCT-2教材总库的索引行截图

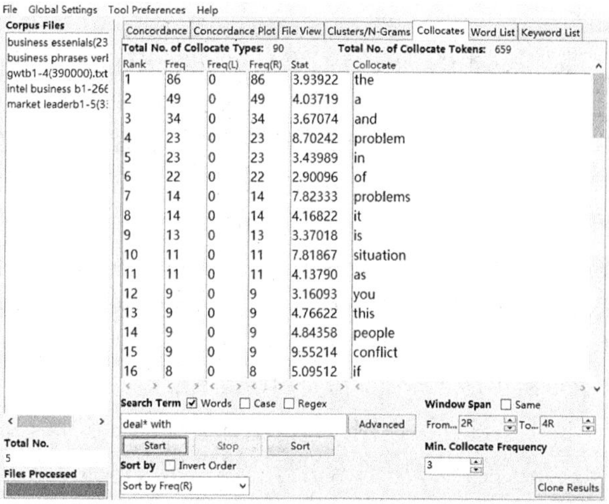

图5.34　DEAL with在BCT-2教材总库的搭配词表截图

表5.4　DEAL with右搭配名词的语义范畴分类

	问题事务类		人员机构类		商务活动类	
序号	名词	频数	名词	频数	名词	频数
1	problem	37	customer	12	paperwork	6
2	situation	11	people	9	training	6
3	conflict	9	company	6	work	6
4	complaint	8	employees	6	employing	5
5	crisis	6	businesses	4	selling	5
6	issues	6	firms	3	communication	3
7	stress	6	labor	3	order	3
8	questions	5	staff	3	products	3
9	emergencies	4			hiring	3
10	events	4				
11	case	3				
12	interruptions	3				
13	risk	3				
合计 105 次，占比 55%			合计 46 次，占比 24%		合计 40 次，占比 21%	

教学实施：

步骤1： 教师展示图5.33的一批DEAL with索引行，引导学生观察其右边的搭配词并归纳其结构范式（如DEAL with + N/NP）。

步骤2： 教师展示DEAL with右侧2词到4词跨距内的搭配词表（如图5.34），现要求学生对其中的名词并做语义内容分类（如problem、situation可归入事务问题类，customer、people可归入人员机构类，paperwork、training可归入商务活动类）；然后展示先前已归好的30个高频名词（见表5.4），让学生归纳DEAL with与不同类别名词共选时所表达的意义有何不同（例如，后接公司机构类名词时表"与……做生意"；后接问题事务类名词时表示"处理或应对问题或困境"）。

步骤3： 请学生继续关注图5.34搭配词表中的形容词（如difficult和unfavorable），结合图5.35中的索引行，以及图5.33部分索引行中DEAL with前的语境词have to和had to，探讨DEAL with用于"处理问题"时的语用含义（例如，不得不处理的问题通常比较棘手，包括有问题的孩子、难缠的顾客、来自不同民族的员工和种种麻烦事等）。

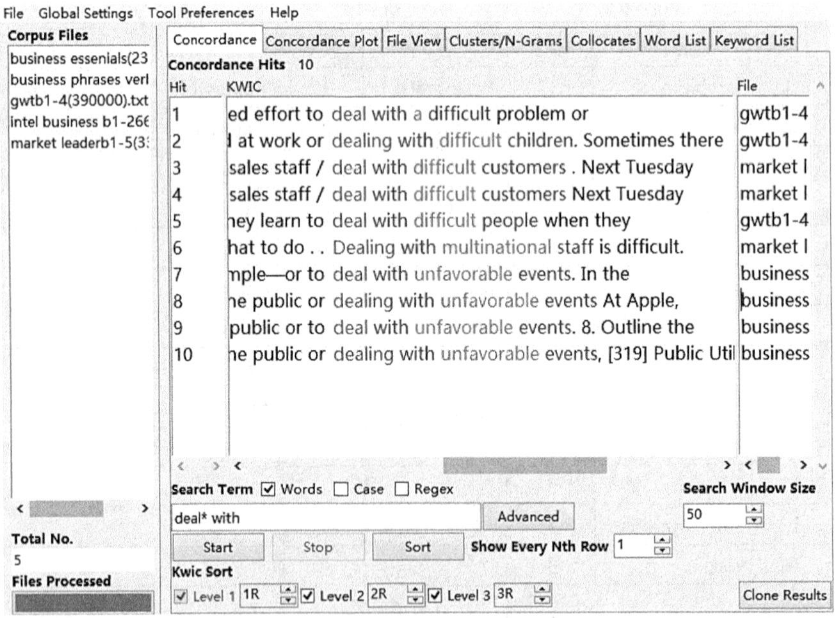

图5.35　DEAL with在BCT-2教材总库中与difficult、unfavorable共选的
索引行截图

步骤4：在学生了解了DEAL with在商务语境中的意义建构模式后，教师提取一批有代表性的索引行设计成填词、释义（paraphrase）与翻译练习题（见图5.36）。

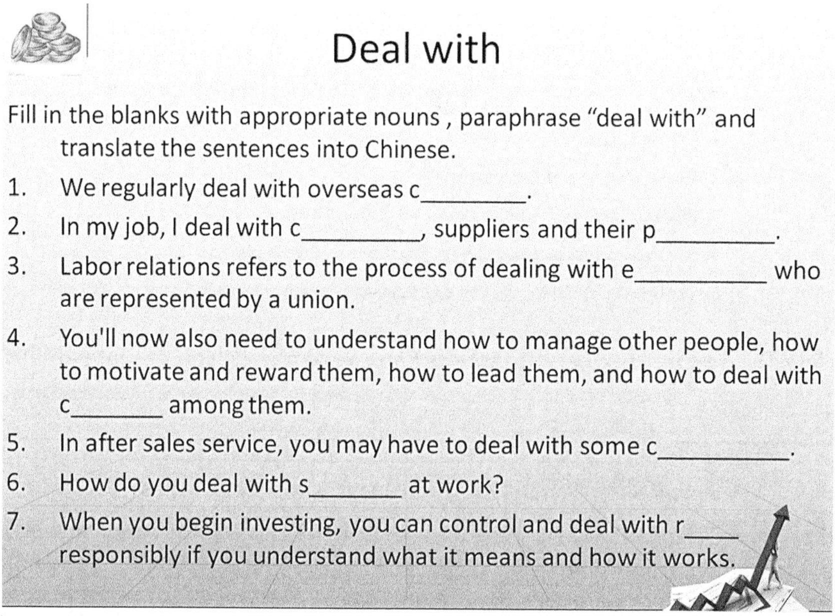

Deal with

Fill in the blanks with appropriate nouns , paraphrase "deal with" and translate the sentences into Chinese.

1. We regularly deal with overseas c_____.
2. In my job, I deal with c_____, suppliers and their p_____.
3. Labor relations refers to the process of dealing with e_____ who are represented by a union.
4. You'll now also need to understand how to manage other people, how to motivate and reward them, how to lead them, and how to deal with c_____ among them.
5. In after sales service, you may have to deal with some c_____.
6. How do you deal with s_____ at work?
7. When you begin investing, you can control and deal with r____ responsibly if you understand what it means and how it works.

图5.36　基于DEAL with索引行加工的填词、释义和翻译练习

设计说明：

图5.36中的空缺的八个词分别为companies、customers、problems、employees、conflicts、complaints、stress和risk，涵盖DEAL with的两大意义模式中的搭配词。其两大意义模式可分别释义为handle（problem）和do business with。翻译时也应有区别，例如句1是可译为"与海外公司<u>做生意</u>"。句2前半句可译为"与客户和供应商<u>打交道</u>"，后半句则可译为"<u>解决</u>他们的问题"。

步骤5：布置学生课后完成《商务短语动词（*Business Phrasal Verbs*）》一书第7到第8页关于deal with的词汇练习（节选见图5.37）。

EXERCISES

A. Using the information above, decide which use of *deal with* is illustrated in each of the following examples. Write the number on the line:

1. We'd prefer to deal with a single supplier. _____
2. Her advice column usually deals with interoffice problems and how to solve them. _____
3. The company will have to deal with several contaminated sites. _____

B. Rewrite the sentences by replacing the underlined word or phrase with the correct form of *deal with* (e.g. *is dealing with*).

1. The bank <u>services</u> a number of US corporations.

2. He likes his job and <u>meeting</u> people.

3. In my field of work, you <u>handle</u> a wide variety of issues.

4. Some companies only <u>offer services to</u> very wealthy people.

5. The translators have <u>processed</u> thousands of pages of documents.

图5.37 《商务短语动词》（*Business Phrasal Verbs*）中的deal with练习截图

案例述评：

本案例凸显商务英语高频短语动词deal with的深度知识教学，类似的短语在《商务英语综合教程》教材中还有货币银行学主题的enter into和领导力主题的comply with等等。短语动词（phrasal verbs）是以动词加上小品词（副词或介词或两者）的结构来表达一个不可分割的完整动词概念（汪榕培 1997），极具口语特征（沈玉刚 2002）。由于其高频而广泛的应用，也成为了英语流利地道的一个标准特征（Alexander 1988：153）。但是，由于其具有同形多义、一义多形与搭配灵活的特征，成为了二语学习者的难点（李全福 2000），中国英语学习者甚至对其有回避倾向（张彬 2007）。曾有学者（Breeze 2012）基于语料库研究发现短语动词是商务话语，尤其是经济金融话语的重要词汇特征。而教科书中的短语动词资源，因其习语性和多义性仅仅是点到为止，往往缺乏系统展示（俞珏 2011）。于是早在2008年Michael Barlow和Stephanie Burdine就基于美国英语商务口笔语语料编纂了《商务短语动词》（*Business Phrasal Verbs*）教材。全书共分65个单元，滚动式介绍并操练了52个高频短语动词。每个动词短语不但基于使用频数厘清不同搭配的短语模式意义，更设置了一批商务语境下使用的各种搭配结构或习语练习。本案例的步骤5使用的正是该书的部分练习。

该案例的设计特点是将deal with作为一个短语意义单位整体习得，尤其重视其使用的语境。教学活动体现了语料库语言学的拓展意义单位分析多个层面：包括步骤1引导学生归纳其搭配词与结构模式DEAL with + N/NP；步骤2通过对搭配词进行语义分类导出不同的语义偏好词所形成的两类意义模式，即"与……做生意"和"处理或应对问题或困境"；步骤3进一步深入探讨DEAL with第二种用法的语用功能（也称"语义韵"，详见Sinclair 2003：187），即"不得不设法应对棘手问题"。最后通过句子填词、释义及翻译等练习巩固目标短语在商务语境中的深度应用知识。活动由始至终都体现商务话语典型情景的语句。

5.3 小结

本章一共展示了七个教学案例。均围绕单元主题，利用多种教学资源（包括《商务英语综合教程》子库、BCT-2教材总库、网络文本或音视频、COCA在线语料库等）和语料库工具AntConc，实施了语料库辅助的商务专题知识构建及语言知识教学活动。其中5.1的案例侧重基于专门话题的主题词和词丛，通过语义范畴分类、语篇图示或专题基础知识框架构建等教学支架，凸显了商务英语专题的核心概念、概念之间的联系以及表达这些核心概念的语言要素。5.2的案例则侧重学科语言知识的深度学习。通过对商务英语多形态短语的拓展意义单位的多层面分析，尤其通过聚焦短语在语境中的词汇、语法、语义和语用共选关系，为学科知识和概念的表述构筑一个语言知识的实用支撑：即恰当地、专业地使用语言资源来表述这些学科知识。

七个案例中对于语料库短语的理念有不同角度的凸显。每一例都是从主题词作为切入点，因为它们特别能够揭示语篇的内容大意，具体到商务英语就是揭示该商务相关专题的基础知识和核心概念。继而超越单词型的主题词表而拓展至基于主题词的多字词丛分析。这是近年来对语篇关键性（keyness）的多种短语型态的探索趋势。因为不论是主题词丛（key clusters）、主题词短语（key phrase）、还是短语框架（Phrase frames）[1]，它们都是以频数驱动的方式提取，再加上形式结构或语篇功能的分类，就能在短语层面上更为准确地揭示语篇更完整、更复杂的意念以及篇章结构的

---

1 其中key clusters指用语料库检索软件按研究者预设长度和频数切点而自动切分提取的N元组（n-gram），详见Bondi（2010：3）。key phrases 指含有一个名词的三字或四字主题词短语，详见Tyrkko（2010：88）。Phrase frames指除了有一个字不同之外，其他字都相同的多字词丛，详见Warren（2010：115）。

典型特点（Bondi 2010：10）。

　　七个案例对短语的处理要求也不尽相同。案例5.1.1的短语基本为语篇主题的相关概念，其提取、识别和分类整合均由教师完成，数量较少，并通过情境语篇帮助学生理解和直接使用。案例5.1.2在专题核心概念短语的基础上补充了体现语篇衔接的短语，为学生产出专题性话语提供教学支架。案例5.1.3则进一步指引学生进行短语深加工（语义范畴分类），细化了对次主题概念的深度理解，并应用于口述主题概念图。案例5.1.4要求学生基于选文主题词拓展词丛进行主旨大意、难点化解和篇章结构特点等语篇分析。案例5.2.1要求学生通过一词多义的短语型式分析做商务英语话语和普通英语的跨体裁对比分析。而案例5.2.2和5.2.3分别对商务英语半技术性词和高频短语动词进行词汇搭配、类连接、语义偏好和语义韵四个层面的深度知识理解练习，并且通过填词、释义和翻译等练习来巩固对短语的认知和应用。

　　七个案例的设计还有一个突出的特点，即教师在课前对语料库资源进行教学加工的大量备课工作。这是当下学习型社会中高校教师的必备素养。从科研者素养看，教师在力行语料库分析、短语识别、范畴分类等过程中不断融入、整合和提升自身的商科知识体系、也不断廓清对短语作为商务话语内容支柱和语言流利度不可替代的关键媒介的认识。从教育者素养看，教师对于如何将语料库短语的教学加工融入到日常主题式教学中，尤其是如何设计与实施各种活动模式，在经历三轮教研的摸索和推进后，也获得了更为清晰的认识和有效的掌控。

第 6 章
语料库辅助的商务英语短语教学效果评价

本章按第4章展示的三轮教研行动的顺序展述语料库辅助商务英语短语教学的效果。效果评估和测试分析包括测试的目标、手段和效果三个部分。其中第一轮主要以语言测试与问卷调查的方式考查学生的短语意识、商科知识和自主学习能力的提升。第二轮主要通过商务概念词项测试考核学生对商科概念和语言知识的理解。第三轮主要通过主题概念图对比分析和主题习作语料对比分析来考查学生商科知识的建构能力和运用主题词语表达主题相关概念的能力。由于学生全程都撰写并提交反思日志，所以本章最后也对学生的日志语料进行分析，作为教学效果的佐证。

6.1 第一轮教研行动效果评价

基于第一轮教研行动的测评是基于行动之前提出的两个假设（详见第4章4.4.3）：

假设1：基于短语的语料库辅助的商务英语主题式教学短期内能促进学生的短语意识和能力的提升，及与主题相关的商科知识的建构。

假设2：基于短语的语料库辅助的商务英语主题式教学能提高学生的自主学习能力。

测试方式主要采用语言测试与问卷调查两种途径。教研者在第一轮教学始末对学生进行了商务英语短语能力测试（前测和后测试题分别参见附录4和附录5），同时在教学结束后一周内通过调查问卷（见附录6）对学生的短语意识、短语能力、商科知识和自主学习能力的自我认知进行调研。

6.1.1 商务英语短语能力测试

6.1.1.1 测试设计形式与目的

教研者按照"商务主题词知识量表"（详见第4章4.4.1）的选词原则从BTC-2教材总库中选取10个目标词汇。这些并非新词，而是学生在已经学习过的商务英语教材中使用的高频主题词。目的是考查学生对目标词在商务语境中的接受性和产出性知识的广度和深度。试题包括单项选择、填空和语篇补全三种题型，一共四道大题，26道题项，每题1分，总分26分。三种题型的形式与目的依次为：

（1）通过单项选择题考查考生是否在特定商务语境中识别（recognize）目标词的搭配结构，如：

You need capital to start a new _____.

A. organization   B. environment

C. opportunities   D. business

（答案是D）

（2）以首字母提示的词语填空题，考查考生能否在商务语境提示下记起（recall）并以拼写形式产出（produce）目标词，如：

In turn, these attitudes usually lead to higher levels of both e_____ motivation and job satisfaction.

（答案是employee）

（3）通过单项选择题从四个目标词搭配结构中选出有语义反差的一个，考查学生对目标词搭配结构的丰富度，如：

A. growing market   B. developing market

C. expanding market   D. declining market

（答案是D）

（4）以语篇补全测试的形式，考核学生能否在图片展示的商务语境下以拼写的形式产出（produce）商务英语高频短语动词，如

This picture describes your daily work. So when asked about your job description, what would you say?

I _____ the customer complaints every day.

（答案是deal with）

6.1.1.2　测试结果分析

表6.1显示，教学班的测试平均分从13.78提高到17.96；配对样本T检验结果显示，前后测成绩有显著差异（p=.000<.05）。也就是说，全班后侧平均分相对于前侧有显著提高。

表6.1　教学班前测和后测配对样本T检验（双尾）

	实验组实验前后短语能力测试				
	N	平均分	标准差	t	p
实验前	23	13.78	3.704	-4.834	.000
实验后		17.96	3.723		

p<.05

但同时也发现：不同语言水平的学习者的短语能力提高程度存在差异。当教研者基于学生的入学前高考英语科目分数，按照30%、40%和30%的比例分成高分组、中间组和低分组；而后分别对照各组学习者在上述短语能力测试的分数，得出结果见表6.2。

表6.2　三组学生前测和后测配对样本T检验（双尾）

	高分组	中间组	低分组
人数	7	9	7
实验前平均分（标准差）	15.29（2.752）	14.00（4.950）	12.00（1.915）
实验后平均分（标准差）	19.57（3.505）	17.78（3.346）	16.57（4.276）
t	-3.333	-3.091	-2.107
p	.016	.015	.080

p<.05

表6.2显示，三个组内的学生平均分均有提高（19.57＞15.29，17.78＞14.00，16.57＞12.00），但高分组和中间组分数的提升有明显差异（高分组：p=.016<.05；中间组：p=.015<.05），而低分组未显示明显差异（p=.080>.050）。由此表明，在同样的教学实验条件下，基于短语的语料库辅助的主题式教学对中高级语言水平的学习者的短语能力的提高更为

显著；而对于低语言水平的学习者的影响不太明显。教研者进一步对低分组的7位学生进行课后访谈并细读他们的反思日志，获得到以下信息：其中仅1人总是有意识地去使用习得到的商务短语，而另6人表示有时或经常这么做；2人表示对于教学实验中教授的语料库的工具已经基本掌握或掌握很好，其他5人表示掌握较差或一般。由此可推测，低分组学生短语能力测试分数提高不大或许与短语意识的提升和语料库自主学习技能的掌握这两者的不理想状况有关。

6.1.2　商务英语短语教学调查问卷

6.1.2.1　调查问卷设计

调查问卷分为两个部分调查学生对自身的短语意识和能力、商科知识以及自主学习能力的报告（见附录6）。第一部分用7道多项选择题回应上述假设1，考查学生在教学实验前后的短语意识和能力及商科知识的提升。1-4题分别考查学生在教研行动前后的短语意识。尽管"意识"在二语习得研究领域是一个有争议的话题，Krashen（1981）在二语习得研究中对"无意识的语言习得"和"有意识的语言学习"之区分确实是广为接受的。Richard（1990：129）认为，"关注"是将输入转化为输出的充分必要条件。他提出意识的三个层面：看到、关注与理解（转化为知识）。本研究因此将短语意识定义为：有意识地关注短语，并通过理解将其转化为知识。基于对短语意识的界定，问卷中的题1-4以学生在学习中关注和理解短语的频率来衡量学生的短语意识。题5考查学生的短语能力提升的自我认知。6-7题考查其对商科知识提升的认知。1-7题的选项均参考Likert五点式自测量表，设计5个层级的选项。1-4题的选项为：A.总是，B.经常，C.有时，D.很少，E.从不；5-7题的选项是：A.完全符合，B.基本符合，C.说不清楚，D.不太符合，E.完全不符合。

调查问卷第二部分设计了8个题项考查学生使用语料库辅助的商务英语短语学习的自主学习能力。从四个变量切入：（1）对于教授的语料库工具和在线语料库平台的掌握程度；（2）在课程内外使用语料库辅助的学习方式的频率；（3）与教师和同学们交流学习语料库辅助方法的频率；（4）在今后的英语和商科学习中使用语料库辅助方法的意愿。因为掌握方法并形成学习习惯和培养短语意识同等重要，只有两者兼备才能持续、有效地进行学习，所以后三者和第一个变量同等重要。具体题项形式同第一部分，采用单选题型，并参考Likert五点式自测量表，设计5个层级的选项。

题12、14和15补充填空，在必要时学生可补充具体信息，如使用语料库的场合、原因及涉及的课程等等。

6.1.2.2　问卷数据分析

第一轮教研行动结束后，教学班23名学生回答了调查问卷，回收有效答卷23份。经过对采集的数据进行分析后有以下四点发现。

（1）学生关注短语的意识有显著提高，但使用短语的意识无明显提升。

来自问卷题1和2的数据显示（见表6.3），教学实验前，学习者在"综合商务英语"课程学习中经常对短语进行关注和理解并不多，仅仅21.7%，即5个学生表示自己经常关注和理解商务话语中的短语结构；43.5%的学生有时关注；其余34.8%的学生则选择很少。但在教学实验之后，已有过半（52.2%）的学生自述在该课程中经常关注；而原先很少关注的学生比例从34.8%骤减为4.3%。

表6.3　教学实验前后学生的商务英语短语意识

	总是		经常		有时		很少		从不	
	人数（个）	比例（%）	人数（个）	比例（%）	人数（个）	比例（%）	人数（个）	比例（%）	人数（个）	比例（%）
前	0	0	5	21.7	10	43.5	8	34.8	0	0
后	1	4.3	12	52.2	9	39.1	1	4.3	0	0

此外，题3数据还显示已有近半数（43.5%）的学生在学习其他课程时也"经常关注"；选择"有时关注"的学生超过半数（56.5%）。

题4调查学生在教学实验后是否有意识去使用短语，因为这是将短语意识转化为短语能力的重要一步。结果是：仅有3位学生（13%）自述"经常"主动使用学过的商英短语，18位（78.3%）选择"有时"，2位（8.7%）选择"很少"。为了更清晰地展现学生短语意识的变化，教研者对教学实验前学生短语意识（题1），分别对实验后学生的短语意识（题2）和短语使用（题4）两者进行T检验。在SPSS输入变量价值时，将5个层级的选项"从不""很少""有时""经常"和"总是"分别赋值为1、2、3、4和5。结果见表6.4。

表6.4　实验前后短语意识配对样本T检验（双尾）

配对	t	df	Sig.（2-tailed）
实验前关注短语的意识–实验后关注短语的意识	-4.746	22	.000
实验前关注短语的意识–实验后使用短语的意识	-.940	22	.357

Sig. <0.05

　　表6.4数据表明，学生关注短语的意识实验前后的差异有显著意义。也就是说，调查问卷中关于短语意识部分的数据验证了上述对表6.3的结果分析，即学生参加了教学实验后，在课堂内外关注商务英语短语意识均有显著提高。但是在输出层面，即主动使用商务英语短语的意识并没有明显变化。这一结果可用二语习得过程的理论框架来解释。正如Gass（1988：200）和Gass & Selinker（2008：481）所指出，二语习得过程由5个概念组成。包括"注意/觉察到的语言输入信息""被理解的语言输入""语言的内化吸收""内隐的语言知识/中介语系统的形成"和"语言输出"（如图6.1所示）。这5个过程环环相扣；但第一个和第二个环节上的意识提高并不意味着第五个环节上也一定有明显提高；是否有最终的输出环节的变化，还有赖于第三个和第四个环节的变化。由此提示教研者在教学任务输入部分的活动设计上加以改进，以促成第五个环节即语言输出层面发生变化。

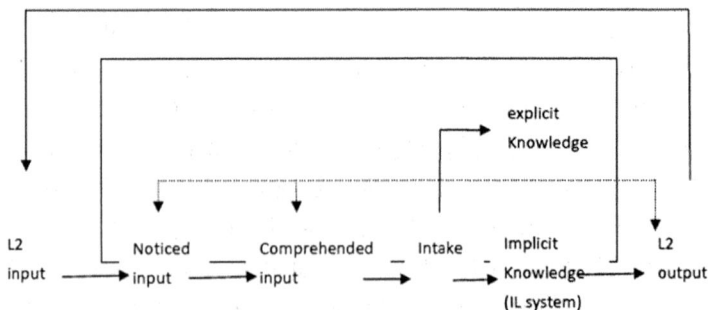

图6.1　二语习得过程图示

（笔者根据Gass & Selinker 2008：481的原图稍作编辑）

（2）大部分学生认同语料库辅助短语教学的方法

题5数据显示（见表6.5），有近70%的学习者基本认同"语料库辅助的教学方法"，认为提高了对商务英语短语的认知、理解和应用的能力；表示"基本不同意"仅有2位。这一结果也印证了之前商务英语短语能力测试中的发现。

表6.5 对商务英语短语能力提升的自我认知

		人数（个）	比例（%）
有效选项	基本不同意	2	8.7
	没有看法	5	21.7
	基本同意	16	69.6
总计		23	100.0

（3）多数学生未认同短语教学能提升商科知识

题6的统计数据显示（见表6.6），仅有8位（34.8%）学生认为语料库短语教学对自身商科知识有明显提升，47.8%的学习者对此没有看法，而4位（17.4%）学生不认同这一点。对于多数学生不认同短语教学能提升商科知识这一发现，可能要归因于第一轮教研行动中的活动设计并不能有效地将商科知识习得融入到基于短语的语料库辅助的商务英语主题式教学模式中，因而问卷中此反馈给下一轮教学设计与评估的改进提供参考。

表6.6 对商科知识提升的自我认知

		人数（个）	比例（%）
有效选项	基本不同意	4	17.4
	没有看法	11	47.8
	基本同意	8	34.8
总计		23	100.0

（4）对语料库辅助教学的反馈基本正面

学生对语料库辅助教学的反馈主要表现在以下四个方面的答题选项。

（a）对于语料库工具和在线语料库平台的掌握程度（题8）

表6.7显示，有9位（39.1%）学生表示掌握良好，11位（47.8%）学生表示掌握一般，仅3位（13.0%）学生表示掌握很差。故从整体来看，大部分学生已基本掌握所教授的语料库工具和在线语料库平台的使用方法和技巧。

表6.7　对语料库工具和在线语料库平台的掌握程度

		人数（个）	比例（%）
有效选项	很好	9	39.1
	一般	11	47.8
	较差	3	13.0
总计		23	100.0

（b）课内外使用语料库辅助的学习方法的频率（题9-12）

表6.8显示，除了"综合商务英语"课程之外，在另两门商务语言类课程，即"商务英语听说"和"商务英语写作"课程中，分别有17.4%和34.8%的学生表示自己高频（总是或经常）使用语料库辅助的方式进行自主学习，分别有26.1%和39.1%的学生表示"有时"使用，而很少或从不使用的学生比例分别为56%和26.1%。从绝对数字上考察，相较于"商务英语听说"课而言，学生在"商务英语写作"课上更为频繁地使用语料库辅助的学习方式。

表6.8　商务语言类课程中使用语料库辅助的学习方法的频率

	总是		经常		有时		很少		从不	
	人数（个）	比例（%）	人数（个）	比例（%）	人数（个）	比例（%）	人数（个）	比例（%）	人数（个）	比例（%）
综	1	4.3	3	13.0	11	47.8	8	34.8		
听			4	17.4	6	26.1	9	39.1	4	17.4
写	2	8.7	6	26.1	9	39.1	4	17.4	2	8.7

另外，有近半数学生（43.5%）自述在"管理学原理"课程中也会经常或有时运用语料库辅助的方式自主学习，见表6.9。

表6.9　管理学原理课程中使用语料库辅助的学习方法的频率

		人数（个）	比例（%）
有效选项	经常	4	17.4
	有时	6	26.1
	很少	5	21.7
	从不	8	34.8
总计		23	100.0

除了以上课程之外，有73.9%的学习者表示他们在本专业其他课程中会使用语料库辅助的学习方式。有的甚至在双学位的商科课程（会计学原理、经济学原理和营销学原理）中也会使用。

（c）与教师和同学们交流学习语料库辅助的方法的频率（题13）

表6.10显示有近三分之二（65.2%）的学生表示"有时"或者"经常"同教师或同学交流语料库辅助的学习方法。

表6.10　与教师和同学交流语料库辅助的学习方法的频率

		人数（个）	比例（%）
有效选项	经常	3	13.0
	有时	12	52.2
	很少	7	30.5
	从不	1	4.3
总计		23	100.0

（d）在今后的英语和商科学习中使用语料库辅助的学习方式的意愿（题14-15）

表6.11显示所有同学都表示会将语料库辅助的方式运用在今后的英语学习中，只是意愿的程度有所不同；而对于商科课程学习也有这种意愿的学生约半数（12人）。

表6.11 在英语和商科课程中继续使用语料库辅助的学习方法的意愿

	总是		经常		有时		很少		从不	
	人数（个）	比例（%）	人数（个）	比例（%）	人数（个）	比例（%）	人数（个）	比例（%）	人数（个）	比例（%）
语	1	4.3	6	26.1	13	56.5	3	13.1	0	0
商	0	0	12	52.2	8	34.8	2	8.7	1	4.4

综合以上各表的调查数据可以总结为以下几点：

第一，大部分学生基本掌握进行自主学习的语料库工具和在线语料库平台的使用技巧。

第二，大部分学生在"综合商务英语"课程中较高频率地使用语料库辅助的方式进行自主学习。在其他商务语言类课程中也会使用，尤见"商务英语写作"课程。在商科课程的学习中，学生适度使用该方法进行自主学习。

第三，大部分学习者会主动向教师和同学交流学习使用语料库的方法和技巧。

第四，绝大部分学习者愿意在今后的英语和商科学习中继续使用语料库辅助的方式进行自主学习。

由此可得出结论，第一轮教研行动有效地提升了学生使用语料库辅助的方式进行自主学习的能力。

6.1.3 第一轮测评小结及反思

第一轮教研行动主要通过测试和调查问卷，辅以课堂观察、日志和访谈等方式（见第四章4.4.3）获得的定量和定性的数据进行分析，得到以下发现：

（1）该模式教学能使学生意识到商务英语短语之重要性，于是开始关注与理解，但是主动使用商务英语短语的意识未有明显提升。

（2）测试显示，该模式能在短期（6周）内明显提升学生（尤其是中高级语言水平学习者）的短语识别能力。

（3）学生对使用语料库辅助学习商务英语知识普遍认同，但对该模式能否明显提升商科知识尚未有一致认可。

（4）该模式下，学生使用语料库方式（工具、资源和平台等）的自主学习能力和意愿较强。

综上所述，这一轮教研行动以内容为依托的商务英语主题式教学宗旨而言，内容构建与语言知识习得的双重目标尚未完全实现。基于本轮的教学及测评反馈（参见本书第4章4.4.3），教研者认为要在第二轮教研行动提出新问题，要对教学方案进行补充，还要在效果评估形式上做出相应调整。

6.2 第二轮教研行动效果评价

鉴于第一轮教学反馈的问题，教研者在第二轮教研行动中针对语料库辅助的商务英语短语教学嵌入主题式教学模式的教学活动设计提出更为具体的三个研究问题（详见本书第四章4.4.4）：

问题1：如何降低第一环节中教学活动的难度使得学生更加积极有效地参与？

问题2：如何有效设计课堂活动促使学生在提升短语能力的同时构建主题相关的商科知识？

问题3：如何有效设计任务类型促使学生更高有效地输出/运用短语？

为了更有效地回应上述问题2，本轮教学评价则改用商务概念词项测试为主要评价手段。

6.2.1　商务概念词项测试

6.2.2.1　测试设计

本研究以BTC-2中约23万词次的《商业概论》教材子库为目标语料（因为这部商务入门类课程教材涵盖商科各重要板块的基础知识，相比另四个教材子库更具基础性和全面性）；以CROWN语料库为参照语料库提取主题词表。参考并扩展Nelson（2000）对商务主题词的语义分类，将头100个主题词进行以下语义范畴分类：

（1）商业组织：business、firm、company、enterprise、corporation等
（2）学科主题：management、accounting、marketing等
（3）商务人员：competitor、CEO、entrepreneur、customer、consumer、
　　　boss、distributor、employee、manager、partner、shareholder、

staff、supplier等

（4）商务活动或事件：business、communication、competition、delivery、development、distribution、investment、payment、takeover、exchange、supply等

（5）商务描述：big、competitive、corporate、financial、global、local、low、International、strategic等

（6）商业环境变化趋势：increase、drop、decline、peak等

（7）政府或央行行为：raise、lower、impose等

（8）商务测量：price、cost、rate、percentage、value、figures、data等

（9）商务行动：pay、achieve、confirm、develop、discuss、improve、manage、receive、provide、sell、send、purchase等

然后从各类主题词中遴选数量相当的若干目标词，设计商务语境中主题词的填空题型（其中给定目标词首字母做提示），如，

Koch's company is Boston Beer, and its flagship p ＿＿＿＿＿＿＿＿ is a premium beer called Samuel Adams.（答案是product）

该项测试的目的是考查学生对基础商务概念的理解及商务主题词的产出能力。在第二轮教研行动之前和之后分别前测40个目标词（见附录7）和后测80个目标词（见附录8），其中前40道题项（简称"后测1"）与前测相同；后40道同类型题项（简称"后测2"）的目标词是按照前测的选词标准提取的另40个主题词。

6.2.2.2　测试结果分析

前测–后测1和前测–后测2两轮配对样本T检验（表6.12）表明，学生后测成绩相较于前测有明显提升。

表6.12　商务概念词项前测和后测配对样本T检验

配对		均值	N	t	df	Sig.（双侧）
对1	前测	17.1	28	-19.513	27	.000
	后测1	30.3	28			
对2	前测	17.1	28	-9.720	27	.000
	后测2	23.9	28			

Sig. <0.05

　　其中，同题测试结果（指后测1）有显著提高，表明学习者经过教学实验后对主题词的产出能力有了明显提升（.000<0.05），不论是由于记忆效应，还是与教学中主题词及短语的反复呈现有关，它都表明学生对商科主题词的认知程度有明显提升。而后测拓展的40题（指后测2）与前测结果相比依然有显著提升，更表明学习者对商务主题词使用能力的提高，因为他们关注、理解并产出前测中并未出现过的目标词。

6.2.2　第二轮测评小结及反思

　　本轮教研行动主要通过商务概念词项测试并辅以课堂观察和教学反馈（学习反思日志分析）方式（见本书第四章4.4.4），主要发现如下：

　　（1）测试显示学生对重要商业概念的理解和表述能力有明显提升。
　　（2）课堂观察与教学反馈显示，新增的课前自由词汇联想构建主题概念图的活动有效激活商务主题相关的重要概念，并促进学生课堂参与度。

　　然而，本轮的测试仅考查学生能否理解商科话题的基本概念，并记住英语表述，但是还不能反映其对商科知识体系及其语言资源的系统了解和综合应用。因此，在第三轮教研行动中，教研者将依据本轮测评的反馈提出更为聚焦的教学问题，并开发更为有效的评估方式。

6.3 第三轮教研行动效果评价

　　鉴于第二轮教学反馈中出现的问题，教研者在第三轮教研行动中针对语料库辅助的商务英语短语教学嵌入主题式教学模式提出更为聚焦教学目标的两个研究问题（详见本书第四章4.4.5）：

　　问题1：如何在活动设计中更加有机地融入商务主题知识与商务英语短语的学习？

　　问题2：如何更全面地评估学生学科知识与语言知识的同步提升？

　　在本轮教研行动中教研者使用了两种新的评估方式：（1）对比分析学生在单元学习前后基于自由词汇联想构建的主题概念图，（2）对比分析学生在单元学习前后基于同一话题的作文语料。

6.3.1　基于自由词汇联想的概念构图

概念构图（concept mapping）源于David Ausubel 在20世纪中提出的同化理论（assimilation theory），以往主要用于科学教学，以增进学科知识理解的教学技术。Ausubel（1963, 1968）依据建构式学习（constructivism learning）的观点，强调先前知识（prior knowledge）是学习新知识的基础框架（framework）。概念构图通过概念外在化（externalization）和搭建新旧知识的桥梁，推进深度学习（Irvin 1995）。除了作为教学技术，还有学者还论证了其同时作为教学评估的有效手段（Novak & Gowin 1984; Novak 1990; William 2004; MacNeil 2007）。他们认为，将某个主题的相关概念及其关系图形化，作为来组织和表征知识的工具。具体操作是将主题概念置于圆圈或方框中，然后用连线将相关的概念或名词连接，需要时在连线上表明两个概念间的意义关系。分析概念图可从其四个要素入手：概念（concepts）、命题（propositions）、交叉连接（cross-links）和层次结构（hierarchical framework）。

6.3.1.1　概念构图活动设计

本研究在第二轮教研行动中，就开始尝试在单元教学的第一个环节即"主题听说热身"开始前请学生独立完成通过自由词汇联想进行主题相关的核心概念构图，激活自己对该主题的已有知识网路，以促进学生在后续的主题听说活动的参与度与有效性。概念在第二轮教研行动中受到了学生的普遍认可，于是教研者在第三轮教研行动中，进一步将其拓展成教学前后分别进行两次相同要求的概念构图。一则作为教学活动形式以可视化的方式呈现其知识体系和概念的重要语言表述，二则通过前后对比可以观测到学生在这两方面的提升。

6.3.1.2　单元教学前后主题概念图对比分析

对比学生在第三轮教研行动各单元教学始末的概念图，发现学后重建的概念图在概念和命题的丰富度明显提高，体现在：（1）主题词和短语的使用数量明显提高；（2）图示节点交叉连接的复杂性和层次结构的多样性也有明显提高。下面分别以货币银行学（money and banking）教学单元同一学生前后两份概念图为例，展示其知识体系及主题词和短语的发展。

entity

value { appreciate / depreciate

(wealth) money (coins, seashell, gold, silver, papes)

income

deposit

principle

buy

bank → interest rate { simple interest rate / double interest rate

risk
return
yield to maturity
nominal interest rate
real interest rate

balance

invest

coupon(discount coupon)

stocks

supply and demand { inflation / deflation

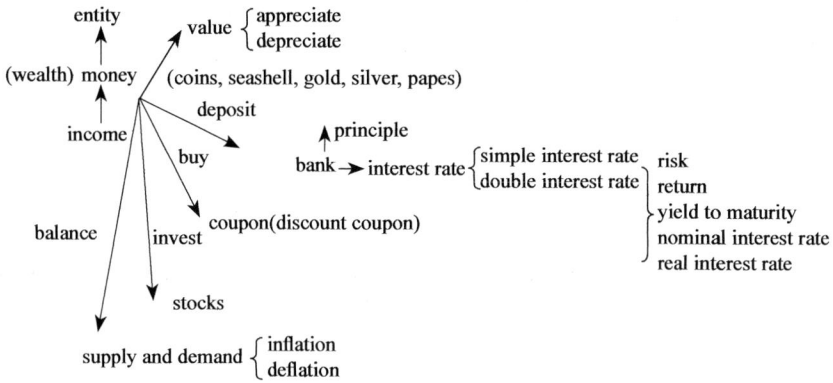

图6.2 学前基于已有知识初建的核心概念图

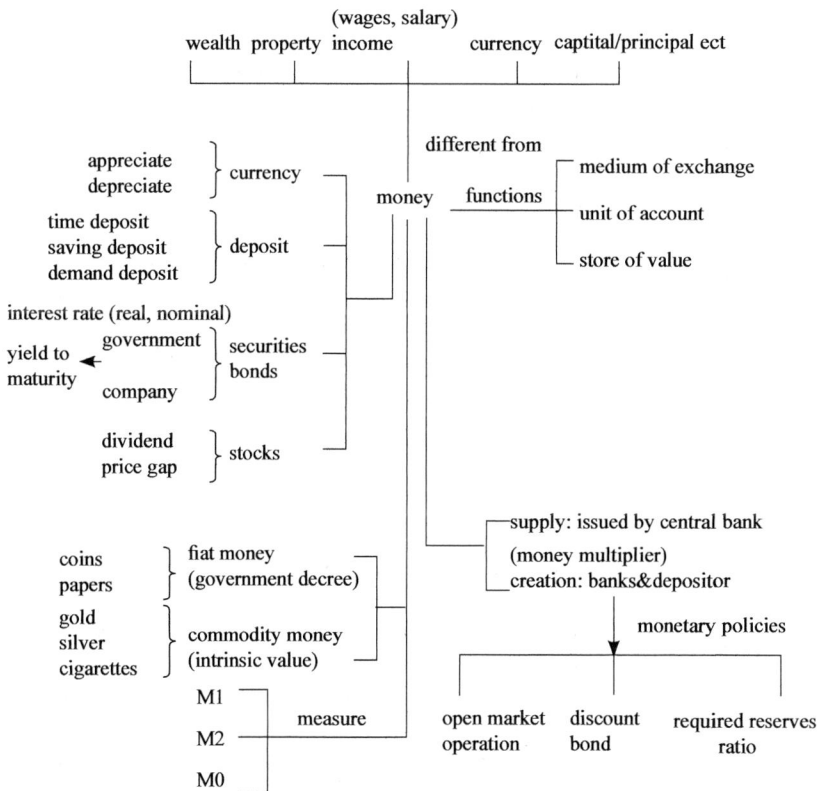

(wages, salary)

wealth property income currency captital/principal ect

appreciate
depreciate } currency

money

different from

functions

medium of exchange

unit of account

store of value

time deposit
saving deposit
demand deposit } deposit

interest rate (real, nominal)

yield to maturity ← government / company } securities bonds

dividend
price gap } stocks

coins
papers } fiat money (government decree)

gold
silver
cigarettes } commodity money (intrinsic value)

M1
M2
M0 } measure

supply: issued by central bank

(money multiplier)
creation: banks&depositor

monetary policies

open market
operation

discount
bond

required reserves
ratio

图6.3 学后重建的核心概念图

对比图6.2和图6.3出现的主题词和主题词拓展词丛的绝对数量，可从量化层面凸显学生在概念构建方面的明显改进，见表6.13和6.14。

表6.13 学前的核心概念图中的要素

要素	数量	详情
概念	24	money, entity, wealth, income, value, coin, seashell, gold, silver, paper, deposit, stock, coupon, discount coupon, bank, principal, interest rate, simple interest rate, double interest rate, risk, return, yield to maturity, nominal interest rate, real interest rate
命题	11	• Money is an entity. • Income can be in the form of money. • Money has value. • Value can appreciate and depreciate. • Money can be deposited in banks. • Money can buy coupon. • Money can be invested in stock. • Force of supply of demand of money can bring about inflation and deflation. • Deposit in banks is principal whose return is decided by interest rate. • Interest rate has the classification of simple interest rate and double interest rate. • Interest rate can also be categorized into nominal interest rate and real interest rate.
交叉连接符号	11	大括号2个，箭头线段7个，小括号2个
层级	4	4级1个，多为2级

表6.14 学后的核心概念构图中的要素

要素	数量	详情
概念	49	money, wealth, property, income, wages, salary, currency, capital, principal, deposit, time deposit, saving deposit, demand deposit, interest rate, real interest rate, nominal interest rate, securities, bonds, government bonds, company bonds, stocks, dividend, price gap, fiat money, government decree, coins, papers, commodity money, intrinsic value, gold, silver, cigarettes, M1, M2, M3, functions, medium of exchange, unit of account, store of value, supply, central bank, money multiplier, creation, banks, depositor, monetary policies, open market operation, discount bond, required reserves ratio

续表

要素	数量	详情
命题	20	<ul><li>Money is different from wealth, property, income, wages, salary, currency, and capital/principal.</li><li>Money can be in the form of currency, deposit, securities like bonds and stocks.</li><li>Money can be fiat money or commodity money.</li><li>Money has the functions of medium of exchange, unit of account, and store of value.</li><li>Money is supplied and issued by the central bank.</li><li>Money is created by banks and depositors.</li><li>Banks are money multiplier.</li><li>Money policies include open market operation, discount bond and required reserves ratio.</li><li>Currency can appreciate and depreciate.</li><li>Deposit can be divided into time deposit, saving deposit and demand deposit.</li><li>Demand deposit's return is decided by interest rate.</li><li>Securities include bonds and stocks.</li><li>Bonds can be issued by government or company.</li><li>The return from bonds is yield to maturity.</li><li>The return from stocks is in the form of dividend and price gap.</li><li>Fiat money is defined by government decree.</li><li>Fiat money could be in the form of coins and paper.</li><li>Commodity money has its intrinsic value.</li><li>Gold, silver, and cigarettes have ever been commodity money.</li><li>Money supplied can be measure in M1, M2, and M3.</li></ul>
交叉连接符号	11	分级大括号14个，小括号5个，线段32（其中1个带箭头）
层级	4	1–4级，多为3–4级

表6.13和6.14分别列举出前后两份概念图中四个要素的使用情况。对比发现，后图在概念和命题的数量上远远高过于前图（49＞24，20＞11），显示丰富度大为提升。而在交叉连接符号的数量及构图的层级上，后图也有绝对优势。显示该生通过基于语料库短语的商务主题教学后，能建构更为完善的知识体系，同时也掌握了表达核心概念和基础知识的重要单词和短语。然而这似乎不足以显示学生对这些学科知识与语言知识的具体应用。因此，本轮的测评还设计了以下主题写作任务。

6.3.2 主题写作

6.3.2.1 主题写作设计

在第三轮教研行动中，学生在每个单元教学之前和之后分别有一次同题作文（见本书第4章4.4.5）。一来给学生在语篇层面运用主题词和短语的机会；二来可用于考查学生对表述重要知识概念的短语的理解和使用能力是否提升。主题作文的题目包括：

（1）货币银行学（money and banking）单元：How to spend your money? Suppose you graduated a couple of years ago, having a steady job of 10,000 yuan RMB for each month, and now your parents funded you 600,000 yuan RMB. Would you like to buy a 2-million-house or save the money into a bank? Justify your choice.

Please supply an appropriate title for your composition and finish your writing within 40 minutes.

（2）投资学（investment）单元：Is it a rational choice to invest in China's real estate?

Some people think that there exists a big bubble in China's real estate market, but others don't think so. Watch the video from CBS NEWS and then write a composition of approximately 350 words on this issue to state your own opinion on:

a. The reasons for soaring housing price

b. Whether there is a real estate bubble in China

c. Whether it is a rational choice to invest in China's real estate

Please supply an appropriate title for your composition and finish your writing within 40 minutes.

教研者将前后两批作文分别建库（简称"前库"和"后库"），大小分别为17, 323和22,054词次。使用LancsBox[1]（Brezina *et al.* 2015）和AntConc软件，对两库进行多维对比分析，包括主题词使用数量、主题词搭配网络和主题词搭配词表等等，分析结果见下节。

---

1 1 LancsBox是英国兰卡斯特大学开发的语料库分析软件，可供用户免费下载和使用。网址参见 http://corpora.lancs.ac.uk/lancsbox/。

6.3.2.2　主题写作语料分析

首先，使用AntConc软件的主题词提取（keyword list）功能，分别以CROWN语料库为参照语料库，按照关键值排序，从前库和后库中分别提取头100个主题词（以下简称前库主题词和后库主题词，详见附录14），并在BTC-2教材总库中选取所有"货币银行学"和"投资学"的语料建"货币银行学和投资学"专题微型语料库，并提取主题词表（按同样参数设置进行提取，简称专题主题词，详见附录14）作为参照主题词表进行对比，结果见表6.15。

表6.15　前后库主题词中出现的专题主题词

前后库共享	前库独有	后库独有
bank, banks, buy, deposit, fund, government, growth, however, income, inflation, interest, investing, investment, investors, is, market, money, pay, payment, price, prices, real, rate, return, value,	debt	economic, risk, supply
共计25个	共计1个	共计3个

表6.15显示，前后库主题词中出现的专题微型语料库中的主题词数量相当，分别为26和28个。除了共享的24个专题主题词，前库独有的loan（贷款）和debt（债务）均是与写作任务内容高度相关的词汇：因为中国一线城市房价高，投资者在贷款买房或进行房产投资时，大多需要申请抵押贷款，构成债务。而后库中独有的主题词economic（经济的）、risk（风险）和supply（供给）则指向了投资分析的第一要素"风险（risk）"和价格决定机制的经济分析（economic）"供给（supply）"和"需求"的关系。由此可见，学生作文的前后库虽在覆盖本专题主题词的类符总数上无差异，但后库的作文在分析投资选择时更全面运用投资分析要素和经济学相关知识（供求关系）进行论证。

进一步选取两库共享的、且是该专题主题词的两个高频实意词price（前库208次，后库278次）和market（前库137次，后库199次）来考查各自搭配词的相貌。教研者先用兰卡斯特大学开发的LancsBox软件的GraphColl功能图示price和market两个主题词在前后库中搭配词的整体图像（见图6.4和图6.5），继而通过AntConc的Collocate功能提取两者的搭配词表（见表6.16对比分析）。

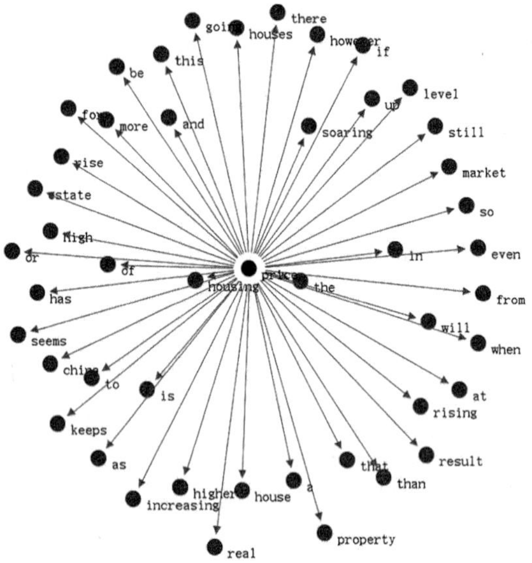

图6.4　前库中price的搭配词网络

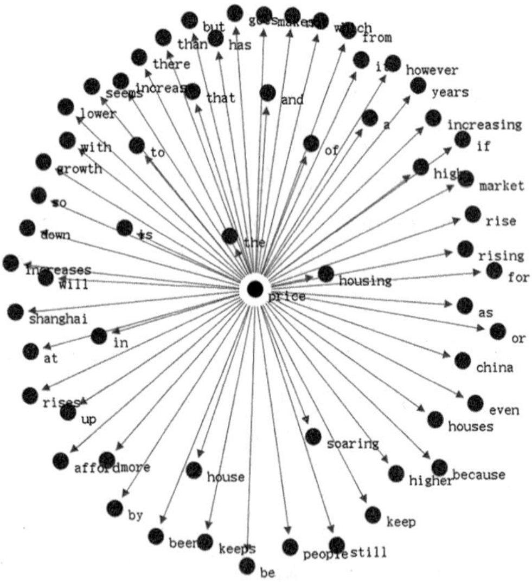

图6.5　后库中price的搭配词网络

图6.4和6.5分别展示price在前后库的搭配词网络（跨距为左4右4，T≥2）。图中心圆点的price是节点词，其向外伸展的、带箭头的线段链接

各个搭配词，线段长短表示与节点词的搭配强度，越短表示搭配越强。直观对比可发现后图比前图的连线更多更密，显示price在后库的搭配词更为丰富；同时，两者的搭配词中的商科主题词数量上的差异可有直观的差异，如前者主要为increase、market、soar和higher，而后者除此之外还有rise、down、lower、growth等。

在GraphColl中进一步点击搭配词中的market（同为专题主题词）可呈现其与price在前后库中的立体共选网络（见图6.6和图6.7）。进一步发现后库（见图6.7）中increase作为price的搭配词有更丰富的词形变体，即除了与前库相同的increasing外，还有increase和increases。而与price搭配的另一个专题主题词market就呈现了更为立体和交错的共选网络（如图6.7所示）。

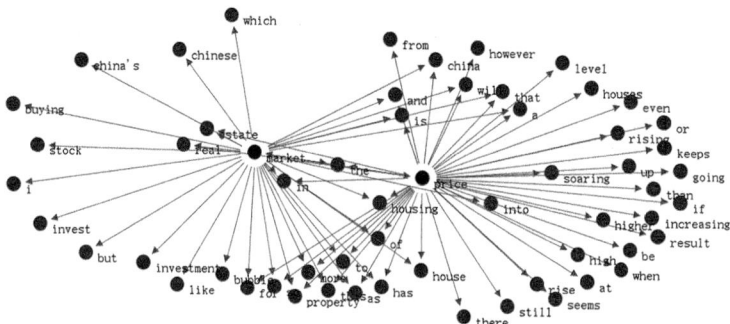

图6.6　前库中price与market的立体共选网络

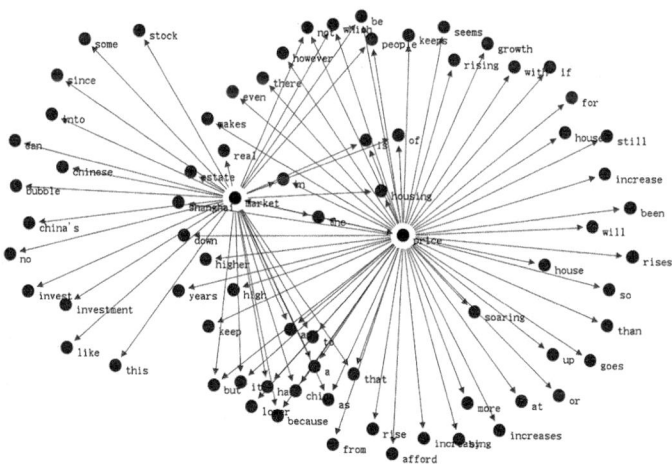

图6.7　后库中price与market的立体共选网络

教研者继而使用AntConc软件中的搭配词（Collocates）检索功能在前库和后库中分别提取price的搭配词表（跨距为左4右4，T≥2），对其搭配词进行更为精确和详尽的对比分析。得知price 在前后库中的搭配词分别为106和130个，提取其中的实义词做词性分类对比，结果如表6.16。

表6.16　前后库中price的实义词类搭配词对比

类别	前后共享搭配词	前库独用	后库独用
名词、代词	China、Shanghai、class、economy、estate、future、gap、growth、house、housing、land、level、market、people、perspective、price、result（17个）	property、origin、share、tier、case、they、risk（7个）	demand、one、inflation、opinion、urbanization、payment、you、index、ratio、he、million、Beijing、thing、past、time、stock、rmb、income、month（19个）
动词类	afford、believe、climb、continue、go、increase、keep、raise、lower、rise rising、skyrocketing、will、can（14个）	control、pay、know、plummet、suppose（5个）	wonder、decrease、fall、curb、should（5个）
形容词、副词、限定词	addition、even、still、current、up、down、first、high、real、many、more、nevertheless、dramatically、extremely、nearly、that、this、my、total（19个）	definitely、today、strange、continuously、constantly、last、middle（7个）	however、recent、especially、nowadays、potential、very、second、unaffordable、continually、hardly、dramatic、likely、another、long、far、much、large、no（18个）
合计	50个	19个	42个

表6.16显示前后库共享price实义类搭配词分别为69个和92个类符。主要包括与写作主题相关的名词（China、estate、house、housing、market、economy、growth等），和价格描述及市场分析相关的动词（climb、go、increase、keep、raise、lower、rise、skyrocketing等），以及描述价格变化波动及分析市场的修饰词（current、up、down、high、dramatically、 extremely、nearly）等。而两者独用的搭配词却有很大差异。首先从独有搭配词种类的总数看，后库是前库的两倍之多（42＞19），其中名词类和形容词类的搭配词类符增数更为明显（19＞7，18＞7）。再从price与搭配词组成的短语内容看，前库与"货币"和"投资"的主题相关的词仅有property（财产）、share（股票）和risk（风险）3个，而后库则有9个，包括：demand（需求）、inflation（通胀）、urbanization（城市化）、payment（支付）、index（指数）、ratio（比率）、stock（股票）、rmb（人民币）和income（收入）。表明后库在描述与分析价格时使用更为丰富的商科的概念，其中包括经济学的供求关系分析、通货膨胀等。

用同样两种工具分析两库共享的高频主题词market，也获得类似的结果，即market不但自身有更为丰富的搭配网络，而且与该专题的其他主题词之间也形成更复杂多样的立体搭配网络。进一步对比分析AntConc提取的market在两库中的搭配词表（跨距为左4右4，T≥2），则更为具体地展现后库在关于"市场"这一概念的语言资源使用及概念探讨的广度和深度上的差异性。表6.17列出两库中market的实义搭配词。

表6.17　前后库中market的实义词类搭配词对比

	前后共享搭配词	前库独用	后库独用
名词、代词	price、bond、investment、return、speculation、stock、money、property、bubble、china、estate、government、house、housing、i、they、we、you、one、people、time（共21个）	profits、rate、investors、savings、actions、future（共6个）	economy、equilibrium、supply、inflation、risk、stability、prosperity、population、experts、case、eyes、it、others、perspective、reason、result、years（共17个）
动词类	be、becoming、booming、buying、can、cause、deal、demand、developing、invest、investing、keep、make、soaring、will（共15个）	break、encourage、leading、needs、save、take（共6个）	rising、control、burst、growing、increase、pay、argue、compared、may、meet、see、seems、speaking（共13个）

续表

	前后共享搭配词	前库独用	后库独用
形容词、副词、限定词	big、chinese、however、local、more、no、not、quickly、real、therefore、still、short、some、that、this、would（共16个）	profitable、stable、dangerous、also、far、private、too（共7个）	thriving、volatile、financial、prosperous、dramatically、relatively、rapid、fast、faster、high、huge、low、up、many、most、my、now、other、quite、rather、second、their、whole、ago、besides、just、least（共27个）
数量	共计52个	共计19个	共计57个

　　表6.17显示前后库共享market实义搭配词主要是与写作任务主题相关的名词（investment、bond、stock、price、money、estate、house、property等），市场行为和市场分析相关的动词（booming、buying、cause、deal、demand、developing、invest、soaring等），以及描述市场变化的修饰词（big、local、quickly、short等）。而两者独用的搭配词也表现出有很大差异。首先，后库独有的搭配词类符总数是前库的三倍（57＞19）；每一种词性的类符数都比前库丰富许多。先看名词类搭配词，前库与"货币"和"投资"的主题相关词仅有profits（利润）、rate（比率）、investors（投资者）和savings（储蓄）4个；而后库则有7个，包括economy（经济）、equilibrium（平衡）、supply（供给）、inflation（通胀）、risk（风险）、stability（稳定性）和prosperity（繁荣）。再看动词类搭配词，前库中的6个动词似与主题相关性不太；而后库的动词却大多与经济与市场描述和分析密切相关，如rising（上涨的）、control（控制）、burst（爆发）、growing（增长的）、increase（增加）、pay（支付）等。最后看形容词类搭配词，前库中仅有profitable（可盈利的）、stable（稳定的）、dangerous（有风险的）3例是对投资选项的修饰性描述语；而后库则有诸如thriving（繁荣的）、volatile（多变的）、financial（财政的）、prosperous（繁荣的）、dramatically（大幅地）、relatively（相对而言）、rapid（迅速的）、fast（快速的）、faster（更快的）、high（高的）、huge（巨大的）、low（低的）、up（向上的）等13个形容词和副词来修饰市场或者描述市场行为。

　　以上对写作前后库中对核心主题词的使用相貌的分析表明学生在教改后能更为深入地、以更丰富多样的短语搭配型式来表述该专题的核心知识概念。尤其体现在后库写作中更多地使用经济学重要概念（如：供求关系的平衡、通货膨胀、稳定性、风险性等）、更丰富地描述市场变化和政府行为（如：上涨、增加、增长、爆发、控制、支付等），并更为生动多样地描述市场变化（如：繁荣的、多变的、迅速地、大幅地、高的、低的、向上的等）。这些都是后库作文在语言资源和商科重要知识融合使用上同步提升的表征。

6.4 学习者反思日志分析

教研者汇集学生在三轮教研行动中撰写的主题单元学习反思日志，建成3万多词次的微型语料库（各轮分别为1.46万、0.65和0.9万词次）。分析的重点落在第三轮中的日志语料，同时也纵向考查三轮之间的变化。例如，在检索学生第三轮反思日志语料的2-4字丛时，发现最高频短语模式：一是"I've/d learned"，后面多接"商务知识和词汇深度知识""如何正确使用商务词汇"等内容（共37例）。二是"a good/better /clearer/thorough等评价类形容词+way/means/method/awareness/understanding/command/comprehension 等方法结果类名词"模式（共36例），多指向语料库辅助的教学方法和技术。另外还有50多例"word + association/mapping/practice"等词丛（即涉及词汇联想、构图或练习），其周边大都相伴helpful/interesting/effective等正面评价类词，如图6.8和图6.9所示。

```
             As far as I am concerned, the  word association and mapping task, which can help
interesting tasks such as group presentation,  word association and writing. To enlarge my scope
      my university life. In terms of the  word association game, I think it helps generate
     a of lexical items such as "portfolio".  Word association is really a good way to
        about this unit. When we are doing  word association, lexical items and knowledge are
  h some exercises concerning ethics, such as  word association mapping and topic writing in the
  iting tasks. Personally speaking, I found the  word association really helpful! When I compare th
  y understand those financial items. Also, the  word association really helps me with building a
 ining of collocation) the other chapters. The  word association task lets me know clear if
          so that I can consolidate it.   The  word association tasks help me structure the knowl
 hing and applying knowledge, especially the  word association tasks. It helps us build up
 riting tasks.    Personally speaking, I find the  word association tasks quite helpful for me to
    . I think the most helpful task was  word association, which provided a overall view on
```

图6.8　word association索引行截图

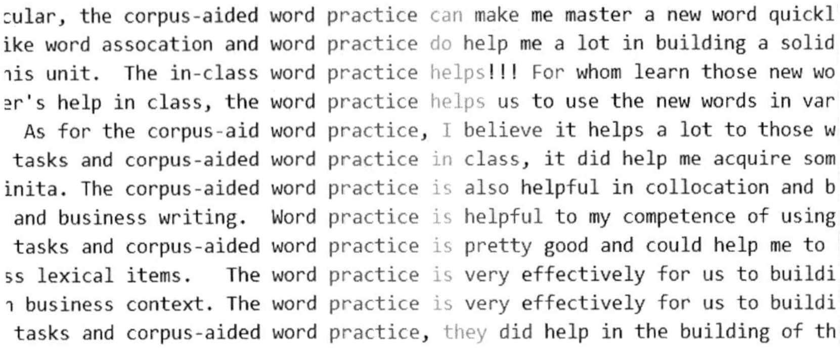

cular, the corpus-aided word practice can make me master a new word quickl
ike word assocation and word practice do help me a lot in building a solid
nis unit. The in-class word practice helps!!! For whom learn those new wo
er's help in class, the word practice helps us to use the new words in var
 As for the corpus-aid word practice, I believe it helps a lot to those w
tasks and corpus-aided word practice in class, it did help me acquire som
inita. The corpus-aided word practice is also helpful in collocation and b
and business writing. Word practice is helpful to my competence of using
tasks and corpus-aided word practice is pretty good and could help me to
ss lexical items.   The word practice is very effectively for us to buildi
n business context. The word practice is very effectively for us to buildi
tasks and corpus-aided word practice, they did help in the building of th

图6.9　word practice索引行截图

从历时分析的角度看，当检索第一轮反思日志语料的2字词丛时，教研者发现由高频词丛I think带出的44例索引行里表达了当时学生对语料库辅助的短语教学褒贬不一（见图6.10）：其中有12例出现good/sufficient/effective/time-saving/stronger desire等词正面评价语料库资源、工具或相关教学活动（如图6.10的第1、11和14的索引行）；但也有12例出现not convenient/confused/difficult/tough等负面评价词（如图6.10的第4、8、13和17的索引行）。

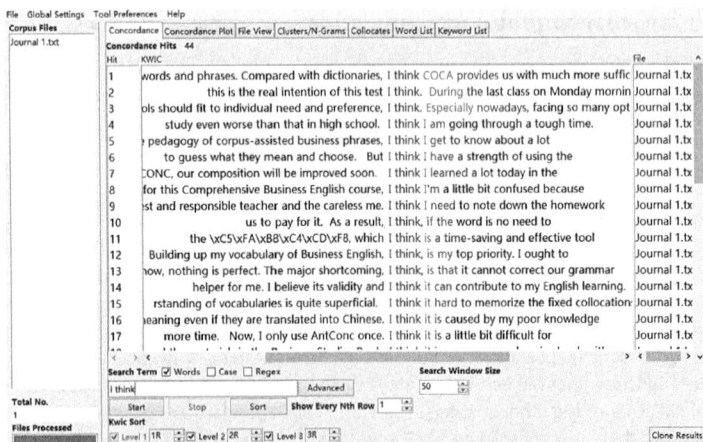

图6.10　第一轮I think索引行截图

相比之下，第三轮日志语料库中共25例I think索引行显示其中有23例（90%）出现了正面评价类共选15次（见图6.11绝大部分索引行）；而仅有

2例（见序号10和13行）反映写作任务量太大和没有小礼物作为激励之类。学生们的积极评价类词语大致可分为三类（见表6.18列举的部分词语）。

Concordance Hits　25

Hit	KWIC
1	learnt the business knowledge in other class, I think CBE class can focus on the business
2	of some very common words, like deal with. I think I am becoming conscious of using these
3	ancial knowledge.　As for the improvement, I think I have deeped the understanding of some
4	should use them. At least better than before, I think. I specially like the group competition, b
5	time can be spent in these 2 chapters, which I think is of great worth.　3. Healthy and Happy
6	ife.　In terms of the word association game, I think it helps generate a linear way of
7	n and business writing.　In my own opinion, I think it took too much time on the
8	, which provided a overall view on the topics. I think it would be better if there is
9	te more words and find out their connection. I think mapping can help me to build up
10	, I hope we can reduce the writing tasks. I think our writing teacher really give us enough
11	s of literature and some economic books, and I think reading helps broaden one's knowledge al
12	actice in class such as word association tasks, I think, such practice indeed help me to some
13	class, in my opinion, is not that fun. I think teacher should give us some small gifts
14	4 did not relate to business so much. And I think that certainly many classmates like and le
15	significant of people's behavior about money. I think the most helpful task was word associatio
16	elative characteristics.　In these two topics, I think the term reports are really helpful, espec
17	edge with my Money and Banking textbooks. I think the text of Business Language is more

图6.11　第三轮I think索引行截图

表6.18　第三轮I think索引行中评价类词语分析

语义类别	示例
整体评价类	better than before of great worth certainly many classmates like and learn a lot really help helpful, most helpful task really interesting quite an improvement effective to help best and most innovative teaching methods
具体得益类	conscious of using these business words correctly deepen the understanding of some specific words in finance broaden one's knowledge about certain field help generate a linear way of thinking，clarifying my understanding of certain topic help me to build up a network or a classification of what I have learned
继续使用类	we can continue using this method

以上三类评价类词语表达了学生从整体上认为语料库辅助的主题教学方法及活动设计有效且有趣，他们的具体收获包括学科知识建构、商务词汇深度知识习得和思维锻炼，而且表示愿意继续使用语料库辅助的学习方法。

综观三轮教研行动的学习者反思日志语料可见：随着语料库辅助的短语教学活动形式的丰富度和有效性的提高，学习者对该教学模式的态度也在随之改变。

6.5 小结

本章依次展示三轮教研行动测评方式和结果具有动态发展的特征。首先是第一轮的调查问卷和商务英语短语能力测试，这种将学生自述结合语言测试的评价模式较为有效地考查学生的短语能力，但由于问卷数据本身存在学生作答时的主观性特征，对于学科知识和语言习得双重目标的实现这一点似未能有效检测。第二轮的商务概念词项测试聚焦商务主题的重要概念及关键术语表达，但似难以对学生的主题学科知识体系进行有效检测；第三轮的主题概念构图和主题写作任务，既能通过主题词和主题词拓展词丛比较全面地展示学生的主题学科知识体系的建构过程，又能考查其语言深度知识的掌握和应用，从而将学科内容与语言进行有机融合，同时还提升学生的思维能力。再加上三轮全程的学习者反思日志分析，则更有力地佐证了之前各种测评结果。

正如有学者指出，语料库辅助短语教学的最大的贡献在于提升学习者的语言敏感意识（Granger 2011：7）。然而要证实和展示学习者语言敏感意识提升的表征却并非易事。国内外曾学者对此做过有益探索，包括Laufer & Hulstijnand（2001：544）提出量化"参与度假设"的途径；Read（2000）提出考查学生掌握词和短语的三大指标；Coxhead（2008：156-158）针对学生使用短语的实际问题设计大学生问卷和访谈表；邓飞和何安平（2015：92-101）调查大学生语料库课程作业中的词丛形式的术语使用频数，等等。本章展示的测评手段既借鉴了前人的研究成果，又突显了商务英语学科背景下一系列形成性评价手段，包括主题单元始末的主题概念图对比、主题单元习作对比以及学生反思日志跟踪分析等等，力图从教学过程发生的变化诠释学生的认知与能力提升。对此，教研者进一步反思如下：（1）单一种测试和评估手段很难做到双重教学目标的检测，所以要将主题概念构图结合主题习作任务，并辅以学习者反思日志，才能较为全面地评估学习者在学科知识和语言知识上的提升，同时更为微观和细致地了解学生在两方面习得的薄弱点。（2）商务英语短语能力测试和商务概念词项测试，虽然在该教学研究中未能有效地评估双重教学目标的实现，但可作为学习者商务语言能力测评的参考，相信通过后续实验拓展开发出测评学生商务语言能力的更科学的量具。（3）通过跟踪分析学生的反思日志，发现学生除了关注学科知识与语言知识习得双重目标的实现，还提出了自身思维能力的发展。所以，在今后的教研中，如何有效地将学习者思维能力的拓展作为第三个目标维度来指导教学活动设计，将成为后续研究的一个新课题。

第 7 章
总结与展望

本研究从语料库语言学的短语理论与技术出发，结合学科专业教育理论，对高校本科的商务英语课程教学改革开展了历时三年的研究，无论在理论及方法层面，还是在教学应用层面都获得了新的认知和实效成果。

在理论及方法层面，本研究首先廓清了语料库短语研究的内涵，包括语料库的共选理论、拓展意义单位理论、多形态短语理念以及语料库教学加工理念等等。第二，厘清了短语研究的两种范式：即自上而下的以语言理论为指导的传统研究和基于频数的语料库研究两者的各自特点与利弊。更重要的是将二者有机结合应用到证实运用商英学科教研过程中。第三，在教改实践中创造性地将以上理念和技术与现代教育，打通了语料库语言学理论和技术在学科英语教育教学的应用通道。其特色至少有二：一是基于语料库的词丛理念和主题词理念，揭示了商务英语短语的结构特征与功能特征；二是基于商务专题话语的主题词，拓展出多种短语形态分析，从中揭示商英学科知识和语言使用特点。

在教学应用层面，我们广外大商英的语料库教研团队建成了近250万词次的商务英语教材语料库（BTC-1和BTC-2），同时链接亿万词次的网上语料库资源，利用它们实实在在地开展了为期一年共三个轮回的语料库短语辅助商英主题式教学的行动研究，产生了一批语料库短语辅助教学设计评价活动的成功案例。其特色也至少有二：一是将语料库资源和技术常态式地融入日常商务英语教学的全过程；二是同样运用语料库的资源和技术来评价教研行动过程的有效性。

通过本研究，我们还有以下反思。

首先，商务英语短语研究固然离不开商务英语语料库以及提取短语的语料库技术，但更重要的还是研究者具备相关商科的专业知识（business expertise）。唯有如此，方能结合学科背景，对所提取出的商务英语短语进行具有学科深度的解读。也唯有如此，才能较好地开展语料库辅助的商务英语短语教学。限于时间、经费以及我们的商科涵养，本书主要起到抛砖引玉的作用。我们相信，商务英语专业的蓬勃发展，必然会让越来越多的学者探讨语料库应用于商务英语教学的可能领域及潜在价值，让越来越多的教师投入到语料库辅助的商务英语教学中，并让越来越多的学生从中受益。

第二，随着短语在现代语言研究中居于越来越重要的地位，基于频数的短语研究还需要参照、整合传统短语学的某些理性分析视角和概念，进一步改进词语序列提取的技术手段。借鉴和整合传统短语学的视角和概念，并突破词语序列提取的技术瓶颈应是下个阶段语料库研究的重要工作。

第三，本研究中的教改实验，只是涉及商务英语中的一些话题（如领导力、商业伦理、货币与银行等），并没有深入到每个具体的商务学科中（如经济学、管理学、营销学、金融学、会计学、国际商务、人力资源管理等）。未来的研究，必然走向语料库辅助学科英语教学的路径上来。故期待本书的研究成果对商务英语之外的其他学科外语教学与研究也有启迪作用。

参考文献

Altenberg, B. 1998. On the phraseology of spoken English: The evidence of recurrent word-combinations [A]. In A. P. Cowie (ed.). *Phraseology: Theory, Analysis and Applications* [C]. Oxford: Oxford University Press.

Alexander, G. 1988. *Longman English Grammar* [M]. London: Longman.

Ausubel, D.1963. *The Psychology of Meaningful Verbal Learning* [M]. New York: Grune and Stratton.

Ausubel, D. 1968. *Educational Psychology: A Cognitive View* [M]. New York: Rinehart and Winston.

Baker, P. 2004. Querying keywords [J]. *Journal of English Linguistics*, 32 (4): 346-359.

Bargiela-Chiappini, F, Nickerson, C. & Planker, B. 2014. *Business Discourse* (2nd Edition) [M]. Shanghai: Shanghai Foreign Language Education Press.

Bhatia, V. K. 2017. *Critical Genre Analysis: Investigating Interdiscursive Performance in Performance in Professional Practice* [M]. New York: Routledge.

Biber, D., S. Johansson, G. Leech, S. Conrad & E. Finegan. 1999. *Longman Grammar of Spoken and Written English* [M]. London: Longman.

Biber, D., S. Conrad & V. Cortes. 2004. If you look at. . . : Lexical bundles in university teaching and textbooks [J]. *Applied Linguistics* 25, 3: 371-405.

Bondi, M. 2010. Perspectives on keywords and keyness: An introduction [A]. In M. Bondi & M. Scott (eds.). *Keyness in Texts* [C]. Amsterdam: John Benjamins Publishing Company.

Braun, S. 2005. From pedagogically relevant corpora to authentic language learning contents [J]. *ReCALL*17 (1): 47-64.

Breeze, R. 2012. Verb-particle constructions in the language of business and finance [J]. *Language Value*4 (1): 84-96.

Brezina, V., McEnery, T. & Wattam, S. 2015. Collocations in context: A new perspective on collocation networks [J]. *International Journal of Corpus Linguistics* 20 (2): 139-173.

Brinton, D., M. Snow & M. Wesche, 1989.*Content-based Second Language Instruction* [M]. New York: Newburg.

Callies, M. 2009. *Information Highlighting in Advanced Learner English* [M]. Amsterdam: John Benjamins.

Chen, Y. H. & Baker, P., 2010. Lexical bundles in L1 and L2 academic writing [J]. *LanguageLearning & Technology*, 4 (2): 30-49.

Cortes, V. 2004. Lexical bundles in published and student disciplinary writing: Examples from history and biology [J]. *English for Specific Purposes* 23 (4): 397-423.

Cortes, V. 2006. Teaching lexical bundles in the disciplines: An example from a writing intensive history class [J]. *Linguistics and Education*, 17, 391-406.

Cortes, V. 2008. A comparative analysis of lexical bundles in academic history writing in English and Spanish [J]. *Corpora*, 3 (1), 43-57.

Cowie, A. P. 1981. The treatment of collocations and idioms in learners' dictionaries [J]. *AppliedLinguistics* 2 (3): 223-235.

Cowie, A. P. (ed.) 1998. *Phraseology: Theory, Analysis, and Applications* [C]. Oxford: Oxford University Press.

Carloni, G. 2015. *CLIL in Higher Education and the Role of Corpora: A Blended Model of Consultation Services and Learning Environments* [M]. Venice: Edizioni Ca' Foscari.

Coxhead, A. 2008. Phraseology and English for Academic Purpose challenges and opportunities [A]. In F. Meunier & S. Granger (eds.). *Phraseology in Foreign Language Learning and Teaching* [C]. Amsterdam: John Benjamins Publishing Company.

Dai, G. Y. & Liu, Y. 2016. An empirical study on Business English teaching and development in China—A needs analysis approach [J]. *Higher Education Studies* 6 (2): 142-153.

De Cock, S. 1998. A recurrent word combination approach to the study of formulae in the speech of native and non-native speakers of English [J]. *International Journal of Corpus Linguistics*3 (1): 59-80.

Dunning, T. 1993. Accurate methods for the statistics of surprise and coincidence [J]. *Computational Linguistics* 19 (1): 61-74.

Ellis, N. 2008. Phraseology: The periphery and the heart of language [A]. In F. Meunier & S. Granger (eds.). *Phraseology in Foreign Language Learning and Teaching* [C]. Amsterdam: John Benjamins Publishing Company.

Farrell, P. 1990. *A Lexical Analysis of the English of Electronics and a Study of Semi-technical Vocabulary* [R]. CLCS Occasional Paper No. 25. Dublin Trinity College.

Fillmore, C., P. Kay & M. C. O'Connor. 1988. Regularity and idiomaticity in grammaticalconstructions: the case of let alone [J]. *Language*, 64, 501-538.

Firth, J. 1957. A synopsis of linguistic theory, 1930-1955 [A]. In Philosophical Society (ed.), *Studies in Linguistic Analysis, Special Edition of the Society* [C]. Oxford: Blackwell.

Fletcher, W. 2007. KfNgram, accessed 10 April 2018, http://www.kwicfinder.com/kfNgram/kfNgramHelp.html.

Flowerdew, J. 1993. Concordancing as a tool in course design [J]. *System* 21 (3): 231-243.

Flowerdew, L. 2008. The pedagogic value of corpora: A critical evaluation [A]. In Frankenberg-Garcia, A. *et al.* (eds.). *Proceedings of the 8ᵗʰ Teaching and Language Corpora Conference* [C]. Lisbon: ISLA, British Council & Benjamins.

Gass, S. 1988. Integrating research areas: a framework for second language studies [J]. *Applied Linguistics* 9 (2): 198-217.

Gass, S. & Selinker, L. 2008. *Second Language Acquisition: An Introductory Course* [M]. New York and London: Routlege.

Goldberg, A. E. 1995. *Constructions: A Construction Grammar Approach to Argument Structure* [M]. Chicago IL: University of Chicago Press.

Goldberg, A. E. 2003. Constructions: A new theoretical approach to language [J]. *Trends in Cognitive Science, 7*, 219-224.

Goldberg, A. E. 2006. *Constructions at Work: The Nature of Generalization in Language* [M]. Oxford: Oxford University Press.

Granger, S. 1998. Prefabricated patterns in advanced EFL writing: Collocations and formulae [A]. In A. P. Cowie (ed.) *Phraseology: Theory, Analysis, and Applications* [C]. Oxford: Oxford University Press.

Granger, S. 2011. From phraseology to pedagogy: Challenges and prospects [A]. In T. Herbst, S. Faulhaber & P. Uhrig (eds.). *The Phraseological View of Language: A Tribute to John Sinclair* [C]. Berlin: De Gruyter Mouton.

Granger, S. & F. Meunier (eds.) 2008. *Phraseology: An Interdisciplinary Perspective* [C]. Amsterdam/Philadelphia: John Benjamins.

Gries, S. 2008. Phraseology and linguistic theory: A brief survey. In S. Granger & F. Meunier (eds.) *Phraseology: An Interdisciplinary Perspective* [C]. Amsterdam/Philadelphia: John Benjamins.

Howarth, P. A. 1996. *Phraseology in English Academic Writing*. Tubingen: Niemeyer.

Howarth, P. A. 1998. Phraseology and second language proficiency [J]. *Applied Linguistics* 19 (1): 24-44.

Hsu, W. 2011. The vocabulary thresholds of business textbooks and business research articles for EFL learners [J]. *English for Specific Purposes* 30 (4): 247-257.

Hunston, S. 2008. Starting with the small words [J]. *International Journal of Corpus Linguistics* 13 (3): 271-295.

Hunston, S. & Francis, G. 2000. *Pattern Grammar: A Corpus-driven Approach to the Lexical Grammar of English* [M]. Amsterdam/Philadelphia: John Benjamins Publishing Company.

Hunston, S. 2002. *Corpora in Applied Linguistics* [M]. Cambridge: Cambridge University Press.

Hyland, K. 1998. Exploring corporate rhetoric: Metadiscourse in the CEO's letter [J]. *The Journal of Business Communication*, 35 (2): 224-245.

Hyland, K. 2005. Stance and engagement: a model of interaction [J]. *Discourse Studies* 7: 173-192.

Hyland, K. 2008. As can be seen: Lexical bundles and disciplinary variation [J]. *English for Specific Purposes* 27: 4-21.

Irvin, L. 1995. Can concept mapping be used to promote meaningful learning in nurse education? [J]. *Journal of Advanced Nursing* 21 (6): 1175-1179.

Jing, S. 2013. The application of data-driven learning in business English teaching for MBA students in China: A critical assessment [J]. *International Journal of English Linguistics* 3 (1): 171-180.

Johns, T. 1991a. "Should you be persuaded": Two samples of data-driven learning materials [A]. In T. Johns & P. King (eds.). *Classroom Concordancing ELR Journal 4* (pp.1-16) [C]. Birmingham: University of Birmingham.

Johns, T. 1991b. From printout to handout: Grammar and vocabulary teaching in the context ofdata-driven learning [A]. In T. Odlin (Ed.), *Perspectives on Pedagogical Grammar* (pp. 293-313) [C]. Cambridge: Cambridge University Press.

Jones, S. & Sinclair, J. M. 1974. English lexical collocations—a study in computational linguistics [A]. In J. A. Foley (ed.) *J. M. Sinclair on Lexis and Lexicography* (pp. 21-54) [C]. Singapore: National University of Singapore.

Koller, V. 2004. *Metaphor and Gender in Business Media Discourse: A Critical Cognitive Study* [M]. Basingstoke, Hants: Palgrave Macmillan.

Krashen, S. 1981. *Second Language Acquisition and Second Language Learning* [M]. Oxford: Pergamon Press.

Lakoff, G. 1987. *Women, Fire, and Dangerous Things: What Categories Reveal about the Mind* [M]. Chicago, IL: University of Chicago Press.

Laufer, B. & J. Hulstijn. 2001. Incidental vocabulary acquisition in a second language: The construct of task-induced involvement [J]. *Applied Linguistics* 22 (1): 1-26.

Leech, G. 1997. Teaching and language corpora: a convergence [A]. In Wichmann, A. *et al.* (eds.). *Teaching and Language Corpora* [C]. London: Longman.

Lewis, M. 1993. *The Lexical Approach* [M]. Hove, England: Language Teaching Publications.

Lewis, M. 1997. *Implementing the Lexical Approach: Putting Theory into Practice* [M]. Hove, England: Language Teaching Publications.

Li, J. & N. Schmitt. 2010. The development of collocation use in academic texts by advanced L2 learners: A multiple case study approach [A]. In D. Wood (ed.). *Perspectives on Formulaic Language: Acquisition and Communication* [C]. London: Continuum.

Louw, B. 1993. Irony in the text or insincerity in the writer? The diagnostic potential of semantic prosodies [A]. In M. Baker, G. Francis & E. Tognini-Bonelli (eds), *Text and Technology: In Honour of John Sinclair* (pp. 157-176) [C]. Amsterdam: John Benjamins.

MacNeil, M. 2007. Concept mapping as a means of course evaluation [J]. *Journal of Nursing Education* (46) 5: 232-233.

Martinez, R. 2013. A framework for the inclusion of multi-word expressions in ELT [J]. *ELT Journal*67 (2): 184-198.

Martinez, R. & V. Murphy. 2011. Effect of frequency and idiomaticity in second language reading comprehension [J]. *TESOL Quarterly* 45 (2): 267-90.

Martinez, R. & N. Schmitt. 2012. A phrasal expressions list [J]. *Applied Linguistics* 33 (3): 299-320.

McNiff, J. 1988. *Action Research: Principles and Practice* [M]. London: Routledge.

Met, M. 1999. Content-based instruction: Defining terms, making decisions [A]. In *NFLC Reports* [C]. Washington, DC: The National Foreign Language Center.

Moon, R. 1998. *Fixed Expressions and Idioms in English* [M]. Oxford: Clarendon Press.

Nelson, M. 2000. *A Corpus-based Study of Business English and Business English Teaching Materials* [D]. PhD. Dissertation. Manchester: University of Manchester.

Nesselhauf, N. 2005. *Collocations in a Learner Corpus* [M]. Amsterdam: John Benjamins.

Novak, J. 1990. Concept maps and vee diagrams: Two metacognitive tools for science and mathematics education [J]. *Instructional Science* 19 (1): 29-52.

Novak, J. & D. Gowin. 1984. *Learning How to Learn* [M]. Cambridge: Cambridge University Press.

O'Donnell, M., U. Römer & N. Ellis. 2013. The development of formulaic sequences in first and second language writing: Investigating effects of frequency, association, and native norm [J]. *International Journal of Corpus Linguistics* (1): 83-108.

O'Keeffe, A., McCarthy, M. & Carter, R. 2007. *From Corpus to Classroom: Language Use and Language Teaching* [M]. Cambridge: Cambridge University Press.

Paquot, M. 2013. Lexical bundles and L1 transfer effects [J]. *International Journal of Corpus Linguistics* 18 (3): 391-417.

Paribakht, S. & B. Wesche. 1993. Reading comprehension and second language development in a comprehension-based ESL program [J]. *TESL Canada Journal* 11 (1): 9-29.

Partington, A. 2003. *The Linguistics of Political Argument* [M]. London: Routledge.

Pawley, A. & F. H. Syder. 1983. Two puzzles for linguistic theory: Nativelike selection and nativelike fluency [A]. In Richards, J. C. & R. W. Schmidt (eds.) *Language and Communication* [C] (pp. 191-225). London: Longman.

Pickett, D. 1989. The sleeping giant: Investigations in business English [J]. *Language International* 1: 5-11.

Porto, M. 1998. Lexical phrases and language teaching. Forum 36 (3). Available from http://exchanges.state.gov/forum/vols/vol36/no3/p22.htm.

Read, J. 2000. *Assessing Vocabulary* [M]. Cambridge: Cambridge University Press.

Renouf, A. J. & J. Sinclair. 1991. Collocational frameworks in English [A]. In K. Ajimer and B. Altengberg (eds.), *English Corpus Linguistics: Studies in Honour of Jan Svartvik* (pp. 128-144) [C]. Harlow: Longman.

Richard, S. 1990. The role of consciousness in second language learning [J]. *Applied Linguistics* 11 (2): 129-158.

Skandera, P. (Ed.), *Phraseology and Culture in English* (pp. 3-45) [C]. Berlin/ New York: Mouton de Gruyter.

Rizzo, C. & M. Perez. 2015. A key perspective on specialized lexis: Keywords in telecommunication engineering for CLIL [A]. *Proceedings of the 7th International Conference on Corpus Linguistics: Current Work in Corpus Linguistics, Procedia—Social and Behavioral Sciences* [C] 198: 386-396.

Scott, M. & C. Tribble. 2006. *Textual Patterns: Keyword and Corpus Analysis in Language Education* [M]. Amsterdam: John Benjamins Publishing Company.

Shin, Y. & Kim, Y. 2017. Using lexical bundles to teach articles to L2 English learners of different proficiencies [J]. *System*, 69, 79-91.

Simpson-Vlach, R. & N. C. Ellis. 2010. An academic formulas list: New methods in phraseology research [J]. *Applied Linguistics* 31: 487-512.

Sinclair, J. 1966. Beginning the study of lexis [A]. In C. E. Bazell, J. C. Catford, M. A. K. Halliday & R. Robins (eds.). *In Memories of J. R. Firth* [C]. London: Longman.

Sinclair, J. 1991. *Corpus, Concordance, Collocation* [M]. Shanghai: Shanghai

Foreign Language Education Press.

Sinclair, J. 1996. The search for units of meaning [J]. *Textus*, 9: 75-106.

Sinclair, J. 2004. *How to Use Corpora in Language Teaching* [M]. Amsterdam: John Benjamins.

Sinclair, J. 2008. The phrase, the whole phrase, and nothing but the phrase [A]. In S. Granger & F. Meunier (eds.). *Phraseology: An Interdisciplinary Perspective* [C]. Amsterdam: John Benjamins.

Sinclair J. M. & A. Renouf. 1988. A lexical syllabus for language learning [A]. In Carter, R. & M. McCarthy (eds.). *Vocabulary and Language Teaching* [C]. London: Longman.

Sinclair, J. 2003. *Reading Concordances: An Introduction* [M]. London: Longman.

Stephanie B. & M. Barlow. 2008. *Business Phrasal Verbs* [M]. US: Athelstan Publications.

Stubbs, M. 2009. The search for units of meaning: Sinclair on empirical semantics [J]. *Applied Linguistics* 30 (1): 115-137.

Sun, Y. & J. Jiang. 2014. Metaphor use in Chinese and US corporate mission statements: A cognitive sociolinguistic analysis [J]. *English for Specific Purposes* 33 (1): 4-14.

Tyrkko, J. 2010. Hyperlinks: Keywords or key words? [A]. In M. Bondi & M. Scott (eds.). *Keyness in Texts* [C]. Amsterdam: John Benjamins Publishing Company.

VanPatten, B. 2004. Input and output in establishing form-meaning connections [A]. In B. VanPatten *et al.* (eds.). *Form-Meaning Connections in Second Language Acquisition* [C]. Mahwah, NJ: Lawrence Erlbaum Associates.

Warren, M. 2010. Identifying about grams in engineering texts [A]. In M. Bondi & M. Scott (eds.). *Keyness in Texts* [C]. Amsterdam: John Benjamins Publishing Company.

Widdowson, H. G. 2000. On the limitations of linguistics applied [J]. *Applied Linguistics* 21 (1): 3-25.

Widdowson, H. G. 2003. Corpora and language teaching tomorrow [A]. Keynote lecture delivered at the 5th Teaching and Language Corpora Conference, Bertinoro, Italy, July 29, 2002.

Williams, M. 2004. Concept mapping—a strategy for assessment [J]. *Nursing Standard* 19 (9): 33-38.

Willis, D. 1990. *The Lexical Syllabus: A New Approach to Language Teaching* [M]. London: Harper Collins.

Wood, D. 2015. *Fundamentals of Formulaic Language: An Introduction* [M]. London: Bloomsbury.

Wray, A. 2002. *Formulaic Language and the Lexicon* [M]. Cambridge: Cambridge University Press.

Wray, A. 2008. *Formulaic Language: Pushing the Boundaries* [M]. Oxford: Oxford University Press.

鲍文，2013，商务英语学科教师专业发展论［M］。北京：国防工业出版社。

蔡基刚，2010，制约我国大学英语教学方向转移的因素分析,［J］，《外语研究》（2）：40-45。

蔡基刚，2011，CBI理论框架下的分科英语教学［J］，《外语教学》（5）：35-38。

蔡基刚，2013，专业英语及其教材对我国高校ESP教学的影响［J］，《外语与外语教学》（2）：1-4。

曹德春，2011，跨学科构建商务英语理论体系的共同核心——基于北美商务沟通和欧洲商务语篇的跨学科设想［J］，《中国外语》（2）：63-68。

曹合建、朱建忠、陈满生，2008，基于语料库的商务英语研究［M］。北京：对外经济贸易大学出版社。

陈建平，2010，商务英语研究［M］。杭州：浙江大学出版社。

陈琦、高云，2010，学术英语中的半技术性词汇［J］，《外语教学》（6）：42-46。

戴桂玉，2012，商务英语文体研究［M］。上海：上海外语教育出版社。

邓飞、何安平，2015，语料库课程教学对提升学生词块意识的效果研究［J］，《外国语言文学》（2）：92-101。

杜海紫，2013，基于语料库的商务英语口语教学方法研究［J］，《语文学刊》（3）：124-126。

顿官刚，2002，经贸英语词汇的特点及翻译［J］，《山东外语教学》（3）：37-40，57。

高新华、刘白玉，2010，金融危机英语隐喻词汇的翻译［J］，《外语学刊》（5）：119-121。

高霞，2014，中国英语学习者短语能力探究［J］，《现代外语》（6）：863-845。

高霞，2017，基于中外学者学术论文可比语料库的词块使用研究［J］，《外语与外语教学》（3）：42-52。

葛琼，2013，高职学生商务英语信函写作中语块使用研究［D］，硕士学位论文。安徽：安徽大学。

桂诗春、冯志伟、杨惠中、何安平、卫乃兴、李文中、梁茂成，2010，语料库语言学与外语教学［J］，《现代外语》（4）：419-426。

郭桂杭、李丹，2015，商务英语教师专业素质与教师发展：基于ESP需求理论分析［J］，《解放军外国语学院学报》（5）：26-32。

郭云云，2016，语料库辅助高职商务英语ESP词汇教学探讨［J］，《职业技术》（9）：51-54。

何安平，2004，语料库语言学与英语教学［M］。北京：外语教学与研究出版社。

何安平，2008，语料库如何走进课堂教学——原则与方法探究［J］，《中国外语教育》（4）：8-12。

何安平，2009，语料库的"教学加工"［J］，《现代外语》32（2）：214-216。

何安平，2013a，国外语料库语言学视角下多形态短语研究述评［J］，《当代语言学》15（1）：62-72。

何安平，2013b，《语料库的短语理念及其教学加工》［M］。广州：广东高等教育出版。

何家宁，2014，英汉汉英商务口译学习词典编纂原则［J］，《外语教学理论与实践》（01）：82-84。

胡春雨，2004，《语料库与应用语言学》评介［J］，现代外语，2004（3）：323-325。

胡春雨，2011，语料库与商务英语词汇研究［J］，《广东外语外贸大学学报》（2）：55-58。

胡春雨，2012，语料库与商务英语课堂教学［J］，《英语教师》（6）：42-47。

胡春雨，2014a，基于语料库的泡沫隐喻研究［J］，《解放军外国语学院学报》（1）：18-31。

胡春雨，2014b，基于商务英语语料库的RATE搭配特征研究［J］，《北京第二外国语学院学报》（2）：6-12。

胡春雨，2015，语料库文体学视域下的英文商务合同研究［J］，《解放军外国语学院学报》（5）：10-19。

胡春雨、何家宁，2013，基于语料库的商务英语学习词典编纂研究——兼评《牛津商务英语学习词典》［J］，《广东外语外贸大学学报》（6）：38-41。

胡春雨、范琳琳，2016，商务交际中的冲突性话语研究［J］，《外语教学》（2）：12-16。

胡春雨、谭金琳，2017，汉语致股东信中的隐喻及英译研究［J］，《天津外国语大学学报》（1）：25-31。

胡春雨、徐玉婷，2017，基于汉英媒体语料库的"经济隐喻"对比研究［J］，《外语教学》（5）：38-43。

胡春雨、李旭妍，2018，基于语料库的腾讯亚马逊致股东信元话语研究［J］，《外语学刊》（1）：24-32。

黄莹，2012，元话语标记语的分布特征及聚类模式对比分析［J］，《外国语文》（4）：84-90.

雷春林，2006，内容教学法与复合型外语专业教学——以商务英语教学模式为例［J］，《外语电化教学》（3）：32-38。

李丽，2010，CBI教学理念融入商务英语教学的有效性研究［J］，《北京第二外国语学院学报》（8）：74-79。

李全福，2000，英语短语动词的特点及教学方法［J］，《雁北师范学院学报》（1）：50-51，60。

李文中，2004，基于COLEC的中介语搭配及学习者策略分析［J］，《河南师范大学学报》（5）：202-205。

李文中、濮建忠，语料库索引在外语教学中的应用［J］，《解放军外国语学院学报》（2）：20-25。

梁茂成，2008，中国大学生英语笔语中的情态序列研究［J］，《外语教学与研究》（1）：52-58。

梁茂成，2009，微型文本在外语教学中的应用［J］，《外语电化教学》（3）：8-12。

梁茂成、李文中、许家金，2010，《语料库应用教程》［M］。北京：外语教学与研究出版社。

林添湖，2001，试论国际商务英语学科的发展［J］，《厦门大学学报（哲社版）》（4）：143-150。

林添湖，2005，加强理论建设是商务英语学科继续发展的根本出路［J］，《国际商务研究》（2）：1-7。

刘法公，2009，中国从无到有的商务英语学科［J］，《外语界》（6）：10-16。

刘法公，2015，论商务英语专业培养目标核心任务的实现［J］，《中国外语》（1）：19-25。

陆军、卫乃兴，2014，短语学视角下的二语词语知识研究［J］，《外语教学与研究》（6）：865-878，960。

马广惠，2009，英语专业学生二语限时写作中的词块研究［J］，《外语教学与研究》（1）：54-60，81。

毛亚英、陈莉萍，2013，国际化背景下以学科内容为依托的大学英语课程体系［J］，《外语研究》（2）：60-63。

濮建忠，2003，英语词汇教学中的类联接、搭配与词块［J］，《外语教学与研究》，（6）：438-445，481。

任朝旺，曾利沙，2016，中英文经济报道中概念隐喻的跨文化性［J］，《广州大学学报（社会科学版）》，（11）：64-69。

石静，2012，Sketch Engine在商务英语词汇教学中的应用［J］，《英语教师》（7）：53-60。

沈玉刚，2002，隐喻意识对英语短语动词习得的作用［J］，《国外外语教学》（2）：15-19。

孙有中、李莉文，2011，CBI和ESP与中国高校英语专业和大学英语教学改革的方向［J］，《外语研究》（5）：1-4。

王冬梅，2009，浅谈语料库在商务英语词汇教学中的作用［J］，《宿州教育学院学报》（2）：143-144。

王卉，2012，航海英语词汇分类与教学［J］，《航海教育研究》（3）：105-107。

王立非、黄湘琪，2011，高校机辅商务英语写作教学系统的研发［J］，《外语电化教学》（11）：37-41，51。

王立非、马会军，2009，基于语料库的中国学生英语演讲话语立场构块研究［J］，《外语教学与研究》（5）：365-370。

王立非、张斐瑞，2015，论"商务英语专业国家标准"的学科理论基础［J］，《中国外语》（1）：13-18。

王立非，叶兴国、严明、彭青龙、许德金，2015，商务英语专业本科教学质量国家标准要点解读［J］，《外语教学与研究》（2）：297-302。

王俊超，2018，中国商务英语教学研究20年可视化分析（1998-2017）
　　［J］，《外国语文》（4）：155-160。

王蔷，2002，《英语教师行动研究》［M］。北京：外语教学与研究出版社。

汪榕培，1997，英语的短语动词［J］，《外语与外语教学》（4）：19-22。

王守宏、刘金玲、付文平，2015，"慕课"背景下以内容为依托的大学英
　　语ESP教学模式研究［J］，《中国电化教育》（4）：97-101，120。

王艳艳、王光林、郑丽娜，2014，商务英语专业人才需求和培养模式调查
　　与启示［J］，《外语界》（2）：34-41。

卫乃兴，2007，中国学生英语口语的短语学特征研究——COLSEC 语料
　　库的词块证据分析［J］，《现代外语》（3）：280-291，329。

卫乃兴，2009，语料库语言学的方法论及相关理念［J］，《外语研究》
　　（5）：36-42。

翁凤翔，2009，商务英语研究［M］。上海：上海交通大学出版社。

许家金、许宗瑞，2007，中国大学生英语口语中的互动话语词块研究
　　［J］，《外语教学与研究》（6）：437-441，481。

徐珺、史兴松，2011，商务英语教学的任务型设计——以《商务沟通》英
　　语课为例［J］，《外语电化教学》（6）：66-71。

严明，2015，"课程—教学—评价"相一致的商务英语专业人才培养模式
　　建构［J］，《外语学刊》（5）：95-98。

俞珏，2011，基于中国学生英语口笔语语料库的英语口语短语动词使用研
　　究［J］，《外语界》（5）：24-30。

曾利沙，2011，基于语境参数观的概念语义嬗变认知机制研究——商务
　　英语时文教学理论与方法［J］，《外语教学》（6）：6-10。

曾利沙，2017，商务翻译研究新探［M］。北京：外语教学与研究出版社。

张彬，2007，英语学习者对英语短语动词的回避现象研究［J］，《解放军
　　外国语学院学报》（6）：60-64。

张立茵，2012，基于在线语料库的商务英语写作实践教学模式研究［J］，
　　《语文学刊》（5）：161-163。

张武保，2014，商务英语专业与学科建设［M］。北京：外语教学与研究
　　出版社。

张佐成，2008，商务英语的理论与实践［M］。北京：对外经济贸易大学
　　出版社。

仲伟合，2013，英语类专业创新发展的探索与突破［A］，《基于多元人才
　　观，探索英语类专业教学的改革与创新》［C］。北京：外语教学与研
　　究出版社。

仲伟合，2014，英语类专业创新发展探索［J］，《外语教学与研究》（1）：127-133，160。

朱万忠，刘付川，2010，商务英语发展的新契机［J］，《宁波大学学报（教育科学版）》（2）：100-103。

朱文忠，2010，商务英语教学研究［M］。北京：世界图书出版社。

附录

按照Biber *et al.*（2004）的分类体系，我们把BTC中的商务英语短语分为三大类及若干个小类，以下为语料库中出现的类别及举例。

第一大类
Lexical bundles that incorporate verb phrase fragments
（含有动词短语的词丛）

1b.　(connector +) 3^(rd) person pronoun + VP fragment（第三人称＋动词短语）

(1)　*The United States has* often been called a melting pot, where diverse groups from many nations and cultures have melted into a single, more homogenous whole. (BTC—Principles of Marketing)

(2)　*It is important to* distinguish between a product idea, a product concept, and a product image. (BTC—Principles of Marketing)

1c.　Verb phrase with non-passive verb（非被动式动词短语）

(3)　*You need to understand* leverage so that you can control risk and magnify returns for the firm's owners and to understand capital structure theory so that you can make decisions about the firm's optimal capital structure. (BTC—Principles of Managerial Finance)

1d.　Verb phrase with passive verb（被动式动词短语）

(4)　Several examples of specific questions concerning disabilities that should and should not be asked in employment interviews *are shown in the* following chart. (BTC—Human Resources Management)

(5)　They attract consumer attention, offer strong incentives to purchase, and *can be used to* dramatize product offers and boost sagging sales. (BTC—Principles of Marketing)

1g. discourse marker + VP fragment（话语标记语+动词短语）

(6) 15-2 *What is the* relationship between the predictability of a firm's cash inflows and its required level of net working capital? How are net working capital, liquidity, and risk of insolvency related? (BTC—Principles of Managerial Finance)

(7) ***What happens to the*** money supply when the Fed raises the discount rate? (BTC—Principles of Economics)

第二大类
Lexical bundles that incorporate *dependent clause* fragments
含有从属小句结构的词丛

2c. *If*-clause fragments（*If*从句）

(8) *If the price of* wine is $3 per glass and the price of cheese is $6 per pound, what is the marginal rate of substitution at this optimum? (BTC—Principles of Economics)

2d. (verb/adjective) to-clause fragment（动词/形容词）+ to 不定式

(9) Using the inputs shown at the left, you should find the growth rate *to be 6.96%,* which we round to 7%. (BTC—Principles of Managerial Finance)

第三大类
Lexical bundles that incorporate *noun phrase* and *prepositional phrase*
含有名词短语和介词短语的词丛

3a. (connector +) Noun phrase with of-phrase fragment含有of的名词短语

(10) Dealing with the stress and honoring *the value of the* shuttle program are helping employees to maintain morale and optimism while facing a new frontier. (BTC—Human Resources Management)

(11) Persistent growth in *the quantity of money* supplied leads to continuing inflation. (BTC—Principles of Economics)

3b. Noun phrase with other post-modifier fragment有后置语修饰的名词短语

(12) Persistent growth in *the quantity of money* supplied leads to continuing inflation. (BTC—Principles of Economics)

(13) A lower price level reduces the interest rate, encourages greater spending on investment goods, and thereby increases the quantity of *goods and services demanded.* (BTC–Principles of Economics)

(14) Suppose the government sets the license fee equal to *the difference between the* domestic price and the world price. In this case, all the profit of license holders is paid to the government in license fees, and the import quota works exactly like a tariff. (BTC—Principles of Managerial Finance)

3c. Other noun phrase expressions其他类型的名词短语

(15) This theory of interest-rate determination will help explain the downward slope of *the aggregate-demand curve,* as well as how monetary and fiscal policy can shift this curve. (BTC—Principles of Economics)

(16) In turn, this might lead to *an increase in the* company's stock price, making it easier for the company to raise additional capital from investors in the future by issuing new stock. (BTC—Principles of Management)

3d. Prepositional expressions介词短语

(17) *In the United States* alone, federal, state, and local governments contain more than 88,000 buying units that purchase more than $1 trillion in goods and services each year. (BTC—Principles of Marketing)

(18) A second is that *in the long run,* Monsanto's insect-resistant crops might make matters worse because over time insects will evolve resistance to the "natural pesticides" engineered into Monsanto's plants, rendering the plants vulnerable to a new generation of "superbugs." (BTC—Principles of Management)

附录2　BTC中商务英语短语的功能类别及例证

　　按照Hyland（2008）的分类体系，我们把BTC中的商务英语短语按功能分为三大类及若干个小类，以下为语料库中出现的类别及举例。

话题类

(1) *The aggregate-demand curve* slopes downward for three reasons. (BTC—Principles of Economics)

(2) They also buy an incredible variety *of goods and services*. (BTC—Principles of Marketing)

量化类

(3) Bananas are not the only item in Chiquita's product line, but they are by far the most important, representing over *50 percent of the* company's sales. (BTC—Principles of Management)

(4) For example, Amazon.com offers the Kindle Fire tablet computer, which sells for less than *40 percent of the* price of the Apple iPad or Samsung Galaxy. (BTC—Principles of Marketing)

描述类

(5) The major factors that affect the cost, which is the rate of interest paid by the bond issuer, are the bond's maturity, *the size of the* offering, the issuer's risk, and the basic cost of money. (BTC—Principles of Managerial Finance)

(6) A firm does not have to pay out all its earnings to households in the form of interest and dividends. (BTC—Principles of Economics)

结构类

(7) The six projects are listed *in the following table*, along with their initial investments and their IRRs. Using the data given, prepare an investment opportunities schedule (BTC—IOS). (BTC—Principles of Managerial Finance)

(8) That is, it involves entire supply chain management-managing upstream and downstream value-added flows of materials, final goods, and related

information among suppliers, the company, resellers, and final consumers, as *shown in Figure 12.5.* (BTC—Principles of Marketing)

定位类

(9) But with an unfair labor practices strike, the workers who want their jobs back *at the end of the* strike must be reinstated. (BTC—Human Resources Management)

(10) *At the same time,* some of these countries have the most promising markets for the goods and services MNCs offer. (BTC—Principles of Managerial Finance)

框架类

(11) That advice didn't stop William B. Harrison Jr., the current CEO of J.P. Morgan Chase, from receiving $15 million to $20 million in pay, bonuses, and stock options *for each of the* past few years. (BTC—Principles of Managerial Finance)

(12) The three product divisions are still assigned profitability goals, whereas the marketing and sales division is evaluated *on the basis of* sales growth. (BTC—Principles of Management)

融入类

(13) *As we will see* in the next section, if managers have a strong ethical foundation, they are far less likely to take actions that damage stakeholder interests. (BTC—Principles of Management)

(14) *You need to understand* factors affecting dividend policy because you may want to argue that the firm would be better off retaining funds for use in new marketing programs or products, rather than paying them out as dividends. (BTC—Principles of Managerial Finance)

(15) The company *should be able to* answer yes to all three R-W-W questions before developing the new-product idea further. (BTC—Principles of Marketing)

立场类

(16) The employee owns the plan and keeps it even if the employee leaves

the company. ***It can be used to*** further one's education, perhaps in order to move to a different job in the company. (BTC—Human Resources Management)

(17) More often than not, these customers visit casinos for an evening, rather than staying overnight at the hotel, and they ***are more likely*** to play at the slots than at tables. (BTC—Principles of Marketing)

过渡类

(18) "Truth-in-savings laws," ***on the other hand***, require banks to quote the annual percentage yield (BTC—APY) on their savings products. (BTC—Principles of Managerial Finance)

(19) *In other words, the* team plans, organizes, and controls work activities with little or no direct involvement of someone with higher formal authority. (BTC—Principles of Management)

结果类

(20) If the firm's financial leverage would actually remain unchanged *as a result of* the proposed acquisition, would this alter your recommendation in part A? Support your answer with numerical data. (BTC—Principles of Managerial Finance)

附录3　商务主题词知识量表

Instructions: This paper is composed of two parts: personal information and a self-report test on your vocabulary knowledge scale of 10 key Business English words.

Personal information

姓名：＿＿＿＿＿＿＿＿　　　高考英语分数：＿＿＿＿＿＿＿＿

Self-report Test

Report your vocabulary scale: please choose the <u>MOST</u> suitable one for you from the following 5 scales on each word and fill in the gap after the word. If you choose (5), then you have to fill in the gap of (4).

(1) I don't remember having seen this word before.

(2) I have seen this word before, but I don't know what it means.

(3) I have seen this word before, and I think it means ＿＿＿＿＿＿＿. (synonym or translation)

(4) I know this word. It means ＿＿＿＿＿＿＿. (synonym or translation)

(5) I can use this word in a collocation structure in Business English: ＿＿＿＿＿＿＿. (write a phrase)

Example:

Funds (4)<u>基金</u>(5) <u>mutual funds</u>

(1) manager ＿＿＿＿＿＿＿＿＿＿＿＿＿＿＿＿＿＿＿＿＿＿＿

(2) employee ＿＿＿＿＿＿＿＿＿＿＿＿＿＿＿＿＿＿＿＿＿＿

(3) business ＿＿＿＿＿＿＿＿＿＿＿＿＿＿＿＿＿＿＿＿＿＿＿

(4) market ＿＿＿＿＿＿＿＿＿＿＿＿＿＿＿＿＿＿＿＿＿＿＿＿

(5) describe ＿＿＿＿＿＿＿＿＿＿＿＿＿＿＿＿＿＿＿＿＿＿＿

(6) access ＿＿＿＿＿＿＿＿＿＿＿＿＿＿＿＿＿＿＿＿＿＿＿＿

(7) raise ＿＿＿＿＿＿＿＿＿＿＿＿＿＿＿＿＿＿＿＿＿＿＿＿＿

(8) financial ＿＿＿＿＿＿＿＿＿＿＿＿＿＿＿＿＿＿＿＿＿＿＿

(9) sale ＿＿＿＿＿＿＿＿＿＿＿＿＿＿＿＿＿＿＿＿＿＿＿＿＿＿

(10) ownership ＿＿＿＿＿＿＿＿＿＿＿＿＿＿＿＿＿＿＿＿＿＿

附录4　商务英语短语能力前测

Instructions: This paper is composed of two parts: personal information and a test on your phrase ability in Business English. THANK YOU FOR YOUR COOPERATION.

Personal information

姓名：＿＿＿＿＿＿　　　　　高考英语分数：＿＿＿＿＿＿

1. **Multiple choices: Please choose the <u>BEST</u> answer from four choices to make each statement complete and correct. (8*1')**

(1) You need capital to start a new ＿＿＿.
   A. organization　　B. environment　　C. opportunity　　D. business

(2) An integrated ＿＿＿ strategy ensures that the Four Ps blend together so that they are compatible with one another and with the company.
   A. marketing　　B. business　　C. corporate　　D. functional

(3) This diagram ＿＿＿ transformational and charismatic perspective on leadership.
   A. tells　　B. describes　　C. informs　　D. hints

(4) Speedy delivery and easy ＿＿＿ to technical support is certainly a benefit.
   A. approach　　B. access　　C. gain　　D. road

(5) The various government interventions, such as ＿＿＿ bailouts, represented strategies to restore economic stability.
   A. economic　　B. economical　　C. financial　　D. budget

(6) The most common application allows buyers to enter a system to see which products are available for order and delivery. But if those products are outdated, then the ＿＿＿ can be closed.
   A. browse　　B. sale　　C. order　　D. website

(7) The master partner retains at least 50 percent ＿＿＿ and runs the business, while minority partners have no management voice.
   A. ownership　　B.priority　　C. holdings　　D. possessions

(8) If companies ＿＿＿ prices, the Fed will ＿＿＿ interest rates more, so profit margins will get squeezed.
   A. raise　　B. improve　　C. enhance　　D. increase

2. **Gap filling: Complete the following sentences by filling it with a word or phrase. (8*1')**

(1) In turn, these attitudes usually lead to higher levels of both e_____ motivation and job satisfaction.

(2) During a downturn in the b_____ cycle, people in different sectors may lose their jobs at the same time.

(3) These results, called a demand and supply schedule, are obtained from m_____ research, historical data, and other studies of the market.

(4) List and d_____ at least three of these strategies.

(5) Designed for business travelers, most guest rooms include a Courtyard Suite with high-speed Internet a_____, meeting space, and a_____ to an exercise room, restaurant and lounge, swimming pool, and 24- hour a_____ to food. (the same words for three gaps)

(6) General Motors and Chrysler, suffering grave f_____ losses in 2008, needed to demonstrate that they can survive and repay the bridge loans received from the US Department of the Treasury.

(7) While eBay sellers hope for a high price, they sometimes are willing to give up some profit in return for a quick s_____.

(8) In recent years, several issues have grown in importance in the area of corporate o_____, including joint ventures and strategic alliances, employee stock o_____ plans, and institutional o_____. (the same words for three gaps)

3. Look at the words and phrase below. Underline the odd one out. (8*1')

(1) A. growing market   B. developing market
    C. expanding market   D. declining market

(2) A. swamp a market   B. corner a market
    C. flood a market   D. saturate a market

(3) A. international market   B. domestic market
    C. overseas market   D. worldwide market

(4) A. sluggish market   B. stable market
    C. flat market   D. volatile market

(5) A. launch a product   B. bring out a product
    C. introduce a product   D. exhibit a product

(6) A. employee ownership   B. employee participation

     C. employee leasing   D. employment buyout

(7) A. sales analysis   B. sales assistant

     C. sales budget   D. sales channel

(8) A. business angle   B. business analyst

     C. business consultant   D. business guru

4. Discourse completion test (2*1')

(1) This picture describes your daily work. So when asked about your job description, what would you say?

I _____ the customer complaints every day.

(2) At the promotion conference of your new product of your company, you meet with one of your former business associates. When asked "What are you doing here", what will you respond?

I am here _____ my company's new product.

附录5　商务英语短语能力后测

Instructions: This paper is composed of two parts: personal information and a test on your phrase ability in Business English. THANK YOU FOR YOUR COOPERATION.

Personal information

姓名：＿＿＿＿＿＿＿　　　高考英语分数：＿＿＿＿＿＿＿

1. **Multiple choices: Please choose the BEST answer from four choices to make each statement complete and correct.**

(1) We have been appointed ＿＿＿ for these products in Australia and New Zealand.

    A. sole distributor　　　　　　　　B. district representative

    C. exclusive commissioner　　　　　D. exclusive broker

(2) During the business meeting, we need to develop a global marketing ＿＿＿＿.

    A. orientation　　B. mix　　C. segmentation　　D. strategy

(3) We can calculate your monthly mortgage ＿＿＿.

    A. payment　　B. installation　　C. debt　　D. loan

(4) Keep your receipt as proof of ＿＿＿.

    A. complaints　　B. purchase　　C. sale　　D. bargain

(5) We needed to expand our product ＿＿＿ under the strategy of Product Development.

    A. portfolio　　B. fame　　C. awareness　　D. life cycle

(6) In 2009, the customer ＿＿＿ was mainly retired people and families, numbers being 100,000 and 90,000 customers respectively.

    A. base　　B. profile　　C. number　　D. composition

(7) The new management techniques aim to improve ＿＿＿ of the company.

    A. ownership　　B. priority　　C. performance　　D. possessions

(8) If this were true, then marketing research would be mainly about collecting data on ＿＿＿ requirements and anticipating their future needs.

    A. clients'　　B. customers'　　C. markets'　　D. competitor

2. **Gap filling: Complete the following sentences by filling it with a word or phrase.**

(1) Most of our sales are through d_____ .

(2) They demanded a wage i_____ of 3 percent.

(3) The government has lifted the p_____ ceiling on petrol, which is a part of p_____ control imposed during the recession. (the same words for two gaps)

(4) There will be a penalty for late p_____ of invoices.

(5) Access to cheap imports raises the p_____ power of consumers in Japan and other countries.

(6) Poorly p_____ management teams will be replaced.

(7) The survey shows that Internet ads significantly increase p_____ awareness.

(8) Product p_____ analysis is used to examine the existing position of the organization's products in their markets to enable better decisions to be made.

3. **Look at the words and phrase below. Underline the odd one out.**

(1) A. authorized distributor   B. sole distributor
    C. exclusive distributor   D. local distributor

(2) A. cut prices   B. lower prices
    C. slash prices   D. diminish prices

(3) A. defer payment   B. refuse payment
    C. make late payment   D. delay payment

(4) A. strong performance   B. solid performance
    C. good performance   D. flat performance

(5) A. product orientation   B. product replacement
    C. editorial film   D. commercials

(6) A. customer satisfaction   B. customer loyalty
    C. customer management   D. customer building

(7) A. level out   B. remain steady
    C. increase slightly   D. plateau

(8) A. pricing strategy   B. corporate strategy
    C. business strategy   D. operating strategy

4. **Read the graph and picture and fill in the gaps with verbal words/ phrases.**

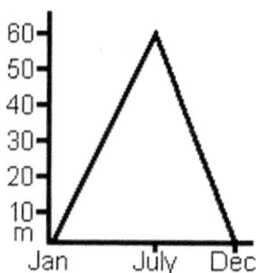

(1) Sales _____ at 60 million dollars in July and then falls sharply during the second half of the year.

(2) The retailer is updating its stores to _____ new customers.?

附录6 商务英语短语教学调查问卷

亲爱的同学：

非常感谢你参与教改项目"语料库辅助的商务英语短语教学研究"！为了进一步了解该教学模式的优势和弊端，请你抽出部分时间填写以下记名问卷。答案没有对错之分，填写时，请根据自己的**实际做法**而非他人的看法。所有资料仅供项目组参考。谢谢你的合作！

中文姓名：＿＿＿＿＿＿＿＿　　　性别：＿＿＿＿＿＿＿＿

第一部分　语料库辅助的商务英语短语教学与短语意识、短语能力和商科知识

1. 在参与教改项目前，我在"综合商务英语"课程的学习中<u>关注和理解</u>商务英语短语（搭配结构、习语等）。
   A. 总是　　　　　　　　B. 经常　　　　　　　　C. 有时
   D. 很少　　　　　　　　E. 从不

2. 参与项目以后，我在"综合商务英语"课程的学习中<u>关注和理解</u>商务英语短语(搭配结构、习语等)。
   A. 总是　　　　　　　　B. 经常　　　　　　　　C. 有时
   D. 很少　　　　　　　　E. 从不

3. 参与项目以后，我在该课程之外<u>关注和理解</u>所接触到的商务话语中的短语（搭配结构、习语等）。
   A. 总是　　　　　　　　B. 经常　　　　　　　　C. 有时
   D. 很少　　　　　　　　E. 从不

4. 参与项目以后，在关注到商务话语中的短语后，我会主动去<u>使用</u>商务英语短语。
   A. 总是　　　　　　　　B. 经常　　　　　　　　C. 有时
   D. 很少　　　　　　　　E. 从不

5. 语料库辅助的商务英语短语教学，<u>提高</u>了我对商务英语短语的<u>认知、理解和应用的能力</u>。
   A. 完全符合　　　　　　B. 基本符合　　　　　　C. 说不清楚
   D. 不太符合　　　　　　E. 完全不符合

6. 语料库辅助的商务英语短语教学，明显提高了我的商科知识水平。

    A. 完全符合   B. 基本符合   C. 说不清楚

    D. 不太符合   E. 完全不符合

7. 我通过语料库辅助的短语教学（课堂学习结合课后自学），商务知识
体系和商务英语短语的习得都有明显进步。

    A. 完全符合   B. 基本符合   C. 说不清楚

    D. 不太符合   E. 完全不符合

第二部分　语料库辅助的商务英语短语教学与自主学习能力

8. 项目中教授的语料库辅助的学习方式（语料库操作软件、语料库或基
于语料库的学习平台等），我已经掌握。

    A. 很好   B. 较好   C. 一般

    D. 较差   E. 完全不会

9. 参与项目后，我在"综合商务英语"课程的各类任务中使用语料库辅
助的学习方式（语料库操作软件、相关语料库或基于语料库的学习平
台等）。

    A. 总是   B. 经常   C. 有时

    D. 很少   E. 从不

10. 参与项目后，我在"商务英语听说"的学习中使用语料库辅助的学习
方式。

    A. 总是   B. 经常   C. 有时

    D. 很少   E. 从不

11. 参与项目后，我在"商务英语写作"的学习中使用语料库辅助的学习
方式。

    A. 总是   B. 经常   C. 有时

    D. 很少   E. 从不

12. 参与项目后，我在"管理学原理"等商科类课程的学习中使用语料库
辅助的学习方式。

    A. 总是   B. 经常   C. 有时

    D. 很少   E. 从不

如你在"管理学原理"之外的其他课程上使用，请具体写明课程名称。

_____

_____

13. 参与项目后，当我有不懂或疑惑时，我会和老师或同学交流语料库辅助的学习方式。

    A．总是   B．经常   C．有时

    D．很少   E．从不

14. 在今后的学习中，我会在英语学习中继续使用语料库辅助的学习方式。

    A．总是   B．经常   C．有时

    D．很少   E．从不

如你的答案是D和E，请简要陈述原因。

_____

_____

15. 在今后的学习中，我会在商科学习中继续使用语料库辅助的学习方式。

    A．总是   B．经常   C．有时

    D．很少   E．从不

如你的答案是D和E，请简要陈述原因。

_____

_____

附录7 商务概念词项前测

Business Lexis Test

Name _____   Class _____   Gender _____

NCEE English Score _____   CBE Score (Year 1) _____

Gap filling: Please fill in the blank with one word based on the context and the given initial letter.

Sample

Koch's company is Boston Beer, and its flagship <u>product</u> is a premium beer called Samuel Adams.

1. B_____ is an organization that provides goods and services to earn profits.

2. Many service and manufacturing companies, especially smaller ones, use functional departmentalization to develop departments according to a group's functions or activities. Such f_____ typically have production, marketing and sales, human resources, and accounting and finance departments.

3. There are three types of business: sole proprietorship, partnership, and c_____.

4. M_____ is the process of planning, organizing, leading and controlling an organization's resources to achieve its goals.

5. A_____ is a comprehensive system for collecting, analyzing, and communicating financial information to a company's owners and employees, to the public, and to various regulatory agencies.

6. Departments may be further subdivided. For example, the m_____ department might be divided into separate staffs for market research and advertising.

7. Accordingly, any stock's value today looks beyond the current price and is based on expectations of the financial returns it will provide to s_____ during the long run.

8. E_____ are people who assume the risk of business ownership.

9. Common titles for top m_____ include president, vicepresident, treasurer, chief executive officer (CEO), and chief financial officer (CFO).

10. Performance Appraisal is evaluation of an e_____'s job performance in order to determine the degree to which he is performing effectively.

11. In general, businesses seek to be close to their customers, to establish strong relationships with their suppliers, and to distinguish themselves from their c_____.

12. Madoff's scheme collapsed when nervous i_____, worried about the economic downturn in 2008, asked to withdraw their money.

13. Indeed, the dramatic price fluctuations that began in mid-2004 have left c_____, government officials, and business leaders struggling to cope with uncertainty about future prices.

14. Salespeople must be adept at performing three basic tasks of personal selling. In order processing, a salesperson receives an order and sees to its handling and d_____.

15. On all economic levels, decisions about what to buy and what to sell are determined primarily by the forces of demand and s_____.

16. A market is a mechanism for e_____ between the buyers and sellers of a particular good or service.

17. To stay afloat, Starbucks is reconsidering all aspects of its marketing strategy, including downsizing the d_____ network of retail stores, refashioning its line of products and prices, and promoting a repositioned Starbucks image.

18. The *board of directors* is a group elected by stockholders to oversee c_____ management.

19. In a s_____ alliance, a company finds a partner in the country in which it wants to do business.

20. Recent signs of recovery for the U.S. auto industry stem from more than f_____ bailouts.

21. E_____ and legal guidelines suggest that hiring and firing decisions should be based solely on the abilities to perform a job.

22. In general, both absolute and comparative advantages translate into

c_____ advantage. Brazil, for instance, can produce and market coffee beans knowing full well that there are few other countries with the right mix of climate, terrain, and altitude to enter the coffee bean market. The United States has comparative advantages in the computer industry (because of technological sophistication) and in farming (because of large amounts of fertile land and a temperate climate).

23. U_____ is the level of joblessness among people actively seeking work in an economic system.

24. M_____ economies rely on capitalism and free enterprise to create an environment in which producers and consumers are free to sell and buy what they choose.

25. A p_____ economy relies on a centralized government to control all or most factors of production and to make all or most production and allocation decisions.

26. Profitability Ratio is a financial ratio for measuring a firm's potential e_____.

27. Consumer taste tests help the firm decide when to introduce new p_____.

28. C_____, therefore, forces all businesses to make products better or cheaper. A company that produces inferior, expensive products is likely to fail.

29. They choose a course of action—buying the stock in anticipation of making a p_____—and then stay with it.

30. Buyers will purchase more of a product as its price drops and less of a product as its price i_____.

31. While taxes are the most obvious way the government r_____ money, it also sells bonds—securities through which it promises to pay buyers certain amounts of money by specified future dates.

32. The recession of 2008-2010 prompted some firms to reduce the wage sand salaries they were paying in order to l_____ costs.

33. To protect domestic firms, Italy i_____ high tariffs on electronic goods. As a result, CD players are prohibitively expensive.

34. Marketing is an organizational function and a set of processes for creating, communicating, and delivering v_____ to customers and for

managing customer relationships in ways that benefit the organization and its stakeholders.

35. The real growth r_____ of the U.S. economic system, therefore, has for the past few years been only modest.

36. Short-term solvency ratios measure a company's liquidity and its ability to p_____ immediate debts.

37. Demand is the willingness and ability of buyers to p_____ a product (a good or a service).

38. Companies with a heightened awareness of social responsibility also recognize an obligation to p_____ opportunities to balance work and life pressures and preferences, help employees maintain job skills, and, when terminations or layoffs are necessary, treat them with respect and compassion.

39. Many enterprises also have missions and mission statements—statements of how they will a_____ their purposes in the environments in which they conduct their businesses.

40. Meanwhile, other streaming video competitors emerge almost daily and who knows when one of these companies might d_____ a new business model that can offset Netflix's current advantages.

附录8　商务概念词项后测

Business Lexis Test

Name _____

Gap filling: Please fill in the blank with one word based on the context and the given initial letter.

Sample

Koch's company is Boston Beer, and its flagship <u>product</u> is a premium beer called Samuel Adams.

Part 1

1. B_____ is an organization that provides goods and services to earn profits.

2. Many service and manufacturing companies, especially smaller ones, use functional departmentalization to develop departments according to a group's functions or activities. Such f_____ typically have production, marketing and sales, human resources, and accounting and finance departments.

3. There are three types of business: sole proprietorship, partnership, and c_____.

4. M_____ is the process of planning, organizing, leading and controlling an organization's resources to achieve its goals.

5. A_____ is a comprehensive system for collecting, analyzing, and communicating financial information to a company's owners and employees, to the public, and to various regulatory agencies.

6. Departments may be further subdivided. For example, the m_____ department might be divided into separate staffs for market research and advertising.

7. Accordingly, any stock's value today looks beyond the current price and is based on expectations of the financial returns it will provide to s_____ during the long run.

8. E_____ are people who assume the risk of business ownership.

9. Common titles for top m_____ include *president, vicepresident, treasurer, chief executive officer* (CEO), and *chief financial officer* (CFO).

10. Performance Appraisal is evaluation of an e_____'s job performance in order to determine the degree to which he is performing effectively.

11. In general, businesses seek to be close to their customers, to establish strong relationships with their suppliers, and to distinguish themselves from their c_____.

12. Madoff's scheme collapsed when nervous i_____, worried about the economic downturn in 2008, asked to withdraw their money.

13. Indeed, the dramatic price fluctuations that began in mid-2004 have left c_____, government officials, and business leaders struggling to cope with uncertainty about future prices.

14. Salespeople must be adept at performing three basic tasks of personal selling. In order processing, a salesperson receives an order and sees to its handling and d_____.

15. On all economic levels, decisions about what to buy and what to sell are determined primarily by the forces of demand and s_____.

16. A market is a mechanism for e_____ between the buyers and sellers of a particular good or service.

17. To stay afloat, Starbucks is reconsidering all aspects of its marketing strategy, including downsizing the d_____ network of retail stores, refashioning its line of products and prices, and promoting a repositioned Starbucks image.

18. The *board of directors* is a group elected by stockholders to oversee c_____ management.

19. In a s_____ alliance, a company finds a partner in the country in which it wants to do business.

20. Recent signs of recovery for the U.S. auto industry stem from more than f_____ bailouts.

21. E_____ and legal guidelines suggest that hiring and firing decisions should be based solely on the abilities to perform a job.

22. In general, both absolute and comparative advantages translate into c_____ advantage. Brazil, for instance, can produce and market coffee beans knowing full well that there are few other countries with the right mix of climate, terrain, and altitude to enter the coffee bean market.

The United States has comparative advantages in the computer industry (because of technological sophistication) and in farming (because of large amounts of fertile land and a temperate climate).

23. U_____ is the level of joblessness among people actively seeking work in an economic system.

24. M_____ economies rely on capitalism and free enterprise to create an environment in which producers and consumers are free to sell and buy what they choose.

25. A p_____ economy relies on a centralized government to control all or most factors of production and to make all or most production and allocation decisions.

26. Profitability Ratio is a financial ratio for measuring a firm's potential e_____.

27. Consumer taste tests help the firm decide when to introduce new p_____.

28. C_____, therefore, forces all businesses to make products better or cheaper. A company that produces inferior, expensive products is likely to fail.

29. They choose a course of action—buying the stock in anticipation of making a p_____—and then stay with it.

30. Buyers will purchase more of a product as its price drops and less of a product as its price i_____.

31. While taxes are the most obvious way the government r_____ money, it also sells bonds—securities through which it promises to pay buyers certain amounts of money by specified future dates.

32. The recession of 2008-2010 prompted some firms to reduce the wage sand salaries they were paying in order to l_____ costs.

33. To protect domestic firms, Italy i_____ high tariffs on electronic goods. As a result, CD players are prohibitively expensive.

34. Marketing is an organizational function and a set of processes for creating, communicating, and delivering v_____ to customers and for managing customer relationships in ways that benefit the organization and its stakeholders.

35. The real growth r_____ of the U.S. economic system, therefore,

has for the past few years been only modest.

36. Short-term solvency ratios measure a company's liquidity and its ability to p_____ immediate debts.

37. Demand is the willingness and ability of buyers to p_____ a product (a good or a service).

38. Companies with a heightened awareness of social responsibility also recognize an obligation to p_____ opportunities to balance work and life pressures and preferences, help employees maintain job skills, and, when terminations or layoffs are necessary, treat them with respect and compassion.

39. Many enterprises also have missions and mission statements—statements of how they will a_____ their purposes in the environments in which they conduct their businesses.

40. Meanwhile, other streaming video competitors emerge almost daily and who knows when one of these companies might d_____ a new business model that can offset Netflix's current advantages.

Part 2

1. We define l_____ as the processes and behaviors used by someone, such as a manager, to motivate, inspire, and influence the behaviors of others.

2. Organizational c_____ is an individual's identification with the organization and its mission.

3. Firms with the highest degree of social r_____ exhibit the proactive stance.

4. A_____ allocation is the proportion of overall money invested in each of various investment alternatives so that the overall risks for the portfolio are low, moderate, or high, depending on the investor's objectives and preferences.

5. A s_____ is a portion of the ownership of a corporation. The company's total ownership is divided into small parts which can be bought and sold to determine how much of the company is owned by each shareholder.

6. A l_____ is a debt that a firm owes to an outside party.

7. Approximately 85 percent of the company's total r_____ comes from advertising.

8. The amount of money that is loaned and must be repaid is called the loan p_____ .

9. Diversification means buying several different kinds of investments to reduce the risk of l_____ if the value of any one security should fall.

10. The high c_____ of gas may also lead to prices going up for other products, ranging from food to clothing to delivery services.

11. By definition, c_____ is completely liquid. Marketable securities purchased as short term investments are slightly less liquid but can be sold quickly.

12. Simply open a new bank a_____ in your name, accept money transfers into it, then forward the money to our customers at locations around the globe.

13. Paper money and metal coins are c_____ issued by the government and widely used for small exchanges.

14. The main function of financial institutions is to ease the flow of m_____ from users with surpluses to those with deficits by attracting funds into checking and savings accounts.

15. If the company fails to make a bond p_____, it goes into default.

16. Using confidential information to gain from a stock transaction is insider t_____. Certain behavior regarding financial representation is also unlawful.

17. The control process begins when management establishes standards, often for financial p_____.

18. One extremely important set of HR challenges centers on workforce d_____—the range of workers' attitudes, values, beliefs, and behaviors that differ by gender, race, age, ethnicity, physical ability, and other relevant characteristics.

19. Another source of returns depends on whether the investment is increasing or decreasing in dollar value. Price a_____ is an increase in the dollar value of an investment.

20. If we want to discuss something we tell the secretary beforehand, and she puts in on the a_____. We receive this about a week before the meeting, along with the minutes of the last meeting.

21. For important decisions, if we can't reach a c_____ we have a vote.

22. The Fed, with its goal of economic s_____, uses the money supply to avoid extreme inflation or deflation.

23. For planning, controlling, and decision making, the most important internal financial statement is the b_____—a detailed report on estimated receipts and expenditures for a future period of time.

24. In many markets there is a firm with a much larger market share than its competitors, called a market l_____.

25. B_____ is independent intermediary who matches numerous sellers and buyers as needed, often without knowing in advance who they will be.

26. Online investors buy into and s_____ out of the stocks of thousands of companies daily.

27. Supply is the willingness and ability of producers to o_____ a product or service for sale.

28. Price indexes such as the consumer price index (CPI) m_____ the prices of typical products purchased by consumers living in urban areas.

29. The top managers of a company have to s_____ objectives and then develop particular strategies that will enable the company to achieve them.

30. At large firms, separate departments d_____ with recruiting and hiring, wage and salary levels, and labor relations.

31. Just below top managers are middle managers, including plant, operations, and division managers, who i_____ strategies, policies, and decisions made by top managers.

32. Goal setting helps firms a_____ resources. Areas that are expected to grow will get first priority.

33. Only firms meeting certain minimum requirements—earning power, total value of o_____ stock, and number of shareholders—are

eligible for listing on the NYSE.

34. Scanning the business environment for threats and opportunities is often called e_____ analysis.

35. C_____ Banks are companies that accept deposits that it uses to make loans, earn profits, pay interest to depositors, and pay dividends to owners.

36. The central bank can reduce the reserves by changing the reserve requirements. This reduces the amount of money that banks can create and makes money t_____ or scarce.

37. Existing stocks and bonds are sold in the much larger s_____ securities market, which is handled by such familiar bodies as the New York Stock Exchange.

38. Today's NYSE is a hybrid market that utilizes both floor and e_____ trading.

39. One of the Fed's most important tools in setting m_____ policy is the adjustment of the interest rates it charges member banks to borrow money.

40. Factors affecting the g_____ business environment at a general level include international trade agreements, international economic conditions, political unrest, and so forth.

附录9　微型文本money.txt

What Is Money and What Are Its Functions?

Money is something you've been familiar with throughout your life. In fact, you may already consider yourself an expert on the subject. You regularly use money to measure the value of things you own. You also have some of it in your pocket and in bank accounts. It might surprise you to learn that there's a great deal of disagreement among economists about what money is and how to measure it. Money serves a number of functions, and any definition of money must consider all of its functions.

The four major functions of money are as a medium of exchange, a standard of value, a standard of deferred payment, and a store of value.

A Medium of Exchange. As a generally accepted medium of exchange, money rules out the need for barter, the direct exchange of one item for another. Barter is a very inconvenient means of trading because it requires the double coincidence of wants. A seller with a good or service to offer must search for a buyer who has exactly what the seller desires. For example, if a baker wants meat, he must search for a person who sells meat and wants bread under a barter system. Because money is generally accepted as payment for many purchase, a baker who sells bread for money can use the money to buy meat or anything else he wants.

A Standard of Value. Money provides a unit of account that serves as a standard to measure value. The value of an item is a measure of what a person will sacrifice to obtain it. How much is a two-week vacation in Hawaii worth to you? If you're like most people, you'll probably respond to such a question by valuing the vacation in dollars—way $2,000—rather than in terms of other things (like your car). Whether or not you're conscious of it, you're constantly valuing items in dollars. As a standard of value, money allows the addition of values of many different items as automobiles, repairs, and all other goods and services. The concept of GNP is useless without a standard of value such as the dollar.

A Standard of Deferred Payment. Many contracts involve promises to pay sums of money in the future. The unit of account for deferred payment of debts is also money. If you borrow money to buy a car, the loan contract specifies how much you must pay back every month and the number of months required to satisfy your obligation. However, money serves its function as a standard of deferred payment only if its purchasing power remains fairly constant over time. If the price level rises, the future purchasing power of money over time will go down. Similarly, a decrease in the price level will increase the future purchasing power of money.

A Store of Value. Money can also serve as a store of value that can be quickly converted to good and services. Money as the actual medium of exchange is completely liquid, meaning it can immediately be converted to goods and services without any inconvenience or cost. Other assets that serve as stores of value must first be sold to be converted into a generally accepted medium of exchange. There are often costs and inconvenience associated with liquidating other assets. Holding money as a store of value thus can reduce the transaction costs involved in everyday business.

附录10 微型文本debt.txt

Introduction

Two great mysteries dominate our lives: love and money.

"What is love?" is a question that has been endlessly explored in stories, songs, books, movies, and television.

But the same can NOT be said about the question "What is money?"

It's not surprising that monetary theory hasn't inspired any blockbuster movies. But it was not even mentioned at the schools most of us attended.

For most of us, the question "Where does money come from?" brings to mind a picture of the mint printing bills and stamping coins. Money, most of us believe, is created by the government.

It's true (pause) but only to a point. Those metal and paper symbols of value we usually think of as money are, indeed, produced by an agency of the federal government called the Mint.

But the vast majority of money is not created by the Mint. It is created in huge amounts every day by private corporations known as banks. (long pause)

Most of us believe that banks lend out money that has been entrusted to them by depositors. Easy to picture. But not the truth.

In fact, banks create the money they loan, not from the bank's own earnings, not from money deposited, but directly from the borrower's promise to repay.

The borrower's signature on the loan papers is an obligation to pay the bank the amount of the loan plus interest, or, lose the house, the car, whatever asset was pledged as collateral. That's a big commitment from the borrower.

What does that same signature require of the bank? The bank gets to conjure into existence the amount of the loan and just write it into the borrower's account.

Sound far-fetched?

Surely that can't be true. But it is.

To demonstrate how this miracle of modern banking came about consider this simple story:

The Goldsmith's Tale

Once upon various times, pretty much anything was used as money.

It just had to be portable and enough people had to have faith that it could later be exchanged for things of real value like food, clothing and shelter. Shells, cocoa beans, pretty stones, even feathers have been used as money.

Gold and silver were attractive, soft and easy to work with, so some cultures became expert with these metals. Goldsmiths made trade much easier by casting coins, standardized units of these metals whose weight and purity was certified.

To protect his gold the goldsmith needed a vault.

Soon his fellow townsmen were knocking on his door wanting to rent space to safeguard their own coins and valuables.

Before long, the goldsmith was renting every shelf in his vault and earning a small income from his vault rental business.

Years went by and the goldsmith made an astute observation. Depositors rarely came in to remove their actual, physical gold, and they never all came in at once.

That was because the claim checks the goldsmith had written as receipts for the gold deposited, were being traded in the marketplace as if they were the gold itself.

This paper money was far more convenient than heavy coins, and amounts could simply be written, instead of laboriously counted one by one for each transaction.

Meanwhile, the goldsmith had developed another business. He lent out his gold charging interest.

Well, as convenient claim check money came into acceptance, borrowers began asking for their loans in the form of these claim checks instead of the actual metal. As industry expanded more and more people asked the goldsmith for loans.

This gave the goldsmith an even better idea.

He knew that very few of his depositors ever removed their actual gold. So, the goldsmith figured he could easily get away with lending out claim checks against his depositors' gold, in addition to his own.

As long as the loans were repaid, his depositors would be none the wiser, and no worse off. And the goldsmith, now more banker than artisan, would make a far greater profit than he could by lending only his own gold.

For years the goldsmith secretly enjoyed a good income from the interest earned on everybody else's deposits.

Now a prominent lender, he grew steadily richer than his fellow townsmen and flaunted it. Suspicions grew that he was spending his depositors' money. His depositors got together and threatened withdrawal of their gold if the goldsmith didn't come clean about his newfound wealth.

Contrary to what one might have expected, this did not turn out to be a disaster for the goldsmith. Despite the duplicity inherent in his scheme, his idea did work. The depositors had not lost anything. Their gold was all still safe in the goldsmith's vault.

Rather than taking back their gold, the depositors demanded that the goldsmith, now their banker, cut them in by paying them a share of the interest.

And that was the beginning of banking. The banker paid a low interest rate on deposits of other people's money that he then loaned out at a higher interest.

The difference covered the bank's cost of operation and its profit. The logic of this system was simple. And it seemed like a reasonable way to satisfy the demand for credit.

However this is NOT the way banking works today.

Our goldsmith/banker was not content with the income remaining after sharing the interest earnings with his depositors.

And the demand for credit was growing fast, as Europeans spread out across the world. But his loans were limited by the amount of gold his depositors had in his vault.

That's when he got an even bolder idea. Since no one but himself knew what was actually in his vaults he could lend out claim checks on gold that wasn't even there!

As long as all the claim check holders didn't come to the vault at the same time and demand real gold, how would anyone find out?

This new scheme worked very well, and the banker became enormously wealthy on the interest paid on gold that did not exist!

The idea that the banker would just create money out of nothing was too outrageous to believe, so, for the longest time, the thought did not even occur to people.

But, the power to just invent money went to the banker's head as you can well imagine. In time, the magnitude of the banker's loans and his ostentatious wealth did trigger suspicions once again.

Some borrowers started to demand real gold instead of paper representations. This set off rumours.

Suddenly, several wealthy depositors showed up to remove their gold. The game was up!

A sea of claim check holders flooded the street outside the closed doors of the bank. Alas, the banker did not have enough gold & silver to redeem all the paper he had put into their hands.

This is called a "run on the bank" and is what every banker dreads.

This phenomenon of a "run on the bank" ruined individual banks and, not surprisingly, damaged public confidence in all bankers.

It would have been straightforward to outlaw the practice of creating money from nothing.

But the large volumes of credit the bankers were offering had become essential to the success of European commercial expansion.

So, instead, the practice was legalized and regulated.

Bankers agreed to abide by limits on the amount of fictional loan money that could be lent out. The limit would still be a number much larger than the actual value of gold & silver in the vault. Quite often the ratio was 9 fictional dollars to 1 actual dollar in gold.

These regulations were enforced by surprise inspections.

It was also arranged that, in the event of a run, central banks would support local banks with emergency infusions of gold.

Only if there were runs on a lot of banks simultaneously would the bankers' credit bubble burst and the system come crashing down.

附录11 微型文本marketing.txt

China's Supermarkets Present Export Opportunity

The lightning-fast emergence of supermarkets over the past decade may be the final piece of the China market puzzle. Rising incomes and an expanding urban middle class are setting the stage for China's development as a market for imported foods.

Until recently, many exporters eyeing the Chinese market fled in frustration after encountering a fragmented market made up of thousands of mom-and-pop shops; old-style, open-air markets; and labyrinthine, antiquated wholesale and logistics systems. The old marketing system, controlled by various provincial and city marketing bureaus, consisted of small, fragmented wholesale and retail segments selling local produce; multiple layers of small brokers, wholesalers, distributors and government-licensed importers; and government-run retail outlets.

The good news for food suppliers is that "supermarketization" is transforming China's food sector into a modern retail system. Modern supermarkets, convenience stores, hypermarkets and warehouse clubs, retail formats nearly non-existent in China in the early 1990s—have now captured an estimated 30% of the urban food market and are growing at rates of 30-40% annually.

Chinese supermarkets skyrocketed from just one outlet in 1990 to approximately 60,000 stores, with an estimated $71 billion in sales, by 2003, according to the Chinese Chain Store and Franchise Association (CCFA)②. Growth in the industry that took several decades in the United States and Europe has occurred in a single decade in China. Supermarket sales in Shanghai alone during 2003 were estimated at $5 billion, equivalent to half of Shanghai's retail food sales.

Supplier Benefits

The new supermarket sector is a boon to exporters for two reasons:

The way they sell to consumers: Supermarkets, engaged in fierce competition with other types of outlets for the Chinese consumer's dollar, are eager to carry new products to meet consumer demand for quality and product diversity. Some advertise exotic products to get customers in the door.

The way they buy from suppliers: Supermarket chains employ centralized, high-volume distribution systems that give exporters a larger target with fewer distribution layers to navigate. Procurement modernization is increasing the advantage of suppliers that can deliver quality products in a timely and price-competitive fashion. These factors should give foreign food suppliers a better chance to compete in the Chinese marketplace.

Sources of Supermarket Sector Momentum

The sector includes a number of different store formats: small chain convenience stores selling primarily canned goods and beverages and/or snack and convenience foods; standard supermarkets; hypermarkets that sell a full range of consumer goods, from clothing and electronics to bicycles; and large warehouse clubs. The large formats account for the lion's share (95%) of sales in the modern retail sector; convenience stores garner only 5%. These market shares are expected to continue for the foreseeable future.

Supermarkets began developing in the early 1990s in Shanghai and several other major cities, where they were encouraged by local governments. The largest Chinese supermarket chains started out as government-operated department stores and marketing bureaus in Shanghai. Multinational chains from Europe, Japan, and the United States provided a second major impetus in the development of the sector in the mid-to late 1990s in the most prosperous coastal cities, including Shanghai, Guangzhou and Shenzhen. Supermarket development took off in other large cities such as Beijing in the late 1990s.

Although about 80% of China's supermarkets are in the eastern region, all major chains have aggressive expansion plans targeting medium and small cities, central and western provinces, and rural areas. And while multinational companies at present have about 40% of the sector's sales, domestic companies such as Lianhua and Hualian have developed quickly.

Local governments are actively encouraging the transition to supermarkets by shutting down wet markets (traditional street markets) and in some cases converting them into supermarkets. In 2004, China's Ministry of Commerce announced a five-year plan to develop a rural retail network of chain supermarkets and express stores in small towns, pushing the supermarket format into China's vast rural hinterland.

Supermarkets Displace Traditional Markets

Supermarkets enjoyed initial success with packaged foods and processed food staples like rice, flour and cooking oil. Supermarkets and convenience stores have also played a key role in boosting consumption of milk products, other beverages, snacks and convenience foods. Chinese consumers have traditionally bought most of their fresh foods—vegetables, fruits, and meats—from wet markets. Vendors in wet markets sell generic produce grown on local farms or purchased from wholesale markets. Before the supermarket explosion, they usually purchased canned and packaged foods from small mom-and-pop stores, roadside kiosks or the food product sections of government department stores.

Supermarkets are rapidly gaining a competitive edge over these traditional retailers. They offer a cleaner, more comfortable and convenient shopping environment. Quality is generally better and more standardized. In the case of packaged foods, shoppers do not have to haggle over prices, and they can trust product measures and units. Supermarkets offer a wider array of products than do traditional shops. Refrigerated, frozen and ready-to-eat foods are available; almost 90% of urban Chinese households now have home refrigerators. However, many shoppers continue to purchase fresh produce from wet markets while making weekend trips to the supermarket for other items. They prefer the freshness, low prices and personal interaction at wet markets for fresh fruits and vegetables.

Nevertheless, supermarkets are quickly taking over the fresh produce segment of the market as well, by matching wet market prices and offering superior quality and sanitation. An important measure of their initial success is that Chinese supermarkets now sell roughly $4 billion worth of fruits and vegetables to Chinese consumers—about twice China's exports in that category to the rest of the world. That is, the internal "supermarket market" is already large and dynamic, rivaling exports from China, and a dynamic market for imports to China.

Imports Arrive

Imported foods, until recently a rarity in China, are now widely available in Chinese supermarkets. Washington apples, California oranges and wines, lychees from Thailand, butter from New Zealand and cheeses from France are commonly found on supermarket shelves. Supermarkets feature many international food brands, such as Kellogg's cereals, Hormel sausages and hot dogs, Lay's potato chips, Nestle and Danone milk products, McCormick jellies and Skippy peanut butter, many of which are manufactured locally, albeit sometimes with imported ingredients.

China's growing middle class (estimated at 200-300 million persons, out of a population of 1.3 billion) has the purchasing power to afford imported foods, but this crucial market segment has been kept largely out of the reach of food exporters by the combination of China's antiquated marketing system and high trade barriers. But China cut tariffs, import licensing requirements and state trading monopolies as a result of its entry into the WTO (World Trade Organization) in 2001. Lower trade barriers are a first step to opening the Chinese market at its borders and ports, but a competitive, efficient domestic marketing system is necessary to get imported products from entry points to the Chinese consumer. That's where supermarkets come in.

Supermarkets are bringing world-class procurement systems into China, giving potential exporters a bigger target to aim for and knitting together market segments fragmented by geography and other factors. Supermarket chains are establishing large, centralized distribution centers that draw products from throughout China, and from elsewhere in Asia, Oceania, the Americas and Europe. Multinational logistics firms are now operating in China, whose WTO commitments mandate that the country open its market to foreign companies engaged in wholesaling and distribution in 2004.

The integration of China into multinational retail chains may open more avenues to its market. The world's largest food retail chains—such as Wal-Mart, Carrefour, Metro and Tesco—are now buying from and selling to China. Wal-Mart's procurements from China are already so huge that the amount exceeds the gross national product of many countries, and Wal-Mart's sales in China are increasing as well.

The largest Chinese food retailer, Lianhua, has started to open stores in Europe with the intent of developing into a retailer that can buy and sell in both domestic and foreign markets. Suppliers able to establish themselves in the procurement system of a multinational chain may have easier access to the China market.

附录12 "N+that (clause)" 微型文本（仅随机展示其中的30例）

1. _VBZ based_VVN on_IN the_DT idea_ NN that_IN/that any_DT given_VVN person_ business essentials(231000).txt 0 1

2. Hat_NP ._SENT Another_DT business_NN hat_ NN that_IN/that many_JJ people_NNS wear_ business essentials(231000).txt 0 2

3. _VBN a_DT surging_JJ global_JJ economy_ NN that_IN/that until_IN recently_RB caused_ business essentials(231000).txt 0 3

4. _NN theft_NN ,_, yet_RB another_DT indication_ NN that_IN/that gas_ NN was_VBD becoming_ business essentials(231000).txt 0 4

5. _DT standards_NNS of_IN business_NN conduct_ NN ,_, that_IN/that a_DT society_NN is_ business essentials(231000).txt 0 5

6. included_VVN as_RB well_RB ._SENT Note_ NN that_IN/that the_ DT concept_NN of_ business essentials(231000).txt 0 6

7. _PP will_MD lose_VV the_DT money_ NN that_IN/that it_PP spent_ VVD making_ business essentials(231000).txt 0 7

8. _MD "_`` lose_VV "_" the_DT extra_JJ profit_ NN that_IN/that it_PP could_MD have_ business essentials(231000).txt 0 8

9. oligopoly_NN ,_, and_CC monopoly_NN ._SENT Note_ NN that_IN/ that these_DT are_VBP not_ business essentials(231000).txt 0 9

10. _RB dominated_VVN by_IN one_CD producer_ NN that_IN/that other_ JJ firms_NNS cannot_ business essentials(231000).txt 0 10

11. _VVN in_IN producing_VVG the_DT food_ NN that_IN/that we_PP needed_VVD ._SENT business essentials(231000).txt 0 11

12. _VVG power_NN parity\xA1\xAAthe_NNS principle_ NN that_IN/that exchange_NN rates_NNS are_ business essentials(231000).txt 0 12

13. _NP Power_NP Parity_NP the_DT principle_ NN that_IN/that exchange_NN rates_NNS are_ business essentials(231000).txt 0 13

14. _VBZ the_DT amount_NN of_IN money_ NN that_IN/that the_DT government_NN owes_ business essentials(231000).txt 0 14

15. _DT private_JJ borrowing_NN and_CC investment_ NN that_IN/that increase_NN productivity_NN ._SENT business essentials(231000). txt 0 15

16. declines_NNS ._SENT Keeping_VVG in_IN mind_ NN that_IN/that

our_PP$ definition_NN of_ business essentials(231000).txt 0 16

17 y_RB increase_VV further_RBR ._SENT Unemployment_ NN that_IN/ that results_NNS from_IN this_ business essentials(231000).txt 0 17

18 area_NN ._SENT List_NN each_DT store_ NN that_IN/that you_PP see_VV and_ business essentials(231000).txt 0 18

19 ce_NN ._SENT Background_NN Information_NN Assume_ NN that_ IN/that you_PP own_VVP a_ business essentials(231000).txt 0 19

20 QUESTIONS_NP 1._CD Discuss_NP the_DT role_ NN that_IN/that various_JJ inducements_NNS other_ business essentials(231000). txt 0 20

21 _PP deal_VV with_IN business_NN behavior_ NN that_IN/that we_PP regard_VVP as_ business essentials(231000).txt 0 21

22 _VBP the_DT standards_NNS of_IN behavior_ NN that_IN/that guide_ NN individual_JJ managers_ business essentials(231000).txt 0 22

23 _JJ Ethics_NP standards_NNS of_IN behavior_ NN that_IN/that guide_ NN individual_JJ managers_ business essentials(231000).txt 0 23

24 uations_NNS ._SENT Suppose_VV ,_, for_IN example_ NN ,_, that_ IN/that our_PP$ manager_NN loses_ business essentials(231000). txt 0 24

25 _DT single_JJ most_RBS effective_JJ step_ NN that_IN/that a_DT company_NN can_ business essentials(231000).txt 0 25

26 _DT firm_NN sends_VVZ a_DT signal_ NN that_IN/that it_PP expects_ VVZ ethical_ business essentials(231000).txt 0 26

27 _JJ about_IN the_DT potential_JJ liability_ NN that_IN/that employee_ NN e-mail_NP business essentials(231000).txt 0 27

28 _IN particular_JJ ,_, to_TO the_DT extent_ NN that_IN/that an_DT organization_NN acknowledges business essentials(231000).txt 0 28

29 _RP for_IN the_DT simple_JJ reason_ NN that_IN/that people_NNS still_RB need_ business essentials(231000).txt 0 29

30 \xA1\xAAto_NN a_DT felony_NN charge_ NN that_IN/that it_PP had_ VHD mishandled_ business essentials(231000).txt 0 30

附录13 微型文本premium.txt

In April 2000, the Anglo-Dutch Unilever NV announced it would buy flagging Ben and Jerry's stocks for 43.50 a share, a large premium over the previous day's closing price of 434.93.

CSN, one of Latin America's large fully integrated steelmakers, is offering €5.75 a share for 100 per cent of Cimpor's capital, a premium of 5 per cent on Thursday's closing price.

The eau-de-cologne is positioned as a premium fragrance. It is priced at the top end of the market.

The other assistant manager, meanwhile, has urged just the opposite approach: raise room rates by at least 20 percent and sell food to rescue workers and hospitals at a premium price.

One will always find a Rolex in an upmarket distribution outlet and at a premium price.

Can Starbucks reposition the brand so it appeals to the convenience market without tarnishing the company's premium image?

They get the right to promote their chocolate products not only as "fair-trade" but, often, as "organic" products as well—categories that typically command premium retail prices.

In fact, FLO pays an even higher premium on organically certified cocoa—$200 instead of $150 per ton—and the extra cost, of course, shows up in retail prices.

If insurance for additional amount and/or for other insurance terms is required by the Buyers, prior notice to this effect must reach the Sellers before shipment and is subject to the Sellers' agreement, and the extra insurance premium shall be for the Buyers' account.

Ask for two premium economy tickets to New York on 4th June, returning on 9th June.

When Citibank introduced its credit card in the Asia-Pacific region, it launched it sequentially and tailored the product features for each country which maintaining its premium positioning.

For loyal buyers of Godiva premium chocolates, performance includes such sensory delights as aroma, flavor, color, and texture.

Historically, building a brand was rather simple. For that, consumers were prepared to pay a premium.

It's definitely "no frills", but I'm always willing to pay a premium for business class, so long as it isn't exorbitant.

The hotels place a premium on customer satisfaction.

Premium sales-promotion technique in which offers of free or reduced-price items are used to stimulate purchases.

Mmm, I suppose we could offer some free content. Then make readers pay a subscription for premium content—extra materials like DVD workout programmes—that sort of thing.

"Often fair trade is sold at a premium," he charges, "but the entire premium goes to the middlemen."

For lovers of upscale coffee products, Starbucks has long been the standout brand with a premium image as the "home of affordable luxury."

附录14　主题写作分析相关主题词表

货币银行学和投资学专题主题词表（头100个）

前库主题词	专题库 主题词	后库主题词	前库主题词	专题库 主题词	后库主题词
afford	amount	according	is	**inflation**	keep
apartments	are	afford	it	institutions	land
are	assets	are	live	**interest**	large
bank	b	**bank**	living	**investing**	living
banks	bank	**banks**	lower	**investment**	lower
believe	banking	because	**market**	investments	**market**
bubble	**banks**	bubble	may	investor	means
burst	bond	burst	means	**investors**	middle
buy	bonds	**buy**	middle	**is**	million
buying	**buy**	buying	million	its	**money**
can	buyers	can	**money**	loan	month
China	by	cannot	month	loans	more
Chinese	c	China	more	low	mortgage
choice	capital	Chinese	mortgage	many	my
choose	cash	choice	my	**market**	not
cities	com	choose	parents	markets	parents
class	commercial	cities	**pay**	**money**	**pay**
crisis	common	class	**payment**	mutual	**payment**
debt	companies	demand	people	of	people
demand	company	**deposit**	policy	or	policy

续表

前库主题词	专题库 主题词	后库主题词	前库主题词	专题库 主题词	后库主题词
deposit	countries	<u>economic</u>	**price**	p	**price**
doubt	credit	economy	**prices**	**pay**	**prices**
economy	currency	estate	profit	**payment**	purchase
estate	current	**fund**	profits	percent	put
fund	<u>debt</u>	future	purchase	**price**	**rate**
future	**deposit**	**government**	purchasing	**prices**	rather
ghost	deposits	great	**rate**	**rate**	rational
government	different	**growth**	rational	rates	**real**
growth	dividend	high	**real**	**real**	reasons
have	each	higher	reasons	reserve	**return**
high	<u>economic</u>	house	result	**return**	<u>risk</u>
higher	electronic	houses	**return**	<u>risk</u>	rmb
house	example	housing	rising	s	salary
houses	exchange	**however**	rmb	savings	save
housing	fed	huge	salary	securities	saving
however	federal	i	save	sell	seems
huge	financial	in	saving	sellers	since
i	firm	**income**	seems	services	soaring
if	firms	increase	since	share	steady
in	for	industry	soaring	shares	still
income	**fund**	**inflation**	steady	stock	<u>supply</u>
industry	funds	instead	still	stocks	the

续表

前库主题词	专题库 主题词	后库主题词	前库主题词	专题库 主题词	后库主题词
inflation	**government**	**interest**	the	<u>supply</u>	there
instead	group	into	there	system	therefore
interest	**growth**	invest	therefore	term	tier
into	**however**	**investing**	**value**	trading	urbanization
invest	http	**investment**	which	u	**value**
investing	important	**investors**	will	**value**	which
investment	**income**	**is**	years	www	will
investors	index	it	yuan	your	years

说明：加粗字体是三个库共享的主题词，单下划线的词语是前库和专题库共享的主题提，双下划线词语则是后库和专题库共享的主题词。

图书在版编目 (CIP) 数据

语料库辅助的商务英语短语教学研究 / 胡春雨，陈丽丹，何安平著 . -- 北京 ：
外语教学与研究出版社，2019.7（2022.2 重印）
（商务英语研究丛书 / 仲伟合总主编）
ISBN 978-7-5213-1068-9

Ⅰ . ①语… Ⅱ . ①胡… ②陈… ③何… Ⅲ . ①商务 - 英语 - 短语 - 教学研究
Ⅳ . ①F7-42

中国版本图书馆 CIP 数据核字 (2019) 第 159421 号

出 版 人　王　芳
责任编辑　李婉婧
责任校对　孔乃卓
封面设计　郭　子　郭　莹
出版发行　外语教学与研究出版社
社　　址　北京市西三环北路 19 号（100089）
网　　址　http://www.fltrp.com
印　　刷　北京九州迅驰传媒文化有限公司
开　　本　650×980　1/16
印　　张　14.25
版　　次　2019 年 8 月第 1 版　2022 年 2 月第 4 次印刷
书　　号　ISBN 978-7-5213-1068-9
定　　价　56.90 元

购书咨询：(010) 88819926　电子邮箱：club@fltrp.com
外研书店：https://waiyants.tmall.com
凡印刷、装订质量问题，请联系我社印制部
联系电话：(010) 61207896　电子邮箱：zhijian@fltrp.com
凡侵权、盗版书籍线索，请联系我社法律事务部
举报电话：(010) 88817519　电子邮箱：banquan@fltrp.com
物料号：310680001

记载人类文明
沟通世界文化
www.fltrp.com